MW00995694

OUT OF PLACE

Out of Place tells a new history of the field of law and society through the experiences and fieldwork of successful writers from populations that academia has historically marginalized. Encouraging collective and transparent self-reflection on positionality, the volume features scholars from around the world who share how their out-of-place positionalities influenced their research questions, data collection, analysis, and writing in law and society. From China to Colombia, India to Indonesia, Singapore to South Africa, and the United Kingdom to the United States, these experts record how they conducted their fieldwork, how their privileges and disadvantages impacted their training and research, and what they learned about the law in the process. As the global field of law and society becomes more diverse and an interest in identity grows, *Out of Place* is a call to embrace the power of positionality. This title is also available as Open Access on Cambridge Core.

LYNETTE J. CHUA is Professor of Law at National University of Singapore and Head of Studies for the Law–Liberal Arts Double-Degree Programme at Yale–NUS College.

MARK FATHI MASSOUD is Professor of Politics and Director of Legal Studies at the University of California, Santa Cruz. He is also a Visiting Professor at the University of Oxford Faculty of Law.

CAMBRIDGE STUDIES IN LAW AND SOCIETY

Founded in 1997, Cambridge Studies in Law and Society is a hub for leading scholarship in socio-legal studies. Located at the intersection of law, the humanities, and the social sciences, it publishes empirically innovative and theoretically sophisticated work on law's manifestations in everyday life: from discourses to practices, and from institutions to cultures. The series editors have longstanding expertise in the interdisciplinary study of law, and welcome contributions that place legal phenomena in national, comparative, or international perspective. Series authors come from a range of disciplines, including anthropology, history, law, literature, political science, and sociology.

Series Editors

Mark Fathi Massoud, University of California, Santa Cruz

Jens Meierhenrich, London School of Economics and Political Science

Rachel E. Stern, University of California, Berkeley

Past Editors

Chris Arup, Martin Chanock, Sally Engle Merry, Pat O'Malley, Susan Silbey

A list of books in the series can be found at the back of this book.

OUT OF PLACE
Fieldwork and Positionality in Law and Society

Edited by

Lynette J. Chua
National University of Singapore

and

Mark Fathi Massoud
University of California, Santa Cruz

CAMBRIDGE
UNIVERSITY PRESS

CAMBRIDGE
UNIVERSITY PRESS

Shaftesbury Road, Cambridge CB2 8EA, United Kingdom

One Liberty Plaza, 20th Floor, New York, NY 10006, USA

477 Williamstown Road, Port Melbourne, VIC 3207, Australia

314–321, 3rd Floor, Plot 3, Splendor Forum, Jasola District Centre, New Delhi – 110025, India

103 Penang Road, #05-06/07, Visioncrest Commercial, Singapore 238467

Cambridge University Press is part of Cambridge University Press & Assessment, a department of the University of Cambridge.

We share the University's mission to contribute to society through the pursuit of education, learning and research at the highest international levels of excellence.

www.cambridge.org
Information on this title: www.cambridge.org/9781009338202

DOI: 10.1017/9781009338219

First published 2024

A catalogue record for this publication is available from the British Library.

Library of Congress Cataloging-in-Publication Data
Names: Chua, Lynette J., editor. | Massoud, Mark Fathi, editor.
Title: Out of place : fieldwork and positionality in law and society / edited by Lynette J. Chua, National University of Singapore, Mark Fathi Massoud, University of California Santa Cruz.
Description: Cambridge, United Kingdom ; New York, NY, USA : Cambridge University Press, 2024. | Includes index.
Identifiers: LCCN 2023029658 (print) | LCCN 2023029659 (ebook) | ISBN 9781009338202 (hardback) | ISBN 9781009338226 (paperback) | ISBN 9781009338219 (ebook)
Subjects: LCSH: Sociological jurisprudence. | Ethnological jurisprudence. | Vulnerability (Personality trait)
Classification: LCC K376 .O98 2023 (print) | LCC K376 (ebook) | DDC 340/.115–dc23/eng/20230929
LC record available at https://lccn.loc.gov/2023029658
LC ebook record available at https://lccn.loc.gov/2023029659

ISBN 978-1-009-33820-2 Hardback

Cambridge University Press & Assessment has no responsibility for the persistence or accuracy of URLs for external or third-party internet websites referred to in this publication and does not guarantee that any content on such websites is, or will remain, accurate or appropriate.

Ξένος ὢν ἴσθι. (Appreciate when you are an outsider.)
—Inscription at the inner chamber of the Temple of
Apollo, 650 B.C.E.

不識廬山真面目
只緣身·在此山中
(You cannot know the real face of Mountain Lu when
you are inside it.)
—蘇軾《題西林壁》

It does not seem important or even desirable to be
"right" and in place … Better to wander out of
place … and not ever to feel too much at
home anywhere.
—Edward W. Said, *Out of Place: A Memoir*

CONTENTS

CONTENTS

CONTRIBUTORS

Leisy J. Abrego is professor in Chicana/o and Central American Studies at the University of California, Los Angeles. She is the author of *Sacrificing Families: Navigating Laws, Labor, and Love Across Borders* (2014) and coeditor of *We Are Not Dreamers: Undocumented Scholars Theorize Undocumented Life in the United States* (2020).

Swethaa S. Ballakrishnen is professor of law at the University of California, Irvine. They are the author of *Accidental Feminism: Gender Parity and Selective Mobility among India's Professional Elite* (2021), coauthor of *Gender Regimes and the Politics of Privacy* (2021), and coeditor of *Invisible Institutionalisms: Collective Reflections on the Shadows of Legal Globalisation* (2021).

Pratiksha Baxi is associate professor at the Centre for the Study of Law and Governance, Jawaharlal Nehru University. She is the author of *Public Secrets of Law: Rape Trials in India* (2014).

Keebet von Benda-Beckmann (1946–2022) was professor emeritus at Martin Luther University Halle/Wittenberg, associate at the Max Planck Institute for Social Anthropology in Halle, and affiliated fellow of the Van Vollenhoven Institute for Law and Development at Leiden University. She was the coauthor of *Political and Legal Transformations of an Indonesian Polity: The Nagari from Colonisation to Decentralisation* (2013).

Margaret L. Boittin is assistant professor at Osgoode Hall Law School, York University. She is the author of *The Regulation of Prostitution in China: Law in the Everyday Lives of Sex Workers, Police Officers, and Public Health Officials* (2024).

Lynette J. Chua is professor of law at National University of Singapore. She is the author of *The Politics of Rights and Southeast Asia* (2022), *The Politics of Love in Myanmar: LGBT Mobilization and Human Rights as A Way of Life* (2019), and *Mobilizing Gay Singapore: Rights and*

Resistance in an Authoritarian State (2014), and is coeditor of *The Asian Law & Society Reader* (2023).

Luis Eslava is research professorial chair of international law at La Trobe University and professor of international law at the University of Kent. He is the author of *Local Space, Global Life: The Everyday Operation of International Law and Development* (2015), and coeditor of *Bandung, Global History, and International Law: Critical Pasts, Pending Futures* (2017) and the *Oxford Handbook on International Law and Development* (2023).

Mark Fathi Massoud is professor of politics and director of legal studies at the University of California, Santa Cruz, and visiting professor at the University of Oxford Faculty of Law. He is the author of *Shari'a, Inshallah: Finding God in Somali Legal Politics* (2021) and *Law's Fragile State: Colonial, Authoritarian, and Humanitarian Legacies in Sudan* (2013).

Sindiso Mnisi Weeks is associate professor of legal studies and political science at the University of Massachusetts, Amherst. She is the author of *Access to Justice and Human Security: Cultural Contradictions in Rural South Africa* (2018) and coauthor of *African Customary Law in South Africa: Post-Apartheid and Living Law Perspectives* (2015).

PREFACE

Positionality in research refers to the disclosure of how an author's self-identifications, experiences, and privileges influence research methods. A statement of positionality in a research article or other publication can enhance the validity of its empirical data as well as its theoretical contribution. However, such self-disclosure puts scholars in a vulnerable position, and those most likely to reveal how their positionality shapes their research are women, ethnic minorities, or both. At this stage of the field's methodological development, the burdens of positionality are being carried unevenly by a tiny minority of researchers. In this book, we spotlight a group of scholars from around the world who shaped the field of law and society through their intentional awareness of how their self-identifications, experiences of marginalization, and professional privileges influenced their research questions, design, methods, and writing about the law. The results of the challenging fieldwork that they conducted have been published elsewhere. In this book, they explain how their experiences of marginality and privilege shaped those influential contributions to the field of law and society.[1]

The authors of the chapters that follow have conducted research on law and society in various places in Australia, China, Colombia, Egypt, India, Indonesia, Myanmar, the Netherlands, Singapore, Somalia and Somaliland, South Africa, South Sudan, Sudan, Taiwan, Thailand, the United Kingdom, the United States, and Vietnam. Their research changed them during their fieldwork and across decades-long careers. As they changed, they approached law and society research differently. They learned to embrace the hard places – both inside and outside – that their research took them, and the surprises that they found in the law, including in the ways it sometimes changes society and sometimes does not. Their experiences are an invitation to all law and society

---

[1] Though "law and society" and "socio-legal studies" have different emphases in different contexts, this book uses the terms interchangeably.

scholars to consider the hard places that we have come from and gone to and how those places have shaped the meanings that we give to the law, how we study the law, and our understanding of law's claims to authority. The authors explain how they work through contradictory ideas, identities, and impulses, and in so doing they challenge the pull toward disciplinary assimilation in law and the social sciences.

In researching and writing this book we learned about the importance of embracing confusion – as well as our conditional and out-of-place identities – especially in places where absolutes seem most efficient or required. Legal research and social science scholarship both traditionally rejected the aphorism that what one sees depends on where one sits. But the scholars in this book specify where they sit precisely to share what and how they see. They show that life at the margins of a place or a disciplinary field – an "out of place" positionality – allows them to see what those at the center may not see. They are outsiders looking in, bringing fresh ideas from their fieldwork in different political contexts. This cultural turn – a subjective turn – has taken place in legal scholarship, journalism, and across the social sciences. It has created space for authors to reflect on themselves and, for some of them, to insert themselves, their backgrounds, and their experiences into their work. They are methodologically self-conscious, bridging rigorous empirical analysis and a commitment to justice. And when law and society scholars do this, they are transforming the field.

* * *

Out of Place began as a conversation between the editors about how doing fieldwork has enhanced our contributions to the study of law and our lives as individuals. We could not have considered this project without experiencing the kindness of hundreds of people who gave us their time during our own fieldwork. We also could not have completed this project without being inspired by the law and society scholars who bring their fieldwork and positionality into this book: Leisy Abrego, Swethaa S. Ballakrishnen, Pratiksha Baxi, Keebet von Benda-Beckmann, Margaret L. Boittin, Luis Eslava, and Sindiso Mnisi Weeks.

We presented earlier versions of this project at workshops we organized at National University of Singapore and the annual meeting of the Law and Society Association, where we benefitted from the insights of Penelope Andrews, Amr Shalakany, and Kathryne Young. Massoud also presented earlier versions of Chapter 1 at All Souls College

(University of Oxford), the American Bar Foundation, the University of British Columbia Faculty of Law, the UC Santa Barbara Legal Humanities Initiative, the UC Santa Cruz Center for Cultural Studies, and at the "Challenging Socio-Legal Methodology" workshop coorganized by the Cardiff University Centre of Law and Society and the University of Oxford Centre for Socio-Legal Studies. Massoud, with Sindiso Mnisi Weeks, organized a workshop, "Out of Place," held at the University of Cape Town. Elements of the Preface and Chapter 1 draw on Massoud's "The Price of Positionality" (*Journal of Law and Society*, 2022).

Funding for research, writing, and a contributors' workshop came from the Singapore Ministry of Education Academic Research Fund Tier 1 [WBS: R-241-000-176-115]. We received supplementary funding from the JY Pillay Global Asia Programme at Yale–NUS College [WBS: E-607-02-0013-01]. Chua thanks Nur Ridhuan bin Abu Baker for assistance, and Wendy Wee and Kris Zhao at the Faculty of Law, National University of Singapore, for administrative support. Massoud thanks the UC Santa Cruz Institute for Social Transformation for research support and Hardeep Dhillon for research assistance. Leisy Abrego, Rachel Cahill O'Callaghan, Patrick Chuang, Vilashini Cooppan, Malcolm M. Feeley, Adam Millard-Ball, Linda Mulcahy, Tom Pyun, and the *Out of Place* contributors provided helpful feedback. Danielle McClellan and Ian Pickett copyedited the manuscript. We thank Matt Gallaway, our editor at Cambridge University Press, as well as Jens Meierhenrich and Rachel E. Stern of the Cambridge Studies in Law and Society. Our colleagues and students at UC Santa Cruz and National University of Singapore provided welcoming spaces for us to research, write, and teach. This book would not have been possible without the kindness of the colleagues, friends, and mentors who shared their experiences with us, including Keebet von Benda-Beckmann (1946–2022).

Lynette J. Chua and Mark Fathi Massoud

CHAPTER ONE

INTRODUCTION
The Power of Positionality
Mark Fathi Massoud

> *Know yourself [because] it is the beginning of all wisdom.*
> – Aristotle

I felt anxiety deep in my stomach as I entered the law professor's office for my tenure-track job interview.[1] It was 2008. I had recently completed my doctorate, and this meeting with a full professor who was also a leading scholar in my field would be pivotal. A "no" vote from him would end my candidacy. I sat across from him, an older white man, ready to discuss my research on human rights. He peppered me with questions about my background, the circumstances surrounding my immigration from Sudan to the United States (US), my childhood experiences, the languages that I spoke growing up, the places that my parents or I had lived, and other personal matters. By the time the interview ended, I had been invited to speak neither about my qualifications – my reasons for applying, my teaching experience, my job talk, my book manuscript – nor about my research and leadership plans were I to be hired. As a lawyer, I knew his direct questions about ethnicity, language, and national origin were prohibited by US employment law and fair hiring practices,[2] but because I was new to the field, needed a job, and wanted to make a good impression, I answered all of them.

---

[1] Elements of this chapter draw on Massoud (2022).
[2] Title VII of the United States Civil Rights Act of 1964 (*29 CFR Part 1601*) prohibits employers from discriminating on the basis of race, color, religion, sex, and national origin.

1

Alone later that night, I cried – not only because I had not wanted to talk about personal matters with this man, but also because I had felt powerless to assert my rights. My vulnerability and fear of not being accepted and not getting a job had replaced my academic preparation and legal training. Though austerity measures led the law faculty to stop this search without hiring anyone, my experience at the interview taught me how scholars exert authority over one another. Asking questions may be a benign way to get to know people in ethnically diverse societies, but it can also spotlight the class and racial privileges that sustain intellectual, socioeconomic, and cultural hierarchies.

Some of us feel like outsiders in our research sites and in academia; both are places dominated by people who do not share our backgrounds. We may find ourselves "out of place" by virtue of our social marginality, unique professional privileges, or both. As this book shows, being out of place – and reflecting on this subject position transparently – provides benefits to law and society scholarship, but it also places burdens on the researchers themselves.

Out of place scholars are typically minorities – through their class background, ethnicity, gender, physical ability, religious beliefs, sexual orientation, and so on. These scholars may find law's power dominated or usurped by able-bodied, gender-normative, heteronormative, and/or majority ethnic or religious populations, often backgrounds and identities to which they do not belong. Feelings of isolation in fieldwork sometimes grow stronger in the academy. Being or feeling different from the majority in a research site or an academic field can compel out of place scholars to think carefully about how their personal backgrounds and experiences shape their research.

Consider the influence of a US Supreme Court nominee's background – their class, gender, race, upbringing, or schooling – in debates over their appointment. Taking a judge's personal background into account is a recognition that factors related to identity and unrelated to legal doctrine shape judicial decisions. Likewise, good lawyering involves using skills learned from law school – such as interpreting precedent, evaluating evidence, and following procedures – and skills learned from life experience. Lawyers unable to recognize how clients, judges, and jurors perceive them are going to struggle. In law and society scholarship, bringing the personal to bear on the research clarifies – or entirely blurs – the boundaries between law, politics, and power.

Academic writing, particularly in the social sciences, was built on the idea of outsiders looking in. However, due to structural inequalities, some people never had the privilege of joining academia because of their class, gender, race, or other minority status, and some of the people who became successful scholars could not share their outsider status. The social theorist Robert Merton, for instance, was born Meyer Schkolnick; he anglicized his name in the early twentieth century during a time when Jewish immigrants faced exclusion from American universities, businesses, and social institutions (Snell 2006). Decades later, a cultural turn in American writing led journalists and scholars to give greater attention to positioning their self-identifications, experiences of marginalization, or professional privileges. The prevalent term for this is "positionality," though several other terms, including "reflexivity" and "standpoint," are also used to refer to similar concepts. While these terms have different genealogies, I see them as interchangeable ways of naming the phenomenon of opening up one's self-identifications – rather than only one's ideas – to criticism.

Scholars of literary theory have labeled this intimate connection between one's lived experiences and theoretical contributions as "autotheory." To them, autotheory is about expressing something that was once inexpressible, including about one's physical body – "the personal made public," as Maggie Nelson discusses it in *The Argonauts* (Nelson 2015, 60). Writing with the self, to Nelson, is both a form of protection and a signal of belonging. For the postcolonial and critical race theorist Vilashini Cooppan, turning to our most intimate sources of knowledge – thinking autotheoretically by connecting ourselves to the arguments that we make – allows us "to think *with* the I, not merely *as* the I" (Cooppan 2021, 587). For Cooppan, recognition of the self is a form of reparation for longstanding social and legal inequalities. It is a starting point for long-run social and legal change in which "a long debt of nonrecognition, historical unseeing, political unresponsivity, closed ears and eyes and hearts, is coming due" (602). Consider the legal scholar Patricia Williams, whose first-person accounts of social marginalization based on gender, race, and class shaped a generation of critical race theory on law's shortcomings (Williams 1991). Consider also the literary historian Saidiya Hartman, who argues that using autobiographical examples as data "is not about navel gazing, it's ... about trying to look at ... one's own formation as a window onto social and historical processes, as an example of them" (Saunders 2008, 5). Conveying personal experiences puts scholars in a vulnerable position,

3

making research and writing more difficult. Such exposure also sparks a rebellion against academic traditions built on a pretense of neutrality – and legal rules built on a pretense of impartiality.

Understanding the conditions under which research creates useful knowledge, and how researchers themselves influence their research, are questions that are as old as the social sciences themselves. This book adds to these questions a distinct and powerful dimension of positionality: one's marginal social position, and the benefits and burdens associated with it. One's sense of marginality may change across places and times. A scholar's ethnic identity may be minoritized in some contexts but not in others, or a working-class immigrant kid may grow up to become a celebrated intellectual employed by a wealthy university. Feeling marginal even in one context of our lives, as all of us do to varying degrees, has important consequences for our research anywhere. Centering a researcher's marginality – their "outsider within status" – adds "excitement to creativity" and enriches academic debate (Collins 1986, S15). My own study (Massoud 2022) of positionality statements appearing in law and society journals found that researchers who occupy marginalized social positions are the most likely ones to be sharing positionality; moreover, many of these marginalized researchers' positionality statements explain how their privileges, and not their marginalization, influenced their research.

To address the connections between positionality, research methods, and law's power, this book brings together a globally diverse group of law and society scholars who share a marginalized, or out of place, positionality in their research. In the chapters that follow, they explain how their identities, backgrounds, and experiences transformed their research and themselves, during and after fieldwork, and across some-times decades-long careers. They discuss what they learned about the law by virtue of being and working out of place.

Out of Place offers an antidote to those who see law as a set of abstract rules. Positionality shifts attention from the rules to the people who create, enforce, and are subjected to them. This transformation – putting people first in legal studies – increases empathy for research subjects and other researchers. The authors of the chapters that follow have honed these skills. They share their experiences to help early career scholars who are embarking on empirical projects and estab-lished scholars who are retooling their own research. *Out of Place* is designed to encourage collective and transparent self-reflection on positionality and, specifically, marginalization – and to give hope to a rising generation of law and society scholars who may be different from the field's founders in fundamental ways.

A FIELD BORN OUT OF PLACE

If there is any canon that the field of law and society has created since the mid-twentieth century, it is a methodological one. This is because law and society researchers study how the law shapes society often by borrowing or enhancing research methods found in the disciplinary traditions of the humanities and social sciences. Grounded research – traveling to a place to conduct fieldwork, historical research, or interviews – shaped much of our interdisciplinary field's foundation.[3] But this kind of research also shapes law and society scholars as teachers, colleagues, and mentors.

The interdisciplinary field of law and society was born of efforts to connect empirical data with legal studies, often alongside a commitment to addressing inequality. In the US, law and society began as a field of outsiders who felt marginalized by their academic disciplines. The field also grew separately, and earlier, outside of the US. Founded in the 1940s, Japan's law and society association may be the first of its kind. Scholars in Australia, Brazil, China, Egypt, France, India, Indonesia, Mexico, South Africa, and the UK, among other places, have also been producing decades of law and society scholarship. The field's pioneers worked around the world in rapidly changing legal, political, and economic contexts. They distinguished themselves from their law faculty colleagues who were making their careers studying legal doctrine. In other words, law and society scholarship began as an effort by people from different disciplines and in different parts of the world who were professionally out of place and who promoted the benefits of leaving their offices – going out of place – to conduct research.

In the US, many in the first generation of law and society scholars were motivated by a shared desire "to create a more humane, egalitarian society" (Kennedy and Klare 1984, 461). But they also did not write of themselves as fundamentally a group of white men who held significant professional privilege. As the law and society scholar Laura Gómez

---

[3] Political scientists define fieldwork as the purposeful, deliberate, and site-intensive pursuit of "data, information, or insights" (Kapiszewski, MacLean, and Read 2015, 8). Scholars have done fieldwork in-person and virtually (Boellstorff 2008).

noted, the field's "founding generation included no people of color and only three White women – at least partly a reflection of the gender and racial makeup of the professoriat at the time" (Gómez 2012, 222–3). Similarly, nearly all of the twenty-one foundational, "well-known and well-regarded Law and Society research projects" featured in a recent textbook were conducted by white men (Halliday and Schmidt 2009, 7). In this context, explicitly reflecting on positionality would perhaps be too obvious; as Gómez explained, the field's composition meant that US-based scholars of law and society were largely presumed to be white and cisgender male.

Law and society scholars are, of course, more diverse than the pioneering generation, inside and outside the US. Among this new generation are scholars who occupy marginal social positions and who are sharing their positionality. Doing so provides many benefits. It can establish an author's credibility in cases where insider knowledge may be of particular value, such as when a person from a given place, who speaks the local dialect, studies its legal history or legal system. Reflecting on one's positionality can also be a form of knowledge production. It can help scholars to find their inner wisdom, and it can build community among researchers and between researchers and their research subjects, particularly among scholars who identify as members of under-represented or minoritized groups. It can facilitate more open discussion about how racial oppression, gender-based discrimination, and socioeconomic privileges shape research methods and career paths, which creates space for a more diverse generation of scholars to participate in law and society, and to influence the field's development.

However, while positionality provides significant benefits, it comes at a price. When an author consciously blurs the boundaries between the personal and the professional by inserting their experiences into their scholarly work, they open up their ideas and *themselves* to criticism and harm (Medzani 2021; Miled 2019; Galam 2015). That harm may include the devaluation of the scholarly content of the work because, for example, it is therefore presumed not to meet social science standards of neutrality or objectivity. Positionality also requires emotional labor. In some cases, scholars communicate painful memories to their research subjects, reviewers, and readers (Gustafson 2011; Hirsch 2008). Doing so may cause discomfort or – when a scholar is regularly asked to represent and speak about their gender identity or ethnic background rather than their scholarship – exhaustion. At the extreme, researchers who have experienced physical or psychological trauma may retraumatize themselves by retelling their suffering. These harms disproportionately affect historically marginalized groups in academia, including women and people of color.

Moreover, these harms do not merely accrue when marginalized scholars speak about their own positionality; they also accrue when scholars from majority populations do not speak about theirs, because that omission renders positionality peripheral to mainstream law and society scholarship. Normalizing positionality, especially out of place positionality, will involve all scholars in law and society considering how their identities, class backgrounds, and professional privileges shape their motivations, questions, methods, and findings.

In the field of law and society, out of place scholars who are women, ethnic minorities, or both have unevenly carried the burdens of positionality. To provide evidence for this argument, this Introduction proceeds as follows. First, I discuss the benefits of open and principled discussion of positionality, drawing on existing law and society scholarship, including my own. Second, based on a longitudinal empirical study I conducted of positionality in two of the field's oldest journals, I assess who has written about positionality and how and why they have written about it. Third, I reflect upon the costs, particularly for marginalized populations, of disclosing the influence of identities on research and writing. Fourth, I provide an overview of this book and give attention to how an out of place positionality has been building hope for a new generation of law and society scholarship. I conclude by encouraging law and society scholars of all backgrounds to adopt a "position sensibility" by examining and explaining how their own self-identifications, privileges, or experiences shape and challenge research methods.

THE BENEFITS OF POSITIONALITY

Law and society researchers who use empirical methods – particularly qualitative methods such as ethnographic fieldwork, participant observation, and interviews – often invite vulnerable persons to share their backgrounds, emotions, and experiences. Empirical research may therefore involve unequal power relations, especially if researchers reveal little to nothing about themselves while their subjects share intimate stories in order to help the researchers (Rios 2011). Becoming self-aware about their own positionality is a first step that researchers can take towards rectifying this imbalance and building stronger social science methods.

As scholars, our class, educational training, group experience, and membership in minoritized or non-minoritized groups create "cultural frames" through which we ask questions and analyze data (Bell 2016, 320, citing Goffman 1974). Feminist and critical race scholars have argued that it is fundamental to consider how the standpoints of scholars who are members of non-privileged groups influence their approaches to studying law's systemic inequalities.[4] Scholars of intersectionality have shown how people experience multiple, overlapping forms of marginalization – which create privilege in some ways but not in others – depending on their citizenship, class, educational attainment, gender, gender identity, physical abilities, professional position, race, and sexual orientation (Crenshaw 2011, 1991). Building on this feminist and intersectional scholarship, this section outlines five primary benefits of communicating an out of place positionality: establishing connection and credibility, challenging structures of oppression, opening up social science, empowering communities, and communicating privileges.

Establishing Connection and Credibility
Explaining one's positionality allows a reader to understand how data were gathered, who agreed to talk to the researcher, and why they did so. At the beginning of my book, *Law's Fragile State*, I recount how my own background helped me to "build rapport among attorneys, judges, and local activists, who told me they were pleased to see a young man – whose family fled the country never to return – himself come home" to do fieldwork in Sudan (Massoud 2013). Similarly, in my book, *Shari'a, Inshallah*, which was based on fieldwork in the Somali regions of the Horn of Africa, I explained that as an Arab from neighboring Sudan, I felt "welcomed by Somalis who called me their cousin" (Massoud 2021). Though I had prior experience of Sudan and not of Somalia and Somaliland, I thought that it was important to disclose how my self-identification influenced research access at the outset of both books, since their findings are based in part on fieldwork and interviews that I conducted. Likewise, in her article about qualitative research,

---

[4] The feminist and critical race judgments projects offer rewritings of judicial opinions from feminist and racial justice perspectives to show how courts shape law's systemic inequalities (Hunter 2015; Capers, et. al. 2022).

Elizabeth Hoffmann writes that building a "personal connection" with interviewees as well as with readers can help to establish trust and credibility, such as "a divorced mom studying divorced moms ... a female construction worker-turned-sociologist studying women construction workers ... or a law professor studying law students" (Hoffmann 2007, 329, citing Arendell 1997, Paap 2006, and Granfield 1992).

Announcing her positionality at the start of her book *In the Moment of Greatest Calamity: Terrorism, Grief, and a Victim's Quest for Justice*, legal anthropologist Susan Hirsch explains that she studied and participated in legal cases about the 1998 East African embassy bombings, which she had survived. Hirsch sets out to connect with readers by explaining that she writes,

> as [both] an American survivor and the widow of an African victim. I also write from the perspective of a cultural anthropologist ... The book describes my attempts to come to terms with a massive personal and public tragedy ... Above all, I wrote this book to convey my perspective as a victim who turned to law for a response to terrorism and found it as flawed as it was indispensable.
>
> (Hirsch 2008, xv)

The affective nature of Hirsch's opening statements underscores the potential power of positionality. Situating personal experience in relation to empirical research may increase the writer's authority on the topic and help readers to connect with the work at multiple levels: intellectually, professionally, and personally.

Challenging Structures of Oppression

Personal stories challenge oppression, such as when survivors of sexual assault share their stories with policymakers in order to improve laws designed to protect people from gender-based violence (Goodwin 2021; Kershner 2021; Randall 2010). These stories often recount violence that people have suffered because of their perceived race, gender, class, religion, disability, sexual orientation, or other identifications. For this reason, scholars of identity politics have seen such identifications as more than the "descriptive categories of identity applied to individuals"; they are also "elements of social structure [that] emerge as fundamental devices that foster inequality resulting in groups" (Collins 1997, 376).

Communicating our own identifications can challenge structures of inequality and the imperial legacies of academic disciplines. As a graduate student doing fieldwork in the context of Sudan's dictatorship, I gathered hidden, sensitive data on the legal profession from "the dusty bottoms of locked file cabinets" because I was able to connect with open-minded government officials in whose offices those data were kept (Massoud 2013, 235). Socio-legal scholar Nadera Shalhoub-Kevorkian challenges power structures in a different way, by writing about how Israeli settler colonialism influenced not only the arguments in her book *Security Theology, Surveillance and the Politics of Fear*, but also her life as a Palestinian. She wrote the book's preface amid Israeli military bombardments in Gaza in 2014, and in it she reflects on the support that she received from Palestinian family and friends "in spite of all the dispossession around me" (Shalhoub-Kevorkian 2015, p. x). Acknowledging the Palestinian struggle was "the only way," Shalhoub-Kevorkian writes, "to challenge the political economy of war" (Ibid.). Her experience of colonization strengthens her argument about how the law facilitates the Israeli government's surveillance of Palestinians. As Swethaa Ballakrishnen and Sara Dezalay (2021, 5) contend in the introduction to *Invisible Institutionalisms*, "the *reflexivity* of each ... allow[s] for the *dialogue of all*."

Opening Up Social Science
Some social scientists have called on scholars who use qualitative methods to adhere to standards of objectivity, impartiality, and neutrality (King, Keohane, and Verba 1994). These standards grew out of quantitative epistemologies, and they are reified in law. However, a growing number of feminist and critical race scholars have challenged these standards because of the difficulty of cordoning interpretation off from the influence of life experiences, identities, and commitments (Ballakrishnen and Dezalay 2021; Shaw et al. 2020; Gherardi and Turner 2002; Wasserfall 1993; see also the interview with Michael McCann in Halliday and Schmidt 2009). Some of these scholars contend that research relies on interpretation, which itself is shaped by the social, economic, and cultural status of the interpreter. Reflecting on her fieldwork in US military schools, Taylor Paige Winfield writes:

> It is impossible [for an investigator] to fully remove any bias or projection, but the more investigators learn to pay attention to their inner emotions and thoughts, the better they will be able to separate them out from the participants ... and avoid reproducing the "objectifying and imperialist gaze" associated with traditional Western qualitative methods.
>
> (Winfield 2022, 11, citing Kincheloe et al. 2017)

Positionality opens up new forms of social science when scholars index their power relations, showing how they may interpret data via their experiences, privileges, or membership in minoritized groups. In that regard, positionality statements may serve as a bridge between two epistemological areas of law and society scholarship: social-science positivism and critical postmodernism (Cotterrell 2004; Burawoy 1998).[5]

Consider Kaaryn Gustafson, a US law professor who understood that she could not appear neutral during her research interviewing indigent Black mothers receiving welfare payments in California (Gustafson 2011, n. 8). Gustafson is a Black woman who uses a wheelchair, and while conducting fieldwork she was either pregnant or carrying her infant child with her (193). In the methodological appendix to her book *Cheating Welfare: Public Assistance and the Criminalization of Poverty*, Gustafson writes about how her "status ambiguity" prompted the Black American mothers whom she met to deem her nonthreatening. They volunteered personal information to her, sometimes thinking that she could not form a negative judgment of them because of how they viewed her (195). Gustafson sensitizes the reader to the experience of vulnerability. We see her not as an impersonal scholar conducting interviews or reviewing transcripts, but instead as an impassioned interlocutor trying to help readers to appreciate that the tradition of distant objectivity does not fully capture her experience.

Empowering Communities

Some academics write to influence theories or policies. Others write to connect with communities of support that help them to process their own or others' experiences. Such self-awareness often remains unarticulated in mainstream law and society scholarship, which may leave many scholars who see their writing not simply as professional work, but also as a personal and political commitment, feeling out of place. For these scholars, writing about positionality helps them to gain inner strength while they signal their support to other marginalized scholars.

Revealing one's own vulnerabilities can affect empirical work by bringing these concerns to the fore and legitimizing different

---

[5] Philip Selznick, one of the field's US pioneers, reflected in the years before his death on the tension, in law and society scholarship, between positivism on the one hand and what he labeled "a certain amount of postmodern fragmentation and indulgence and lack of coherence" on the other (Cotterrell 2004, 317).

perspectives. Empowerment and community building may begin with sharing experiences of harassment, racism, loneliness, misgendering, presumed incompetence, and "acting white," the majority race of leading North American and European law and society scholars. Such self-revelation ensures that people who might feel similarly also do not feel alone. As a Black woman socio-legal scholar told me while I was researching positionality, "We write our way out of the trauma of our experiences ... not just to help others but partly to help ourselves."[6]

Communicating Privileges

Positionality does not only involve disclosing how our marginalization may have influenced our work; equally important is revealing how our social, economic, or cultural privileges shape the questions that we ask and how we answer them. Our identities are part of the toolkit that we carry with us into theory generation and data-analysis (Reyes 2020). Just as those whom we study use their own "bag of tricks" to guide their interactions with the legal system, reflecting on how we influence and are influenced by our data means understanding the "cultural repertoires" that guide our actions as researchers (Bell 2016, 316–17). These repertoires take shape through the privileges that our perceived identities and insider or outsider status afford to us. Reflecting on his own privileges after a half-century of work, legal scholar Marc Galanter wrote that he started out as "a mid-twentieth-century, middle-class, white American" when he first traveled from the US to India in the 1950s to study its legal system. There, he got what he called his "second legal education" as he turned his academic gaze back onto the US from India to see US law as "wild and unexpected" (Galanter 2021, ix–x).

A researcher's status as an outsider, particularly while conducting fieldwork, may bestow class, gender, or racial privilege. When I did research in South Sudan, my position as an outsider from a US university facilitated meetings with government ministers, judges, diplomats, and United Nations officials, which allowed me to gather data across political and cultural lines (Massoud 2015). Lynette Chua writes, in *The Politics of Love in Myanmar*, that she likewise "embraced" her privilege as a foreigner there, which allowed her to ask "what might have been obvious or stupid questions to ... insiders" while researching

---

[6] Though wishing to remain anonymous, this person gave me consent to publish this quote.

her book on Burmese lesbian rights activism (Chua 2019, 146). Chua says that she was prone to asking "stupid questions" because she was not Burmese and did not identify as a member of the lesbian, gay, bisexual, and trans (LGBT) community. Her outsider status made people comfortable opening up to her and helped her to see events and understand discourses at multiple registers, including as both an empathetic observer and a scholarly interlocutor.

It is difficult to consider, reveal, and describe how class, gender, racial, or other privileges influence our research, and it takes extra skill to explain the uncertainty, pain, and messiness of research processes (Whittingdale 2021; Smith 2021; Halliday and Schmidt 2009). When a researcher candidly discusses their own positionality, their vulnerability can remove the boundaries between the researcher and their research subjects and readers. Of course, it is not likely that positionality statements alone will dismantle the barriers that sustain inequality inside and outside of academia. However, articulating our positionality in print is a step towards explicitly recognizing how these restrictions built the field and whether our research benefits from such barriers or breaks them down.

WHO IS OUT OF PLACE?

The scholars who wrote the chapters that follow have done the hard work of expressing positionality. They draw on their experiences of marginalization, making their vulnerability into a strength. They have placed their trust in Chua and me as the volume editors and in you as the reader. Given the benefits that accrue to the field when scholars disclose their self-identifications, marginalization, and privileges, it would seem to make sense for scholars to do so regularly in their published work. However, this is not yet the case. In fact, as this section will show, at least on the pages of the field's two oldest academic journals, only a small minority of socio-legal scholars actually risk revealing themselves in this manner. Kathleen Blee's assertion that positionality "is often erased from written accounts" of research findings is as empirically true in the 2020s – at least in the field of law and society, one that connects law and social science to social justice – as it was in the 1990s when she wrote it (Blee 1998, 383, cited in Hoffmann 2007, 326). Even more troubling is that the scholars who do write about positionality are overwhelmingly women and ethnic minorities – in other words, those who are also the most likely to be marginalized in the field.

13

To find direct reference to positionality, I analyzed the first fifty-six volumes of the *Law & Society Review* (*LSR*) from 1966 through 2022, and the first forty-nine volumes of the *Journal of Law and Society* (*JLS*) from 1974 through 2022. Together, these are two of the oldest English-language socio-legal studies journals in the world. The *LSR* is the oldest; it is the flagship journal of the LSA. The *JLS* is the longest-established law and society journal in the United Kingdom (UK); it has connections with the UK-based Socio-Legal Studies Association. The results of my study of these two journals provide a baseline for assessing positionality in other law and society journals as well as in books, which necessarily have more space. What I found testifies to the fact that nearly all authors writing for these journals over half a century – to echo the searing words of Edward Said – "were or tried to be cut from the same cloth" (Said 1999, 274).[7]

I searched across all digitized articles from both journals for prominent words used to identify positionality (Table 1.1, see also Wasserfall 1993; Roberts and Sanders 2005; Huisman 2008).[8] In total, I found 28 articles, by 36 authors, that discuss researcher positionality.[9] The authors' racial and gender self-identifications are striking: 22 of the 36 authors identify as white women, nine as women of color, three as men of color, and two as white men. That is to say, women and people of color authored all but two of the 28 articles discussing positionality. Many of them are also minoritized as working class, disabled,

---

[7] As asserted in the *LSR* in 2007, "Assessments ... of grounded theory and theoretical reflexivity ... typically receive some coverage in the better research methods textbooks ... but are seldom, if ever, discussed in ... the field of sociolegal studies" (Treviño 2007, 493).

[8] My initial results, published in Massoud (2022), covered through the third issue of 2021 of both journals and yielded 23 articles that discussed positionality or my related search terms. Since that time, I conducted a new search of the articles published from the fourth issue of 2021 through the fourth issue of 2022. This search uncovered five additional articles – three in the *JLS* and two in the *LSR* – that discuss positionality or my related search terms (Foster and Hirst 2022; Gonzalez, Simon, and Rogers 2022; Leckey 2022; Bunting, Tasker, and Lockhart 2021; Hunter, Roach Anleu, and Mack 2021).

[9] Three papers have three authors identifying their positionalities, three papers have two authors, and one author wrote two of the papers. I excluded various genres – such as presidential addresses and responses; special issues on methods; articles commemorating a scholar's birthday, retirement, or death; and essays in which senior scholars look back on their careers – because these works were meant to provide personal reflections. I also excluded statements describing financial or other conflicts of interest.

TABLE 1.1   Search terms for positionality statements from two
peer-reviewed law and society journals, 1966–2022

Round	Search terms
1	positionality reflexive/reflexivity I identify as my position/identity
2	my class/disability/ethnic/ethnicity/gender/race/racial/sexual/ status as as a(n) African/Arab/Asian/Black/Latino/Latina/Latinx/ethnic/ Muslim/white/non-white/disabled/female/woman/man/male/lesbian/ gay/bisexual/trans/queer/heterosexual/researcher of/person of nonbinary gender identity I write as draw(s) on my insider status/as an insider

Source: Massoud 2022.

immigrants, queer persons, non-native English speakers, or first-
generation university graduates.

   While I conducted iterative searches and developed a systematically
generated sample, the dataset is limited by the search terms and the
journals. However, it is likely true that most of the scholars who have
published in the *JLS* and the *LSR*, especially in the early decades of
both journals, were or are white men, so the proportion of women and
minorities who talk about positionality is much higher than the proportion of white men who do so. This effect is compounded by the fact
that our field has historically been dominated by white men.

   While the concept of positionality is younger than both journals, the
term is at least a generation old, having gained prominence in the early
1990s in feminist and critical race scholarship (England 1994;
Awkward 1995). However, about a third of the twenty-eight articles
that refer to positionality or the related search terms were published
since 2020. While this suggests a rising trend, especially in *LSR* where
most of these articles appeared, it is also a trend that remains
profoundly limited.

   In nearly all of these articles, positionality statements focused on
how the researcher's background and identity may have influenced

access to people and places, including by prompting suspicion or trust. For example, in the oldest article, published in 1978, the author mentioned her positionality as a woman in order to dismiss the effects of her gender on her research (Crowe 1978, 226). Many of the more recent articles discussed power relations between researchers and subjects, including how the privilege of holding a university-based appointment influenced the methods (Cownie 2015, Massoud 2015, Powell and Phelps 2021). One of the authors discussed how his identity as a heterosexual male facilitated access to police officers working in a "heteronormative environment" (Sierra-Arévalo 2021, 80). Other authors focused on their marginalization, including one survivor of trauma and another who reported having an "outsider positionality" in the field of law and society because of her professional writing on critical race theory (Houh 2006, 482). One white male author discussed positionality in the context of his race helping him to access white police officers but blocking his access to their Black colleagues. Across all published articles in the *JLS* and the *LSR*, only two have subheadings on positionality: one of these is titled "Methods and Positionality" (Statz 2021, 16) and the other is "Positionalities" (Gonzalez, Simon, and Rogers 2022, 485). The paucity of these direct references to positionality suggests that the overwhelming majority of scholars writing in our field's leading journals, including minoritized scholars, do not discuss their positionality, an imbalance that this book tries to redress.[10]

Some of my own empirically based articles do not discuss positionality, favoring instead an objective, neutral, or dispassionate scholarly voice (Massoud 2020; 2014; 2011). Reflecting with the benefit of

---

[10] With human subjects research approval from the Institutional Review Board of the University of California, Santa Cruz, I asked the first authors of these 28 articles why they discussed positionality. They gave me varying reasons, including, in their words, "explaining ... why I had access to legally vulnerable people," laying bare the "contingent nature of ethnography," equipping readers "with context that enriches their ... interpretation of what the researcher ... heard or did not," and "exposing ... a perceived disrespect of intersectional scholarship." One author said that it would have felt "wildly irresponsible ... not to grapple with my own identity" as a first-generation university graduate from a rural area working with Indigenous communities. Another author said that "being cognizant of my own privilege was extremely important because of the inherited power dynamics and expectations that exist" in qualitative research. Two authors described to me how their peer reviewers had discouraged exploration of positionality, while another said that the journal editors asked for a fuller methods section that addressed positionality.

hindsight, perhaps I had wanted to foreground the stories of the people whom I had met and the theories that my work had generated. Perhaps I had also not wanted to risk exposing myself to criticism, either for being excessively interested in myself or for "going native" – a disparagement that I received from some senior scholars when starting my doctoral dissertation on human rights activists in Sudan, the country of my birth. As a young scholar hoping to enter and influence a large scholarly field, I adhered to the writing conventions that I had seen in the leading journals.[11] However, the empirical writing of a new generation of more diverse scholars is eroding these traditions.

In some cases, the absence of positionality statements may reflect non-qualitative methods since no socio-legal journal exclusively publishes qualitative work. However, there is nothing to suggest that only scholars who use qualitative methods should consider positionality. Class, gender, and racial privilege or marginalization may influence research design, textual interpretation, and quantitative data analysis just as they may influence qualitative research (Soedirgo and Glas 2021). Even so, women and people of color – who presumably have not written the majority of articles published in our field's journals – are vastly over-represented as authors of articles that discuss positionality in both the *JLS* and the *LSR*.

THE BURDENS OF POSITIONALITY

The intentional choice to discuss positionality may elevate a researcher's authority, but it requires emotional energy, hard work, and skill to overcome significant challenges. Building on the empirical data presented above – which shows that very few articles in two leading journals make reference to positionality, and that those that do are authored almost entirely by women and people of color – this section explains some of the burdens associated with positionality. To paraphrase Emily M. S. Houh's (2006) blistering critique of an introductory law and society reader that failed to incorporate a feminist or critical race perspective, if the field's leading journals are meant to create a

[11] The exception is my 2016 essay, "Ideals and Practices in the Rule of Law," featured in a symposium on my book, *Law's Fragile State*. In this essay, I discuss how a lack of diversity – among the authors whom I was assigned to read in graduate school and the places that those authors studied – formed part of my motivation for studying Sudan (Massoud 2016, 491).

canon of law and society scholarship, what messages are these journals conveying through the glaring absence of explicit reflection on positionality? And, as Houh concludes, more importantly, do we care? (491). I care, for one, because the burdens placed on those who disclose positionality are disproportionately carried by the field's minorities.

Creating Anxiety and Reducing Stamina

Even at the best of times it is challenging to research and write clearly. This challenge is even greater for marginalized persons who are asked to consider and communicate their own positionality. Conducting field-work, for instance, necessitates appreciable emotional strength: arranging interviews, becoming a "sympathetic ear," experiencing survivor's guilt, and dealing with respondents who harass or exert other forms of power over gendered, racialized, or minoritized researchers (Hoffmann 2007, 323). Confronting positionality may yet again painfully remind such scholars of microaggressions encountered in their research or of discrimination experienced in their academic lives. At a workshop that I attended on the topic of "surviving" the academy as socio-legal scholars of color, one young woman spoke of the emotional labor that it took for her "just to work safely" because she needed to focus on trying to "avoid getting cornered or touched by" her department head. An Indigenous professor from North America shared powerfully about how the act of communicating in English – though unremarkable to her colleagues – not only feels to her like a "performance of whiteness" but also functions as a painful reminder of the ongoing destruction of her language and the genocide of her people. A Black professor at an Ivy League university spoke about how students waiting outside a locked classroom thought that she was a member of the janitorial staff whose job it was to unlock or clean the classroom for them.[12] These incidents, while not occurring during fieldwork, stay with people. When they are called upon to communicate positionality, marginalized persons open up their distressing memories to others who might take issue with, critique, or reproduce their trauma.

Reflecting on positionality can generate self-doubt and anxieties, especially for minoritized scholars who conduct empirical research. Kaaryn Gustafson, the law professor who interviewed Black American women receiving welfare payments, felt so much discomfort during her

---

[12] These persons gave me their consent to publish these quotes and experiences here.

research that she admitted her "hesitation to pursue similar research in the future" (Gustafson 2011, 197). Maryam S. Khan experienced anxiety as a socio-legal scholar "systematically called upon to redeem Pakistan's theocratic regime to outside audiences," while also being a woman "actively opposed to" the regime's anti-feminist policies (Khan 2021, 147). Susan Hirsch, the legal anthropologist who survived a terrorist attack, wrote that though her discipline's foundational aim is to pursue knowledge "across differences," perceiving the world from both her own and others' perspectives "felt like a heavy burden" because she "lacked the emotional stamina and training" to interview trauma victims, though she herself was one (Hirsch 2008, xvii). Writing this Introduction to *Out of Place* became a source of personal challenge for me because thoughtfully considering my own positionality is not easy. I am not accustomed to doing it. I was not trained to do it. I was trained *not* to do it. Even in a multicultural society, it feels grueling to share experiences of difference or feelings of isolation.

Making Identity More Important than Theory

Asking scholars to write positionality statements risks reifying the "efficient [yet] provisional identities" that we use in the different spaces that we inhabit in our lives (Said 1999, 84). Even when we report the range and complexity of our positionalities, such a statement can feel incomplete – especially when we have to reduce our positionalities into a sentence or two in an article's methods section. It also risks retraining our scholarly lenses onto certain aspects of an author's multifaceted identifications and experiences rather than focusing on their theoretical and empirical contributions.

To explain how audiences may make identity more important than theory, I return to my own professional experience. My books (Massoud 2021, 2013) were each based on deep historical and empirical research, but when I have given talks on these books, my positionality rather than my scholarship has been the focus of some of my interlocutors. I have fielded questions about being from Sudan in relation to my book on Sudan, and questions about not being from Somalia or Somaliland in relation to my book on Somalia and Somaliland. A colleague recently told me that a white male scholar whom she knows had not been asked about his background when he discussed his fieldwork in East Asia, while she had noticed that I was quite often asked about my positionality when discussing my empirical work. More to the point, the questions that he received focused on his scholarship, while I was

19

asked questions about positionality, which was not the focus of my scholarship. In my case but not in his, people's understanding of the data and theoretical intervention was mediated by their desire to understand positionality. More generally, every question that a scholar is asked about their background is a question not asked about their intellectual contribution.

Edward Said discussed this problem as a process of "challenge, recognition, and exposure" that came from people constantly asking him, "What are you?" He eventually learned to answer that he was, simply, "an American" (Said 1999, 84). He did this to avoid opening up himself and others "to the deeply disorganized state of my . . . history and origins" (Said 1999, 5–6). Shortly before his death, he reflected that his life as a Palestinian-American intellectual raised between Jerusalem, Cairo, and New York "meant not only never being quite right [when confronted by the gaze of other scholars], but also never feeling at ease, always expecting to be interrupted or corrected, to have my privacy invaded and my unsure person set upon. [I was] permanently out of place" (Said 1999, 5–6). Some people might be happy to grant that statements of positionality should be irrelevant to scholarly contributions, but such a posture also maintains an academic status quo in which mainstream scholars are silently presumed to be able bodied, heterosexual, upper class, white, and cisgender male.

Challenging Academic Neutrality

Communicating positionality is difficult for marginalized scholars, especially because academic culture is built upon skepticism and critique. Self-reflection calls into doubt the expectations of modern social science. That is, communicating positionality, depending on its specificity, can jeopardize anonymity and cut against the double-blind peer review process that forms the gold standard of anonymity in social science. A massive amount of research shows that implicit or unconscious bias pervades all fields, from corporate hiring to teaching, healthcare delivery, and police behavior, and it is reasonable to presume that peer review in the field of law and society is not immune to undervaluing the contributions of minoritized scholars (Jolls and Sunstein 2006; Kang et al. 2012 Fitzgerald and Hurst 2017; Staats 2016; Brownstein and Saul 2016). Researchers have suggested that peer reviewers in some historically male-dominated fields hold women to higher standards than men, which leads to longer peer review processes and, in the long term, lower pay and promotion rates for women (Hengel 2017).

Attention to insider and outsider status would help some scholars to clarify their research goals to peer reviewers and build knowledge of the challenges associated with scholars' commitments to the people whom they study and the academic spaces where they try to add knowledge (Young 2020).

Disclosing positionality also cuts against efforts in qualitative research to create repositories that store scholars' raw interview data and field notes. While the goal of these repositories is to promote replicability, scholars' unique positionalities may, in part, shape their interpretations.[13] For many scholars, however, positionality is not merely a part of social science methods; it is the central space from which they produce knowledge. Writing with attention to one's position emphasizes both "the discovery of an identity" and a "sense of participation in a movement [that] renders historical what has … been hidden from history" (Scott 1991, 775–6). Recording positionality alongside interview data may open up social science to these new possibilities.

Reproducing Law's Dominance

The act of positioning oneself may be rebellious, but some scholars and activists caution that it risks reinforcing the power that it is meant to challenge. The feminist historian Joan Scott took up this problem, arguing that socially marginalized people risk reproducing dominance when they make their experiences visible. Narrating one's experiences may "essentialize identity and reify the subject" (Scott 1991, 797). It also precludes "critical examination of the workings of the ideological system itself, its categories of representation … as fixed immutable identities, [and] its premises about what these categories mean and how they operate" (778). Categorizing ourselves and others may create insiders and outsiders. While this can legitimize and elevate personal stories, it can also channel power. The result may be a public performance of identity that puts insider solidarity before healthy debate, or that excludes people whose identities, backgrounds, and experiences do not fit neatly into a prescribed category. To address these issues, the political organizer Maurice Mitchell invites us to refocus attention on the ways that concentrations of wealth, institutional power, and cultural privilege create identity and subjectivity (Mitchell 2022).

---

[13] Qualitative Data Repository, https://qdr.syr.edu. For a critique, see Ellett and Massoud 2016.

People express and understand positionality through particular historical, legal, social, and political contexts. To some scholars, the project of essentializing one's identity and experience is dangerously tied to a hegemonic and American way of categorizing people in the world. Identity in the US is often connected to specific legal ideologies and institutions of ascriptive hierarchy coming out of the country's history of racial classification (Smith 1993). This view of positionality that is tied to US legal categories can miss the ways that some formations of marginalization can coexist and change, such as class, disability, ethnicity, gender, immigration and noncitizenship, religion, and rurality. We may not ever be fully coherent intellectually, politically, psychologically, or emotionally at any one point in our lives, or across the sweep of our lives, which makes positionality unstable.

More consequentially, we must consider whether the invitation to write a statement of positionality – if accepted mostly by white women and people of color – risks reifying gendered and racialized hierarchies. That is, are women and scholars of color complicit with existing power structures by performing difference while white men remain unmarked? Many of us have been taught to disregard our actual or perceived differences, or to hide them to the extent that we are able from those whom we determine to be scholars lacking the experience of extreme social marginalization. The invitation to communicate positionality must not become a requirement, which risks reifying difference. Scholars must be free to withhold their stories as well as tell them, and they must not be forced to discuss or apologize for their positionality.

Without sharing ourselves, however, we risk becoming disembodied thinkers limited by the boundaries set around our field by an earlier generation of law and society scholars. We risk disconnecting ourselves from our own lived experiences, marginalization, privileges, and identifications, even as we appropriate the experiences of our research subjects and then distance ourselves from them in the name of objectivity and neutrality. Such disconnection is a sinister parallel to the ways in which law generalizes, exceptionalizes, and separates unusual behavior and persons from everyday experience, obstructing from view our own contexts and communities (McMillan 2020). In other words, we risk reinscribing the forms of oppression that many law and society scholars have set out to critique.

OVERVIEW OF THE BOOK

I have underscored the importance of balancing positionality's costs and benefits. The remainder of this book proceeds with a sense of hopefulness about the place of positionality in the field's methodological development. In the chapters that follow, eight socio-legal scholars consider and connect with their own positionalities. Given the personal nature of their experiences, they each write in their own styles. What unites their chapters is that they each explain how they found themselves to be out of place, how they confronted, understood, and adopted that subject position, and how they shaped their understanding of the law and their contributions to the field by virtue of being out of place. They explain positionality across the lifespan of the research process (Abrego) and its constituent steps, including fieldwork within a specific research site (Mnisi Weeks and Boittin), fieldwork across multiple projects (Chua), long-term fieldwork in courtrooms (Baxi), building theory (Ballakrishnen and Eslava), and multi-sited fieldwork across a multi-decade career (von Benda-Beckmann).

Their work provides three broad lessons about an out of place positionality. First, they never took their identities for granted at any point in the research process. This lesson is important for everyone precisely because, as Ballakrishnen explains in Chapter 7, some of us do not have the luxury of not thinking about our identities. Scholars who write about and discuss positionality, especially those unaccustomed to doing it, must thus do so with care and consideration.

Second, they did not shy away from hybridity and confusion whenever they considered their positionality. Identities and subject positions are conditional. The scholars in this book who used qualitative methods found themselves inside and outside of place in a multiplicity of ways, often simultaneously, and at different points in the research process, all of which is hard to compartmentalize. This can lead to ambiguity and discomfort. However, as their writing shows, being out of place, and accepting that positionality with gratitude, can also create a growing sense of confidence and authority. While being vulnerable is not easy, it is a significant part of the research and writing process.

Third, the authors in this book embraced fluidity, multiplicity, and ambiguity not just in their personal and professional lives but also in the law. Reflecting on identities and experiences created space for these authors to understand how the law constrains or opens identities. Law and society research has long shown that the law does not exist simply

23

in courts or their official records. It exists in people's ordinary consciousness and behavior (Ewick and Silbey 1998). The power of positionality comes when out of place scholars welcome themselves into
spaces where they initially may not have felt welcomed.

The scholars in this book are early career, mid-career, and senior
scholars in the field of law and society. We hold different advanced
degrees in anthropology, law, political science, socio-legal studies, and
sociology. Collectively, we resist the urge to see "outsiderhood [as] a
characteristic way of inventing ... Americanness" (Moore 1987, ix).
We come from and work in at least ten countries on four continents,
and we do fieldwork in other places too. Most of us are also immigrants,
living and working in countries different from those of our births. Four
of us self-identify as women of color, two as white women, two as men
of color, and one as a gender nonbinary person of color. Some of us
come from the working class or rural areas. We all hold faculty
appointments at major universities. The privileges of our faculty
appointments have given us the time and resources to do what we
love – research, teach, and write – and to reflect upon positionality,
which contributed to making this book a reality.

Chapter 2, Leisy Abrego's "Research as Accompaniment," provides a
critical reflection on how she conceptualizes, conducts, analyzes, writes
up, and presents her research projects. As a "mestiza from a working-
class background," Abrego does not have the luxury of deciding to
distance from or "intellectualize" oppression. However, she sees colleagues who come from majority groups do this with relative ease.
Abrego is a sociologist who studies how legal violence is perpetrated
against migrants and its effects on their legal consciousness. She is also
an advocate for refugee rights. In her chapter, she explains her identity
as both an immigrant in the US from Central America and a scholar of
immigrant rights and experiences. She feels called to commit herself to
the rigorous standards required for social science and moreover to the
rigorous standards required for meaningful empathy with her study
participants and readers. Although much of her work is qualitative,
she has chosen, for instance, not to interview migrants languishing in
US border detention facilities but instead to draw attention to their
plight by obtaining and analyzing government documents that provide
evidence of US imperialism. Abrego writes that she welcomes "the
grainy truths that arise in ... embodied research and people-centered
analysis." This perspective also influences how she studies immigration
law. Being an out-of-place scholar empowers Abrego "to eschew any

false premise of the law's objectivity and to view multiple angles of a law, its creation, and implementation, while also understanding how it shapes people's public and more intimate behaviors." The result is pathbreaking and interdisciplinary scholarship that is "simultaneously humanizing and rigorous," and that fosters community through an "accompaniment" with immigrants rather than a study of immigrants.

Chapters 3 and 4 bring us into the experience of being out of place in the specific context of fieldwork. Chapter 3, "'Pretty and Young' in Places Where People Get Killed in Broad Daylight," by Sindiso Mnisi Weeks, turns on its head Abrego's notion of closeness and proximity. Specifically, Mnisi Weeks reflects on the tension she felt when other scholars identified her too closely with her study participants, who like her are Black South Africans. Their shared background seemed to taint or decrease her scholarly credibility, she writes. While this perspective of being a young African woman studying other young African women gives her some insider status, it also shapes how other academics see her, how study participants see her, and how she has come to see herself. Mnisi Weeks is a scholar of gender, Indigenous rights, and constitutionalism in South Africa, as well as race in the United States. However, her marginalized identity in the law sapped her authority in the centers of patriarchal power where the law resides – both in the communities she has studied and in the academy whose "default representative is a white, middle-aged, European and/or American male locked in a single discipline." Adding to this for African scholars is the fact that "the formal law's understanding of the customary law of . . . African people has been based on articulations of such by white, male anthropologists of European or American nationality or ancestry." Mnisi Weeks's intersectional identities and positionality, however, are precisely what allowed her to study and show how social and legal injustice are never far apart, as they weave their way into and out of the rural courts and traditional justice forums that she studied in KwaZulu-Natal.

Chapter 4, Margaret L. Boittin's "Out of Place when Studying China's Sex Industry," explains how being out of place can paradoxically put one back in place – or exactly where one needs to be to achieve their research goals and values. Boittin is a lawyer and US-trained political scientist who works in a Canadian law faculty. She explains how being out of place is relative. She may not be out of place in North America as "a white woman with blond hair and blue eyes," but she was obviously out of place when she was studying sex workers in China.

While being out of place in China was "draining to the core," she writes that embracing this outsider status also became the source of her strength during fieldwork and later in the academy. Like Abrego's "accompaniment," Boittin found empathy with her study participants during her fieldwork, not only with the sex workers who navigated assault and harassment but also with the police officers and public health agents who found themselves "in positions of surprising precarity and weakness as they navigate their professional responsibilities to implement prostitution policies." But being a woman studying sex work also shoved her into a "methodological and substantive periphery" of law, political science, and China studies. This made not just her research but also herself face higher levels of scrutiny. Boittin's scholarship, however, has successfully traversed the disciplinary boundaries that she had been taught to avoid crossing. Boittin concludes with a reminder about the exhaustion of being out of place but also with gratitude to the many respondents – sex workers, their clients, and police officers – who felt comfortable with her precisely because she was an outsider.

Chapter 5 is Lynette J. Chua's "Feeling at Home Outside: Embracing Out-of-Placeness in the Study of Law and Resistance." Chua is a scholar of law and social movements originally from Malaysia, educated in Singapore and the US, and working in Singapore. She says that across these diverse contexts she has "always been drawn to being, and [has] always been out of place." Chua reflects on how her out of place positionality enabled her to write two books. For both books, *Mobilizing Gay Singapore* and *The Politics of Love in Myanmar*, Chua embraced her own status ambiguity by holding in balance both an insider status (as an Asian person who had lived and worked in Southeast Asia) and an outsider status (not being Singaporean or Burmese, nor part of the gay rights movement in either place). It was her own out of place positionality that she says first drew her to "out-of-place movements," which allowed her to see "the strength of human agency to forge resistance against [legal] odds." While being out of place in so many ways "can become wearisome," it is also what enabled her to see the importance of emotions and relationships for human rights activists, a central theme of Chua's work on Myanmar.

Chapter 6, "Out of Place in an Indian Court: Notes on Researching Rape in a District Court in Gujarat (1996–1998)," by Pratiksha Baxi, is a reflection on the "unsafe" and "painstaking work" of observing rape trials. Baxi, a leading sociologist of gender, learned Indian law and medical jurisprudence on her own during her fieldwork, through conversations with lawyers, observing trials, and reading books. However, her outsider status as a nonlawyer and as a woman led various people in the courtrooms where she conducted fieldwork to "scold" her for studying rape trials. She witnessed how sexism gave the law its power. The "judicial hierarchy was foundationally sexist," she writes, because "male desire was inserted in the place of law" in legal arguments and judgments. The out of place feeling from fieldwork followed her long afterward, like a trauma. Though her fieldwork took place more than two decades earlier, the "anger and grief" never went away. They were instead "deferred to writing." She writes that after her fieldwork she "was not in my own skin. I was out of place in the university and home felt unfamiliar ... Law had interpolated the intimate." However, she concludes, that "If law's attachment to cruelty continues to mark the self, then the ability to love and be in solidarity is the necessary condition for living with the field."

Chapters 7 and 8 turn to the ways that an out of place positionality builds socio-legal and cultural theory. Chapter 7 is Swethaa S. Ballakrishnen's "At Odds with Everything Around Me: Vulnerability Politics and Its (Out of) Place in the Socio-Legal Academy." Ballakrishnen, who uses nonbinary pronouns, is a sociologist of law and globalization who studies, among other things, inequality and identity in the legal profession. They identify as "a global south queer [with] 'local north' advantages." Their chapter considers how identity and vulnerability – and not merely ideas – build critical legal theory. Specifically, Ballakrishnen argues that complicated legal and social hegemonies create outsider status, but the process of making hidden identities visible creates closeness, camaraderie, and change in our scholarship. Data, like identity, is not neutral, though both are often valorized in that way. And the law, Ballakrishnen writes, is also very much like identity in that both are "predicated on trust, exchange, and power, and each, when moderated with self-reflexive vulnerability, hold within them the capacity to belong, break-open, and build anew."

Chapter 8, Luis Eslava's "Trigueño International Law: On (Most of the World) Being (Always, Somehow) Out of Place," uses the framework of this book to build an "out of place" theory of international law. Eslava, a scholar of international law and development, draws on postcolonial legal theory, history, and ethnographic research in Latin America and elsewhere to show how the field of international law produces and is produced by "out of placeness." The result is an international legal order that has, for five hundred years, "continually wrecked and disciplined" people and places, especially in the Global South. Eslava sets up his "out of place" theory of international law by analyzing three moments in which he has come to understand how international law wreaks so much havoc on global culture. First, he uses the idea of a *trigueño* identity ("part-Indigenous, part-African, and part-Spanish") to explore, autoethnographically, the fluidity of life in the South. Second, he explains how international law cannot adequately account for the disorder that it produces in the Global South and the Global North. Finally, he points scholars towards seeing that being out of place is fundamentally about dislocation, which is both a global reality and a sensible ethical position for contemporary interdisciplinary scholarship.

Chapter 9, "Becoming a Familiar Outsider: Multi-sited and Multi-temporal Research in Plural Legal Contexts," concludes the book. In it, the legal scholar Keebet von Benda-Beckmann reflects on forty-five years of ethnographic fieldwork on legal pluralism in Indonesia and the Netherlands. In her fieldwork, and across her career, von Benda-Beckmann writes, she would begin as a "total stranger" and then slowly turn into a "familiar outsider." She felt out of place as a lawyer in social science and as the descendant of a Dutch colonial sugar plantation administrator. She often conducted fieldwork with her husband, which meant that "We came as a family and had to divide our time between research and the children." Von Benda-Beckmann, who died before this book's publication, reminds us all that across a long and successful career, simply "being there" is ultimately what shapes our relationships and our ability to find "remarkable continuity" in the law across times and places.

Good, interdisciplinary research and fieldwork are not easy. Writing for an interdisciplinary audience is even more challenging. I learned from the contributions in this volume about the importance of not ignoring the place of the self during the research and writing process. Paying attention to our own lived experiences, marginalization, and privileges may help us to understand or own outsider status to our research subjects, and the ways that we also render our research subjects into outsiders. When we appreciate the power of positionality, we retrain our lens onto how law acts rather than what law says. We can see more clearly the imperfect and sometimes dangerous processes by which any person, powerful or weak, claims authority. It is important, then, for each of us to ask what hard places our experiences and our research have taken us to, and how those hard places have shaped the meanings and work of the law.

CONCLUSION

Drawing on empirical research and professional experiences in the field of law and society, including my own, this Introduction has described the benefits and burdens associated with communicating positionality, particularly an out of place positionality. While the benefits – establishing credibility, promoting diversity, and empowering marginalized scholars – accrue to the global law and society community, the burdens – increasing anxiety, shifting attention away from theoretical contributions, and reproducing dominance – are disproportionately borne by a small minority of scholars. Correspondingly, the scholars for whom articulating positionality may have little to no cost are also those who do not do it.

Law and society scholars would do well to adopt what I call a "position sensibility" by recording privileges and vulnerabilities throughout their research and writing processes, as the authors do in the chapters that follow. A sustained inquiry into positionality in law and society reminds scholars that humans, not abstract rules, are the heart of a legal process, and that balancing rules and personhood improves scholarship as it does adjudication (Noonan 2002). Regularly considering positionality also helps to frame theoretical contributions, which renders positionality statements a more structured and integrated part of our methods. For some scholars, this could mean explaining how their marginalization overlapped with that of their research subjects, which helped or hindered their study in distinctive ways. For others, this could mean exploring how privilege – for instance, being a well-paid professor employed by an elite university – provided them with the space, time, and resources to perform a certain kind of research.

Positionality can be a primary motivator of some scholarship, so it is important for those in a majority to consider it with care and to avoid co-optation. Transgender persons and those who identify as gender-fluid or gender nonbinary often advocate for the regular sharing of personal pronouns (such as they, she, and he) even when a cisgender person's pronouns may seem obvious. Likewise, disclosing positionality is not only a part of the conversation; for many people, it "is a conversation" in itself (Ballakrishnen and Dezalay 2021, 22).

Understanding identity and group experience is more crucial now than ever when studying the systemic pressures facing our societies. I write this Introduction to *Out of Place* during a time of roiling social change: Black Lives Matter, #MeToo, and renewed struggles against settler colonialism in North America, populism in Europe, and human rights abuses across all continents. As these social movements have shown, a counter-hegemonic productivity comes from exposing people to worlds other than their own. Such contemporary struggles have also created enemies in high places. In the US, for example, a remarkable effort has begun to stop the teaching of critical race theory, a field that intersects with law and society.[14] The adversarial legal framework and its reverence for an impartial or "blind" justice may be hostile to the expressions of positionality at the heart of contemporary social movements. However, the long arc of the law – as much law and society scholarship has shown – can and does bend towards justice.

References

Arendell, Terry. 1997. "Reflections on the Researcher–Researched Relationship: A Woman Interviewing Men." *Qualitative Sociology* 20: 341.

Awkward, Michael. 1995. *Negotiating Difference: Race, Gender and the Politics of Positionality*. Chicago: University of Chicago Press.

Ballakrishnen, Swethaa, and Sara Dezalay, eds. 2021. *Invisible Institutionalisms: Collective Reflections on the Shadows of Legal Globalisation*. Oxford: Hart.

Bell, Monica C. 2016. "Situational Trust: How Disadvantaged Mothers Reconceive Legal Cynicism." *Law & Society Review* 50: 314.

Blee, Kathleen M. 1998. "White-Knuckle Research: Emotional Dynamics in Fieldwork with Racist Activists." *Qualitative Sociology* 21: 381.

Boellstorff, Tom. 2008. *Coming of Age in Second Life: An Anthropologist Explores the Virtually Human*. Princeton, NJ: Princeton University Press.

Brownstein, Michael, and Jennifer Saul, eds. 2016. *Implicit Bias and Philosophy, Volume 2: Moral Responsibility, Structural Injustice, and Ethics*. Oxford: Oxford University Press.

Bunting, Annie, Heather Tasker, and Emily Lockhart. 2021. "Women's Law-Making and Contestations of 'Marriage' in African Conflict Situations." *Law & Society Review* 55(4): 614.

Burawoy, Michael. 1998. "Critical Sociology: A Dialogue between Two Sciences." *Contemporary Sociology* 27(1): 12–20.

[14] In 2021, for instance, the Kansas Board of Regents asked state universities for a list of courses that include critical race theory, and other US states followed suit (Shorman and Bernard 2021).

Capers, Bennett, Devon W. Carbado, R. A. Lenhardt, and Angela Onwuachi-Willig. 2022. *Critical Race Judgments: Rewritten U.S. Court Opinions on Race and the Law*. Cambridge: Cambridge University Press.

Chua, Lynette J. 2019. *The Politics of Love in Myanmar: LGBT Mobilization and Human Rights as a Way of Life*. Stanford, CA: Stanford University Press.

Collins, Patricia Hill. 1986. "Learning from the Outsider Within: The Sociological Significance of Black Feminist Thought." *Social Problems* 33(6): S14.

———. 1997. "Comment on Hekman's 'Truth and Method: Feminist Standpoint Theory Revisited': Where's the Power?" *Signs* 22(2): 375.

Cooppan, Vilashini. 2021. "Skin, Kin, Kind, I/You/We: Autotheory's Compositional Grammar." *ASAP/Journal* 6(3): 583.

Cotterrell, Roger. 1986. "Law and Society: Notes on the Constitutions and Confrontations of Disciplines." *Journal of Law and Society* 13(1): 9.

Cotterrell, Roger. 2004. "Selznick Interviewed: Philip Selznick in Conversation with Roger Cotterrell." *Journal of Law & Society* 31(3): 291.

Cownie, Fiona. 2015. "The United Kingdom's First Woman Law Professor: An Archerian Analysis." *Journal of Law and Society* 42(1): 127.

Crenshaw, Kimberle Williams. 1991. "Mapping the Margins: Intersectionality, Politics, and Violence against Women of Color." *Stanford Law Review* 43(6): 1241.

———. 2011. "Twenty Years of Critical Race Theory: Looking Back to Move Forward." *Connecticut Law Review* 43(5): 1253.

Crowe, Patricia Ward. 1978. "Complainant Reactions to the Massachusetts Commission against Discrimination." *Law & Society Review* 12(2): 217.

Ellett, Rachel, and Mark Fathi Massoud. 2016. "Not All Law Is Public: Reflections on Data Transparency for Law and Courts Research in Africa." *APSA African Politics Conference Group* 12(2): 8.

Erlanger, Howard S. 2005. "Organizations, Institutions, and the Story of Shmuel: Reflections on the 40th Anniversary of the Law and Society Association." *Law & Society Review* 39(1): 1.

England, Kim V. L. 1994. "Getting Personal: Reflexivity, Positionality, and Feminist Research." *The Professional Geographer* 46(1): 80.

Ewick, Patricia, and Susan Silbey. 1998. *The Common Place of Law*. Chicago: University of Chicago Press.

Foster, Deborah, and Natasha Hirst. 2022. "Doing Diversity in the Legal Profession in England and Wales: Why Do Disabled People Continue to Be *Unexpected?*" *Journal of Law and Society* 49(3): 447.

Fitzgerald, Chloë, and Samia Hurst. 2017. "Implicit Bias in Healthcare Professionals: A Systematic Review." *BMC Medical Ethics* 18: 1.

Galam, Roderick G. 2015. "Gender, Reflexivity, and Positionality in Male Research in One's Own Community with Filipino Seafarers' Wives." *Forum: Qualitative Social Research* 16(3).

Galanter, Marc. 2021. "Where the Wild Things Are: India as Legal Education." Foreword. In *Invisible Institutionalisms: Collective Reflections on the Shadows of Legal Globalisation*, edited by Swethaa Ballakrishnen and Sara Dezalay, vii–x. Oxford: Hart.

Gherardi, Silvia, and Barry Turner. 2002. "Real Men Do Not Collect Soft Data." In *The Qualitative Researcher's Companion*, edited by A. Michael Huberman and Matthew B. Miles, 81–100. Thousand Oaks, CA: Sage.

Goffman, Erving. 1974. *Frame Analysis: An Essay on the Organization of Experience*. Cambridge, MA: Harvard University Press.

Gómez, Laura E. 2012. "Looking for Race in All the Wrong Places." *Law & Society Review* 46(2): 221.

Goodwin, Michele. 2021. "I Was Raped by My Father. An Abortion Saved My Life." *The New York Times*, November 30, 2021. www.nytimes.com/2021/11/30/opinion/abortion-texas-mississippi-rape.html.

Gonzalez, Shannon Malone, Samantha J. Simon, and Katie Kaufman Rogers. 2022. "The Diversity Officer: Police Officers' and Black Women Civilians' Epistemologies of Race and Racism in Policing." *Law & Society Review* 56(3): 477.

Granfield, Robert. 1992. *Making Elite Lawyers: Visions of Law at Harvard and Beyond*. New York: Routledge, Chapman and Hall.

Gustafson, Kaaryn S. 2011. *Cheating Welfare: Public Assistance and the Criminalization of Poverty*. New York: New York University Press.

Halliday, Simon, and Patrick Schmidt, eds. 2009. *Conducting Law and Society Research: Reflections on Methods and Practices*. Cambridge: Cambridge University Press.

Hengel, Erin. 2017. "Publishing while Female: Are Women Held to a Higher Standard." *Cambridge Working Paper in Economics 1753. Faculty of Economics*. Cambridge: University of Cambridge.

Hirsch, Susan. 2008. *In the Moment of Greatest Calamity: Terrorism, Grief, and a Victim's Quest for Justice*. Princeton, NJ: Princeton University Press.

Hoffmann, Elizabeth A. 2007. "Open-Ended Interviews, Power, and Emotional Labor." *Journal of Contemporary Ethnography* 36(3): 318.

Houh, Emily. 2006. "Still, at the Margins." *Law & Society Review* 40(2): 481.

Huisman, Kimberly. 2008. "'Does This Mean You're Not Going to Come Visit Me Anymore?': An Inquiry into an Ethics of Reciprocity and Positionality in Feminist Ethnographic Research." *Sociological Inquiry* 78: 372.

Hunter, Rosemary. 2015. "The Feminist Judgments Project: Legal Fiction as Critique and Practice." *International Critical Thought* 5: 501.

Hunter, Rosemary, Sharyn Roach Anleu, and Kathy Mack. 2021. "Feminist Judging in Lower Courts." *Journal of Law and Society* 48(4): 595.

Jolls, Christine, and Cass R. Sunstein. 2006. "The Law of Implicit Bias." *California Law Review* 94(4): 969.

Kang, Jerry, Mark Bennett, Devon Carbado, Pamela Casey, Nilanjana Dasgupta, David Faigman, Anthony Greenwald, Justin D. Levinson, and Jennifer Mnookin. 2012. "Implicit Bias in the Courtroom." *UCLA Law Review* 59(5): 1124.

Kapiszewski, Diana, Lauren M. MacLean, and Benjamin L. Read. 2015. *Field Research in Political Science: Practices and Principles*. Cambridge: Cambridge University Press.

Kennedy, Duncan, and Karl Klare. 1984. "A Bibliography of Critical Legal Studies." *Yale Law Journal* 94(2): 461.

Kershner, Isabel. 2021. "Stabbed 20 Times by Her Husband, She Now Fights Laws Favoring Abusers." *The New York Times*. December 3, 2021. www.nytimes.com/2021/12/03/world/middleeast/israel-shira-isakov-domestic-violence.html.

Khan, Maryam S. 2021. "Islamic Review in Pakistan." In *Invisible Institutionalisms*, edited by S. Ballakrishnen and S. Dezalay, 147–67. Oxford: Hart.

Kincheloe, Joe L., Peter McLaren, Shirley R. Steinberg, and Lila D. Monzo. 2017. "Critical Pedagogy and Qualitative Research: Advancing the Bricolage." In *The SAGE Handbook of Qualitative Research*, edited by Norman Denzin and Yvonna Lincoln, 418–65. Thousand Oaks, CA: Sage.

King, Gary, Robert Keohane, and Sidney Verba. 1994. *Designing Social Inquiry: Scientific Inference in Qualitative Research*. Princeton, NJ: Princeton University Press.

Leckey, Robert. 2022. "Child Welfare, Indigenous Parents, and Judicial Mediation." *Journal of Law and Society* 49(1): 151.

Massoud, Mark Fathi. 2011. "Do Victims of War Need International Law? Human Rights Education Programs in Authoritarian Sudan." *Law & Society Review* 45(1): 1.

2013. *Law's Fragile State: Colonial, Authoritarian, and Humanitarian Legacies in Sudan*. Cambridge: Cambridge University Press.

2014. "International Arbitration and Judicial Politics in Authoritarian States." *Law & Social Inquiry* 39(1): 1.

2015. "Work Rules: How International NGOs Build Law in War-Torn Societies." *Law & Society Review* 49(2): 333.

2016. "Ideals and Practices in the Rule of Law: An Essay on Legal Politics." *Law & Social Inquiry* 41(2): 489.

2020. "The Rule of Law in Fragile States: Dictatorship, Collapse, and the Politics of Religion in Post-Colonial Somalia." *Journal of Law and Society* 47: S111.

2021. *Shari'a, Inshallah: Finding God in Somali Legal Politics*. Cambridge: Cambridge University Press.

2022. "The Price of Positionality: Assessing the Benefits and Burdens of Self-Identification in Research Methods." *Journal of Law and Society* 49 (S1): S64.

McMillan, Nesam. 2020. *Imagining the International: Crime, Justice, and the Promise of Community.* Stanford, CA: Stanford University Press.

Medzani, Justice M. 2021. "Positionality Statement on Studying Male Victims of Intimate Partner Abuse in Zimbabwe: A Research Note." *International Journal of Social Research Methodology* 24(3): 387.

Miled, Neila. 2019. "Muslim Researcher Researching Muslim Youth: Reflexive Notes on Critical Ethnography, Positionality, and Representation." *Ethnography and Education* 14(3): 1.

Mitchell, Maurice. 2022. "Building Resilient Organizations." *The Forge.* https://forgeorganizing.org/article/building-resilient-organizations.

Moore, Laurence R. 1987. *Religious Outsiders and the Making of Americans.* Oxford: Oxford University Press.

Nelken, David. 1998. "Blinding Insights? The Limits of a Reflexive Sociology of Law." *Journal of Law and Society* 25(3): 407.

Nelson, Maggie. 2015. *The Argonauts.* Minneapolis, MN: Graywolf Press.

Noonan, John T. 2002 [1976]. *Persons and Masks of the Law: Cardozo, Holmes, Jefferson, and Wythe as Makers of the Masks.* Berkeley and Los Angeles: University of California Press.

Paap, Kris. 2006. *Working Construction: Why White Working-Class Men Put Themselves and the Labor Movement in Harm's Way.* Ithaca, NY: Cornell University Press.

Powell, Amber Joy, and Michelle S. Phelps. 2021. "Gendered Racial Vulnerability: How Women Confront Crime and Criminalization." *Law & Society Review* 55(3): 249.

Randall, Melanie. 2010. "'Sexual Assault Law, Credibility, and Ideal Victims': Consent, Resistance, and Victim Blaming." *Canadian Journal of Women and the Law* 22(2): 397.

Reyes, Victoria. 2020. "Ethnographic Toolkit: Strategic Positionality and Researchers' Visible and Invisible Tools in Field Research." *Ethnography* 21(2): 220.

Rios, Victor. 2011. *Punished: Policing the Lives of Black and Latino Boys.* New York: New York University Press.

Roberts, John Michael, and Teela Sanders. 2005. "Before, During and After: Realism, Reflexivity and Ethnography." *The Sociological Review* 53: 294.

Said, Edward W. 1999. *Out of Place: A Memoir.* New York: Random House.

Saunders, Patricia J. 2008. "Fugitive Dreams of Diaspora: Conversations with Saidiya Hartman." *Anthurium: A Caribbean Studies Journal* 6: 5.

Savelsberg, Joachim J., Sida Liu, Carroll Seron, Terrence Halliday, Calvin Morrill, and Susan Silbey. 2016. "*Law & Society Review* at Fifty:

A Debate on the Future of Publishing by the Law and Society Association." *Law & Society Review* 50: 1017.

Scott, Joan. 1991. "The Evidence of Experience." *Critical Inquiry* 17(4): 773–97.

Shalhoub-Kevorkian, Nadara. 2015. *Security Theology, Surveillance and the Politics of Fear.* Cambridge: Cambridge University Press.

Shaw, Rhonda M., Julie Howe, Jonathan Beazer, and Toni Carr. 2020. "Ethics and Positionality in Qualitative Research with Vulnerable and Marginal Groups." *Qualitative Research* 20(3): 277.

Shorman, Jonathan, and Katie Bernard. 2021. "Kansas Universities Asked to Compile List of Courses that Teach Critical Race Theory." *Kansas City Star*, June 4, 2021. www.kansascity.com/news/politics-government/article251898553.html.

Sierra-Arévalo, Michael. 2021. "American Policing and the Danger Imperative." *Law & Society Review* 55(1): 70.

Smith, Jessica. 2021. "Journeying the Everyday of Civic Space: Movement as Method in Socio-Legal Studies." *Journal of Law and Society* 48: S59.

Smith, Rogers M. 1993. "Beyond Tocqueville, Myrdal, and Hartz: The Multiple Traditions in America." *American Political Science Review* 87(3): 549.

Snell, Joel C. 2006. "Robert Merton Dies at 92." *College Student Journal* 40: 250.

Soedirgo, Jessica, and Aarie Glas. 2021. "Towards Active Reflexivity: Positionality and Practice in the Production of Knowledge." *PS: Political Science & Politics* 53(3): 527.

Staats, Cheryl. 2016. "Understanding Implicit Bias: What Educators Should Know." *American Educator* 39: 29.

Statz, Michele. 2021. "On Shared Suffering: Judicial Intimacy in the Rural Northland." *Law & Society Review* 55: 5.

Treviño, Javiar A. 2007. "Theory and Methods in Socio-Legal Research, Edited by R. Banakar and M. Travers." *Law & Society Review* 41: 493.

Wasserfall, Rahel. 1993. "Reflexivity, Feminism and Difference." *Qualitative Sociology* 16: 23.

Whittingdale, Eleanor. 2021. "Becoming a Feminist Methodologist while Researching Sexual Violence Support Services." *Journal of Law and Society* 48(S1): S10.

Williams, Patricia J. 1991. *The Alchemy of Race and Rights: Diary of a Law Professor.* Cambridge, MA: Harvard University Press.

Winfield, Taylor Paige. 2022. "Vulnerable Research: Competencies for Trauma and Justice-Informed Ethnography." *Journal of Contemporary Ethnography* 51(2): 135–70.

Young, Kathryne M. 2020. "Understanding Illegality: Tests and Trust in Sociolegal Fieldwork." *Journal of Organizational Ethnography* 9(2): 223–36.

RESEARCH AS ACCOMPANIMENT

Reflections on Objectivity, Ethics, and Emotions

*Leisy J. Abrego**

I am a Salvadoran immigrant scholar in the United States. This means that I have lived and built a research career in the country whose settler-colonial government funded the civil war and benefited from the conditions that displaced my family from our birthplace. Consequently, and by design, I am always already positioned by others as being out of place. As a mestiza from a working-class background, I represent a notably small demographic in US academia, one whose ability to properly conduct research and to produce insightful work is often in question. For example, when I asked a professor for a letter of recommendation for a travel grant to conduct graduate research in El Salvador, he responded: "Make sure you are not just going to hang out with family." And when as a research assistant I submitted multiple interview summaries to the Principal Investigator of a project, her response was genuine shock each time at my ability to conduct incisive interviews and to write clearly and perceptively. She did not expect someone who looked like me to excel at these skills, even though I was close to completing a PhD at the time. Such reminders of my marginalized positionality and of the associated assumptions others place on

* I wish to thank the generous and thoughtful participants of the workshop, "Out of Place: Power, Person, and Difference in Socio-Legal Research" organized by Lynette J. Chua and Mark Fathi Massoud. The conversations were generative and gave me freedom to reflect deeply on my trajectory in academia. I am also grateful to Flori Boj Lopez and Karina Alma for incisive comments on an earlier draft, and to Carlos Colorado for his consistent support.

me have punctuated my journey and continue to contextualize my work: they taught me not to invest in presumed rules of research, including canonical approaches in the field of law and society.

It is not surprising that there are few others who share aspects of my social location as knowledge producers in academia. As sociologist Steven Osuna notes:

> Through a racialized, gendered, and especially class-specific project, academic institutions have privatized and restricted knowledge production to elites and those from the upper classes. Any knowledge production by the lower orders of society has been interpreted as illegitimate, backward, or nonscientific, thereby allowing the knowledge produced through academic institutions by intellectuals to mask power relations through claims of objectivity and positivism.
>
> (Osuna 2017, 27–8)

Indeed, many saw me as inherently less capable than others. In their eyes, my social location placed me outside of who may be trusted to uphold the revered values of objectivity, positivism, and even basic competence as a scholar. These professors communicated to me that they saw me as being out of place in a PhD program, but their actions were also instructive in other ways: I learned early on that my work as a socio-legal scholar should never aim to maintain an academic hegemony that in its development, excluded me and others like me.

Much of the underpinning of methodological training in sociology underscored similar marginalization. Patterns in funding, publication, awards, and assigned readings privileged quantitative approaches because they were perceived as systematic, replicable, and scientific (Luker 2008). On the other end of that spectrum of the notion of validity, scholars of color doing qualitative work – especially when invested in social justice – were deemed unable to capture "the truth" because we were too close to our research subjects, always already too "biased" (Gupta and Ferguson 1997). Never mind that "outsider" scholars have a history of egregiously biased and harmful misrepresentations of communities of color (Carbado and Roithmayr 2014).

Qualitative methodology curricula also established the expectation that good qualitative research required a start and end date, with the goal of entering and exiting "the field" in ways that minimized emotional entanglements. What happens when you live in "the field" and your goals expand beyond academic knowledge production? In this chapter, I reflect on how, given my social location, I have navigated these expectations across the arc of the research process in multiple studies. It is a methodological appendix of sorts that scrutinizes two decades of qualitative work in the intersecting fields of international migration and law and society; and it calls for a reassessment of the potential value of our intellectual work.

ACCOMPANIMENT IN ACADEMIA

Now that I teach in a department of Chicana/o and Central American Studies, I rarely deal with the raced and classed forms of rejection common in sociology or law and society spaces. Visits to other departments and campuses, however, remind me of how social location can vastly inform one's approach to research. I enjoy giving talks to different audiences. I am energized by the intellectual engagement that opens possibilities for new directions in my analysis.

But sometimes these interactions are difficult. At a visit to an elite private US university, for example, a few white male graduate students training in qualitative social science research joined some faculty members and me for dinner. In the midst of savoring the delightful organic food, I noticed myself starting to feel physically ill in reaction to some of the students' commentary. One student stated that qualitative work is great because you can hear the gruesome stories about violence in migrants' lives, but you have the reprieve of theory to make sense of what they have gone through and distance yourself through it. Another agreed and added that writing was the best part of being a scholar because it removes him from the violence and permits him to organize and intellectualize it.

I felt ill because I know my own experience and that of many US scholars of color. We cannot fully distance ourselves from the structures that produce violence; intellectualizing is not the end goal. Instead, we are deeply committed to people's well-being just as much as, and often more than, to the advancement of a field. We are aiming to be in accompaniment.

As Barbara Tomlinson and George Lipsitz explain (2019, 23) when they draw from the ideals and practices of the Salvadoran martyr Oscar A. Romero, accompaniment is "a disposition, a sensibility, and a pattern of behavior. It is a commitment based on a cultivated capacity for making connections with others, identifying with them, and helping them." For Romero, accompaniment meant making the needs of the most powerless and most oppressed – the people most likely to be left out – into *everyone's* first priority. It entailed asking questions before acting, taking inventory of multiple forms of social exclusion, and learning how to be people who do not succumb to the dominant norms of an acquisitive, aggressive, and antagonistic world.

(Tomlinson and Lipsitz 2019, 25)

Scholars who are members of the majority racial group, who benefit from patriarchy and white supremacy, have the privilege of intellectual-izing and distancing, and are more likely to be endorsed as appropriately objective and rigorous. Indeed, academia exists in and often reproduces the "acquisitive, aggressive, and antagonistic world." Scholars who choose to counter the rules of objectivity and rethink notions of rigor (Hale 2008), are invested as co-creators of a process of transformation, often making the most oppressed their priority. This requires humility, carries immense responsibility, and can make writing feel paralyzing (Negrón-Gonzales 2014).

My practices of accompaniment stand in opposition to settler-colonial standards of objectivity(Morgensen 2012), but my work is rigorous in ways that matter beyond academic norms. This becomes evident to others through the emotional nature of the work. My practices of accompaniment give me access to people's lives in ways that can evoke deep emotions from study participants, readers, and audience members.

At my talks, people often ask me how I deal with the painful stories I document. Depending on who is asking, this question and ensuing conversations can signal different concerns. In my experience, white students are trying to make sense of how to follow the prescribed rules of "objectivity" while aiming to unearth deep insights about human experiences. Similar questions from working-class students of color, however, suggest a desire to understand how one maintains emotional well-being when the research so persistently reveals the kind of suffering that hits close to home. In each of these instances, though based on different priorities, audiences read me as being out of place in academia: one group for not being objective enough; the other for being too close to the institution's demands to do good work on behalf of the commu-nity. After two decades of research, I have come to understand that it is precisely my marginalized positionality as an out-of-place scholar that permits me to negotiate all such expectations to produce socio-legal work that is simultaneously humanizing and rigorous.

This chapter is about how the framework of accompaniment allows me to process the emotions of conducting law and society research. I find that by centering the emotional well-being of the most oppressed – study participants and readers from similar communities – research becomes a way to foster community because it allows people to engage in emotional ties with one another. I contend that a socio-legal researcher's positionality also entails an *emotional* positioning and that emotions, rather than their denial through an expectation of "objectivity," produce more honest and ethical research. Notably, my commitment to accompaniment blurs the presumed division between researcher and study participants.[1]

RESEARCH TOOLS FOR ACCOMPANIMENT

> The late poet-warrior, Audre Lorde, warned that the master's tools will never dismantle the master's house. As with any theoretical premise, Lorde's caveat is useful only if the elements – whose paring away enables its elegance and urgency – are added back, so that the general truth of the abstraction has concrete meaning for day-to-day life. The issue is not whether the master uses, or endorses the use of, some tool or another. Rather, who controls the conditions and the ends to which any tools are wielded?... The house must be dismantled so that we can recycle the materials to institutions of our own design, usable by all to produce new and liberating work.
>
> (Gilmore 1993, 70)

I have a PhD in sociology. There is no question that I was trained to use "the master's tools." Most of my research projects to date have drawn on in-depth interviews with immigrants in various legal statuses in the United States. Analyzing their words and using a comparative strategy to underscore common narratives by legal status, I aim to capture how US foreign and immigration policies centrally shape the everyday lives of migrants. It is my social location guided by goals of accompaniment that permit me to use "the master's tools" to my own ends, in "new and liberating" directions.

I conduct research in a notably anti-immigrant political and discursive context in which immigration policies are often violently enforced

---

[1] I wish to credit Karina Alma and Floridalma Boj Lopez for encouraging me to make these points more explicitly and boldly.

(Menjívar and Abrego 2012). As a member of one of the racial groups that is most explicitly targeted by such immigration policies in the United States, I am firmly aware of the intimate ways in which enforcement spreads fear and uncertainty in immigrant communities. Interviews allow me to learn directly from those who are targeted, whose voices and experiences are too often excluded or misrepresented in public discourse. From the conception of a project to the recruitment of participants, to the interactions during each interview, and through the dialectical process of analysis – all aspects and stages of my work are deeply informed by my social location, a commitment to humility, and goals of accompaniment.

I am both the thoroughly trained social science scholar who designs studies methodically to leverage the analytical power of comparative research, and I am the Salvadoran immigrant whose relatives and close friends suffer daily the complex consequences of the very systems that I analyze. My out-of-place status as a socio-legal scholar allows me to prioritize my own and my research participants' humanity above a questionable expectation for objectivity in the research process. To conduct thorough and humane law and society research (indeed, to even consider these equal priorities), I perform academic accompaniment in the tradition of Oscar A. Romero. For every project, therefore, I prioritize the most oppressed. This demands a layered process; every stage of research and analysis requires humility and different strategies to help me ethically manage emotions and information while capturing what is at stake for immigrant communities.

Conceptualizing a Project

Because of who I am, because I migrated as an undocumented child, because my family was forced to flee a war that was being funded and promoted by the US government to uphold a capitalist system that undermines the well-being of the majority of Salvadorans in El Salvador and abroad (Abrego and Villalpando 2021), I seek out research projects that help me understand how humans suffer, adapt, and live in the face of systemic, often legally condoned injustice. I remember how it felt as a child to interact with immigration authorities: we had to wake up before dawn, make our way through city streets and highways to get downtown and stand in line outside of the federal building before it opened, without any guarantee that we would be seen that day. If we were lucky, the line of people waiting was not yet too long and we were able to get a number to be seen.

Inside, we were sent through barren halls and into a waiting room that would soon be filled with other anxious people. We all sat quietly on uncomfortable chairs. My family walked in together when called into small offices. Sometimes we were treated kindly, or at least neutrally, and we were relieved. Often, we were treated poorly. Though it must have been difficult for my parents to remain quiet in the face of such disrespect, we did not question anything because our fates were in the hands of the people who asked my parents prodding questions. I vividly recall that even after we got legal permanent resident status, any time we crossed the border and returned to the United States, my parents were nervous at the point of inspection. The border authorities there also had the right to talk to us as they wished, to presume the worst of us.

This knowledge is embodied and powerfully lodged inside of me. In hindsight, it is not surprising that I seek out research projects that center the law as a powerful site of production of violence. I initially entered into the practice of empirical research, however, without a conscious awareness of how my lived experiences were shaping my academic interests. Instead, like most social scientists, I aimed to begin the research process guided by a carefully constructed research question. While I often revisit and revise my research question multiple times throughout the duration of a project, even after the conclusion of the analysis, I also believe that a solid research question best helps to guide research. I arrive at this research question through a dialectical process that takes into account the questions raised in the literatures on law and society and immigration, and places them in the context of what I witness to be pressing issues in the day-to-day lives of the people who are targeted by changing laws and dominant discursive contexts.

With a foot in academia and another in working-class immigrant communities, being out of place generates research questions that demand nuanced answers. It is not enough to generate theory for the sake of theory; it is necessary to also produce knowledge that reflects carefully and justly contextualized immigrant realities and informs immigrant rights movements. Conceptualizing a project as accompaniment, therefore, requires some understanding of the state of the academic field(s) of interest and a deep familiarity with the processes, practices, and emotions of the people and communities in question.

It has been a long process of learning and unlearning. In 2001, when I embarked on my first empirical project, I was taking graduate courses on immigration. The emphasis in much of that literature was on the concept of assimilation – the idea that after a generation or more, the immigrant stock (immigrants, their children, and grandchildren) would look statistically just like the average middle-class white population (Gordon 1964; Park 1950). Implicitly, immigrant "success" was understood in that literature as approximation to whiteness. Measuring assimilation involved looking closely at national origin and racial groups' average levels of educational attainment; at what percentage of each group were completing college; their average wages; and, most problematic in my mind, how many were intermarrying with whites (Osuji 2019). Implicit in this approach was the idea that "successful" immigrants were good enough to be accepted into white families. Most research questions derived solely from that literature were about measuring groups' socio-economic attainment and whites' acceptance of them.

At the same time as I was reading that literature, I was spending time with high school youth at a community-based organization. What began as a class requirement to conduct an ethnography ended up becoming an important space in which to practice research as accompaniment. Immigrant students taking a video-making class taught me about the challenges they faced in their poorly resourced schools and, in some cases, as they came to learn that they were undocumented. Toward the end of that academic year – my first year in graduate school – another youth organization started meeting in the same space as the video-making class and some of the youth in the first class joined the group. Mostly undocumented, they were organizing to try to influence public policies in the state of California. I attended all the meetings, gave rides to some of the participants, and joined them as a chaperone on a bus trip to the state capitol over 350 miles away. Through my research, I developed short bios of some of the students that activists then presented during legislative visits to lobby for the passage of Assembly Bill 540, a policy that would make it possible for undocumented students to afford college in California. Having gotten to know a group of students who would benefit from the passage of the bill, I became invested in their political fight, at the same time that I needed to conduct research for my master's thesis.

The immigration literature suggested that "success" for these migrants would be to attend college, but it did not account for the fact that state and federal policies *impeded* college attendance for undocumented youth. Still new to the practice of empirical research and academic writing, I devised a research question that safely (within the master's house) centered the notions that were prominent in assimilation literature. I tried to answer the research question: how do undocumented children of immigrants experience assimilation? I designed a study that used interviews to compare the migration, schooling, and neighborhood experiences, as well as the future plans of children of immigrants in three legal categories: US citizen, legal permanent resident, and undocumented. The comparative strategy allowed me to, on the one hand, underscore their many shared experiences as working class and poor Latino immigrants up until high school graduation, and on the other, reveal their starkly divergent future plans and college prospects due to legal status (Abrego 2006). My status as a researcher steeped in immigrant communities allowed me to recognize the missing factor of legal status, and later to develop a focus on the legal, social, and political construction of "illegality" that effectively hinders what migration scholars were counting as "success."

Recruiting Study Participants
Being an out-of-place scholar and an immigrant from a working-class background committed to accompaniment also informs how I approach the people who participate in my research. Unlike traditional researchers who are taught that their research projects (and career) take precedence over the desires of "human subjects" (for a similar observation, see González-López 2010), in the tradition of Romero, I understand my work as needing to center the well-being of participants. I grew up in a poor neighborhood where outsiders sometimes came to conduct research without explaining to us what they were doing. Too young to understand who was behind such projects, I do remember feeling uncomfortable with their assumptions about my community. In hindsight, I wonder if those researchers and outsiders thought they were improving our neighborhoods, maybe even empowering us. If they did, they were mistaken. Their lack of humility and unwillingness to include us in the process prevented any sense of ownership or empowerment for us.

These experiences contextualize how I understand my responsibilities as a researcher. I do not feel comfortable entering a project presuming that the benefits to my career and to the vague notion of a socio-legal scholarship field are sufficient to override the discomfort or potential harm that my research could bring to the individual people who participate.[2] I am aware of the intricate ways that laws shape people's intimate and complex lives, and I do not want to open up difficult conversations without offering something in return.

Early in graduate school, before I had children or work responsibilities, I was able to spend ample time getting to know people and assisting in their various efforts prior to requesting interviews. In my first empirical project, for example, I spent countless hours not only attending meetings and providing rides, but I also helped edit students' college application essays and wrote letters to politicians to share findings from my work along with a request for policy changes to benefit the youth I was writing about. I did much of the same for my second research project. Still involved in the immigrant rights movement, I began to see changes in how students presented themselves and how they understood their place in US society after a change in law granted them greater access to higher education. I was conscientious in my decision not to request interviews with them until after I had helped a few of them navigate higher education, serving as an unofficial mentor and making myself available whenever they sought me out.

To date, I continue to accompany the immigrant rights movement. With added responsibilities, however, I have only managed to stay in touch through social media with many of the people who participated in my first two projects. Time constraints no longer allow me to be present to the same degree or in the same ways as when I was a graduate student. My approach now includes applying for sufficient funds to provide monetary compensation to people who are willing to share their stories with me. For one project, for example, I was able to secure enough funding to pay each study participant US$50 per interview (Abrego 2018b). While traditional researchers sometimes question the ethics of providing monetary incentives (Fisher and Anushko 2008), I understand people's time, stories, and energy to be valuable and because most of the people I interview are also exploited workers, I know that this sum will minimally help offset financial need. I view these payments as the least I can do to thank them for sharing their stories and knowledge. I get to learn directly from them – the experts of their own experiences.

---

[2] There are important, broader discussions about ethics in social science research that are beyond the scope of this chapter, but merit close attention, as well (Fisher and Anushko 2008).

Conducting Interviews

Once people have agreed to participate in an interview with me, the next part of the process is to approach our interaction mindfully and with humility (González-López 2011). This practice is something I learned while conducting interviews and not through my formal academic training. In 2001, during my first study, I had a striking moment that underscored the different sets of rules and expectations in research. I had just completed my first year in graduate school and after spending several months volunteering as a teaching assistant in a video-making class, I asked the students if I could interview them for my master's thesis.

The youth in the class knew me well by then and happily agreed to participate. During the interviews, all the students expressed an understanding of their family's migration as central to their lives; shared that they had witnessed violence in their communities; and noted a severe lack of resources in their schools. Expecting that there would be many clear distinctions in their experiences by legal status, I was starting to worry that the differences were not evident in their narratives. Finally, during one interview, when sharing his hopes for the future, an undocumented student began to cry. Internally, my first response was a sense of relief and even excitement because his emotions would help confirm my hypothesis.

My mind raced thinking about how I could leverage this interview and his tears to strengthen my findings. This would allow me to make a clear connection in my thesis between the youth's experiences and the legal categories that I was arguing mattered centrally in the process of immigrant integration. The student went on to talk about how disoriented he felt to have recently learned of his undocumented status as a sixteen-year-old. He had difficulty focusing in school and wondered how life would be in the future. Would he be able to achieve any of the goals he had envisioned for himself? My next emotion was shame. Excitement was not an acceptable feeling in the face of a scared teenager's tears. How could I prioritize my thesis over this young man's well-being? Why did I, even for a second, think that my academic goals superseded the emotional well-being of the people living through the challenges I was studying?

To this day, I am ashamed of my one-time excitement in the face of another person's pain. I vowed to never allow academia's rules and expectations to devalue study participants' and my own humanity. To that end, I work hard to create a comfortable conversational atmosphere in every interview. An interview is, after all, just a specific kind of human interaction, and in any conversation human beings develop a relationship, even a very brief one, that determines how we feel and how we respond to one another. Here too, Romero's centering of the needs of the oppressed, is a guiding framework for research.

Providing accompaniment as a scholar requires humility and a pres- ence of mind to understand even in indirect language the law's conse- quences in people's lives, even when they do not actually name the law as the culprit of their problems. For example, even though few children of migrants I interviewed in El Salvador were familiar with the term for Temporary Protected Status (TPS), they described the sadness that invaded them when they knew that their parents had work permits (and presumably a stable legal status) but had not returned. They expected parents to demonstrate their love by visiting them, but these expectations were based on incorrect understandings of the law. Having lived experiences in communities with many undocumented and temporarily protected immigrants, I understood the role of the law in their families' separation.

Many of these conversations and realizations are painful for study participants to revisit. Therefore, I also always remind inconsolable interviewees that we can stop the conversation whenever they want. We can take a break or end the interview if talking is too difficult. I sometimes cry with them. Despite expectations of "objectivity" and replicability (that would require me to ask questions in the exact same way of every single study participant), I do not hold back. If I feel like reaching out and lightly touching their arm to console them, I do so. Sometimes, I can sense that my crying will only make the situation more difficult, either because they are trying to be strong or because it will make them more emotional, so instead I offer comforting words or gestures. Here, it is important not to make the situation about me. The interviewee should not be expected to do the emotional labor of consoling the researcher.

I have worried about harming study participants in the process of trying to tell a more holistic analytical story about their lives while offering them little in the way of concrete and immediate rewards for their time, stories, and vulnerability. Most often, however, people have told me after the interview that it felt good to share and release some of the pain they carry. They are grateful for the opportunity to be heard with compassion. This alleviates my fear that interviews may be too emotionally extractive, and, after multiple studies, I recognize that the

47

rewards may not ever be directly tied to those who initially shared their words with me, but that there can be a more collective sense of healing and justice for those who later read the words and feel identified, even empowered, by the stories.

Given the intimacy of interviews, however, this is not always the most appropriate method to conduct socio-legal research on the consequences of US foreign and migration policies. Since 2014 when Central American unaccompanied youth were arriving to the United States and being detained inhumanely in large numbers, my mind and heart have been with these asylum seekers. As a Salvadoran immigrant, I find it deeply distressing to see the images of the squalid and lethal conditions so many people, including transgender folks, women, and children, have been confined to over the last several years.

Amid ongoing disputed and contemptible changes in immigration policies, these migrants' current conditions are cataclysmic. My socio-legal researcher skills and the interview space that I am able to create, no matter how mindful and humane, will not lessen their dire immediate needs. Unable to volunteer at the border for prolonged periods, I feel that it is exploitative to request interviews with asylum-seekers who fled dangerously impossible conditions at home, and who have been desperately waiting for months at the northern Mexican border for a chance to plead their case for asylum in the United States. Realistically, even the offer of a financial incentive feels incomplete, as they continue to be dehumanized and unprotected. Asking them to retell their story of migration while they are in the midst of such devastation feels extractive and abusive – particularly for researchers who descend into the area merely in search of stories to boost their own careers, no matter how "objective" their research design.

In these cases, my interest in uncovering how the legal system produces suffering and inequalities has led me to pursue other methods. While I feel ethically compelled not to request interviews from migrants and asylum-seekers in detention or at the border, I also feel morally compelled to keep shining a light on the ongoing injustice. For this purpose, I have turned to analyzing documents – from the Congressional Research Service, the White House archives, and multiple presidential administrations – to connect the dots between US imperialism, as evident in foreign policies, and the unlivable conditions in Central America that expel migrants and asylum-seekers (Abrego 2017b; Abrego 2018a; Abrego and Hernández 2021; Abrego and Villalpando 2021). In the future, when I turn to other projects,

I hope to return to conducting interviews. As a socio-legal scholar, I find that the greatest insights, both intellectual and practical, come from the very people who live and resist the consequences of the law in their daily lives.

Writing and Analysis

When I do conduct interview-based research, my responsibility as a scholar with the goal of accompaniment requires that I continue to work ethically with the information I collect. After each interview, I often take several days to let people's words and experiences sit with me. This was initially not an intentional part of my process; rather, I came to learn that it was something I needed. In this process, I take the time to imagine their experiences and think often about their strength as human beings who persist through systemic obstacles to try to attain a more stable and happy life. I think about the depth of suffering that some people carry and the lack of empathy of mainstream US society. I write notes about interviewees' gestures, the moments when they took long pauses, when they cried. I write about the emotions I felt during our conversation. And I save all these details to potentially use at the writing and analysis stage of the project. Even when they do not make it into the final draft of a manuscript, those details help me humanize study participants and their stories, and they humanize me while adding depth to my analysis.

When the interviews are done, I have either transcribed the recordings myself or have paid to have them transcribed. At the stage of reading the transcripts to begin the coding process, I once again feel and manage my emotions in order to complete the project. On many occasions, I have cried. Reading the transcripts, even after being present during the interview, often reveals more details that I might have missed the first time around. The crying, in these instances, affirms my humanity and underscores the full humanity of those who I have interviewed, in a process that is not only driven by a sense of academic purpose. I try to be patient with myself as I work through my emotions to eventually get to a point of distance, enough to begin to find and name the patterns, to locate the points of most value for both socio-legal scholarship on immigration and for the immigrant rights movement.

I draw on personal experience to understand the insidious, yet invisible, aspects of law's consequences. Without my embodied knowledge, I may not have sufficient perspective to analyze the words of study participants in the proper context. For example, when people tell me that they are responsible for being undocumented, I emphasize that the settler-colonial legal system simply does not provide the option of legal migration for large numbers of vulnerable people (Speed 2019). When undocumented and poor youth describe themselves as "lazy" and blame themselves for being unable to go to college, I note the timeline of immigration and education policies that contextualize their development and block their college attendance (Abrego 2006). When members of a mixed-status family express feeling hurt at the unequal treatment they receive from their parents, I look beyond individual parenting decisions to consider how the law provides unequal resources for children based on their different legal statuses (Abrego 2016). And when women seemingly make decisions that put their lives in danger, I highlight the legal and economic precarities that limit their options (Abrego 2017a). The parts of me that are marked for marginalization as a scholar simultaneously empower me to eschew any false premise of the law's objectivity and to view multiple angles of a law, its creation, and its implementation, while also understanding how it shapes people's public and more intimate behaviors.

Academic expectations of objectivity unfold in particularly acute ways in law and society research. The study of laws, of a system of rules and regulations, implicitly expects that researchers be particularly "objective" in their study of the legal system. The first time I submitted my work for review to a law and society journal, for example, reviewers requested that I sound more "authoritative" in my writing:

> The work is compelling and the analysis is strong. A significant detractor, however, is the choice of voice and the continual use of I-me- my. . . . it robs the author of her/his legitimacy as a scholar making a profound academic and social argument . . . the author is advised to take her/his spot in academe with conviction. Pronoun and subject choice in this case moves the manuscript in a more informal, less legitimate sphere, unintentionally turning away potential readers and policy makers. . . I found it exceedingly difficult to take the manuscript (and thus the author) seriously due to this choice.

In response to this reviewer's request, I removed about half of these instances, often making sentences sound a bit awkward to my ears. Instead of saying, for example, that "I supplemented the interview data with participant-observation," the published article states, "The interview data is heavily supplemented with participant-observation" (Abrego 2008, 717). The missing words signified that an actual human being conducted the research. It is, therefore, rather telling that an expectation of objectivity makes analysis, at times, more imprecise and always disembodied. In that particular study, none of my conclusions changed, but the reviewer and editor preferred that I not acknowledge my own participation in the work.

Presentations

I am now a full professor and have had the opportunity to present my work hundreds of times. Given my experiences and my commitment to research as accompaniment, presentations have been, at times, particularly difficult, but also incredibly rewarding. It is in the physical exchange of information, in the conversations that happen directly following a presentation that I am able to witness how different audiences receive my work.

Have you ever cried during a research presentation? This was not a possibility we discussed in methods courses in graduate school. Following an expectation of objectivity meant that we would not become emotionally engaged with the people we interviewed, with their experiences or words. Thus, I was not prepared when I first practiced my job talk in my own living room and cried. I practiced it repeatedly until I no longer felt like crying because I worried that I would never be employed if I cried during a job interview. The practicing helped me become distant enough from the suffering I detailed that I could make my analytic points in a standard presentation style in front of audiences.

But then, it happened again. The first time I presented to an audience of Salvadoran youth, at a college conference organized by the college student organization, USEU (Unión Salvadoreña de Estudiantes Universitarios), I read an excerpt from an interview to them in the original Spanish. The mother I had interviewed in California had not seen her daughter in twelve years. With much anguish, she recalled in detail the day she had parted from her daughter to migrate to the United States to provide financially for her family:

> My heart was boiling with sadness. I would watch my daughter play and say, "God, please give me the strength to leave." ... One night I put my daughter to bed and she turned to face the wall. And she always used to hug me, but she did not that day. I think she could sense my

departure . . . and I lay awake crying. And my little girl wakes up and she tells me, "Mami, I want milk (*crying*). I want milk, mami (*crying*)." Those words gave me the strength to [leave]. And I told her, "There is no milk, baby, but I promise I will get you some." And she tells me, "I love you, mami." And I tell her, "I love you too." And she fell asleep until morning . . . That morning, the bus was coming. That was the bus that always sounded the horn loudly at the entrance to the town, and it started . . . I changed my daughter, I put on her pink sandals and I sat her on the table and I told my mother, "Hold her, mom . . . I leave her in your hands. Love her as if she were your own daughter."

(Abrego 2017c: 58)

Although I had already been able to present the same material in English, reading and presenting her words in Spanish to a Salvadoran audience filled me with sorrow and I cried. Horrified, I looked around the room only to find that most people in the audience were also crying. It became an opportunity to acknowledge the pain of these all-too-common family separations in the Salvadoran migrant experience.

That was the last time I cried during a presentation. Instead, I practice and focus on the goal of sharing the material and my analysis with each audience. When I look around the room, however, there are often a few people shedding tears during my reading of interview excerpts. They remind me of the power of study participants' stories and affirm my commitment to them.

I have also been fortunate to hear directly from audience members about how they relate to my work. On one occasion in 2014 at the University of California, Santa Barbara, I gave a talk about how US intervention had played a key role in forcing Salvadorans to flee El Salvador, often leading to family separation. A student I had never met walked up to the front of the room as I was gathering my belongings. The tall, husky young man stood in front of me, wanting to say something, so I looked to engage him. Unlike others who have specific questions about the research, he just asked, "Can I give you a hug?" Surprised, but sensing his sincerity, I said, yes. He gave me a warm, tight hug. Afterward, he told me that his father had been deported to El Salvador when he was only a child. He had grown up with anger, dealing with the turmoil of feeling neglected. Hearing me present my research on how immigration policies play out in other people's lives, he finally understood that his father could not return. It was only in the analytical space of my work that it finally made sense to him that his father's absence did not represent a lack of love, but rather that it was produced by the law and its violent implementation.

As a scholar in search of accompaniment, I bring these experiences into my work. I think of study participants as potential audience members in my presentations and I write with them in mind as much as I write to move and build upon the scholarship on law and society.

CONCLUSION

Credibility in the academic community is based on where people have trained, what degrees they have attained, and how prestigious their publications are, especially in socio-legal work. As an out-of-place scholar, I have been forced to consider these matters. Publications are, after all, the currency of academia. I would not have been employed or tenured without the proper academic qualifications – those things that university committees and administrators can quantify. But what I find most fulfilling in my work is the ability to shape the narrative, highlight the nuances, and underscore the full humanity – my own and that of the study participants who are members of my communities and potential readers of the work. In twenty years, I have learned that even when the exact people I interviewed do not read the final products (often because IRB does not permit me to keep the contact information of interviewees), it may be the case that their children, grandchildren, or other relatives in college classes; or people in very similar life circumstances as them will read their words and feel seen and empowered (see, for example, Sasser 2014). Academic research is both more rigorous and meaningful when our work can reach and faithfully capture the expectations of these multiple audiences (Hale 2008).

Academia presupposes a separation between intellectual and embodied pursuits and prioritizes what feminist scholars and scholars of color critique as a false expectation of objectivity (Collins 1989). An uncritical emphasis on objectivity requires that researchers ignore the messiness of life to categorize people and experiences into dependent and independent variables. Good social science research, in this formulation, is "objective" because it will consistently lead to the same findings, regardless of scholars' social location or emotions. As a scholar with a marginalized positionality, I know this to be false and I welcome the grainy truths that arise in my embodied research and people-centered analysis. I navigate my social location and emotions in detail and at length at every stage of research to serve the purpose of accompanying the very targets of violent laws.

I am constructed as an out-of-place scholar in US academia because I am a Salvadoran immigrant from a working-class background, a subject of US neocolonialism. Using the tools of academia, I make the research process rewarding and more meaningful through accompaniment, by producing work that is more humble, rigorous, and verifiable, not only to the academic community, but – equally importantly – to my own immigrant community, as well. We do this work, we invest time and resources, and we wrestle with the words on the page to weave together stories that will make evident for readers the ways that their own lives, too, are framed within legal structures. When they can see that, and when they can apply that lens to resist in their own lives, out-of-place socio-legal scholars have countered the violent settler-colonial legal system insidiously represented as fair, neutral, and objective; and we have effectively used academic tools in the struggle for justice and liberation.

References

Abrego, Leisy J. 2006. "'I Cannot Go to College Because I Do not Have Papers': Incorporation Patterns of Latino Undocumented Youth." *Latino Studies* 4(3): 212–31.

2008. "Legitimacy, Social, and the Mobilization of Law: The Effects of Assembly Bill 540 on Undocumented Students in California." *Law & Social Inquiry* 33(3): 709–34.

2016. "Illegality as a Source of Solidarity and Tension in Latino Families." *Journal of Latino and Latin American Studies* 8(10): 5–21.

2017a. "Hard Work Alone is Not Enough: Blocked Mobility for Salvadoran Women in the United States." In *US Central Americans: Reconstructing Memories, Struggles, and Communities of Resistance*, edited by Karina O. Alvarado, Ester E. Hernández, and Alicia Ivonne Estrada, 60–76. Tucson: The University of Arizona Press.

2017b. "On Silences: Salvadoran Refugees Then and Now." *Latino Studies* 15(1):73–85.

2017c. *Sacrificando familias: Navegando leyes, trabajo y amor a través de las fronteras*. San Salvador: Universidad Evangélica de El Salvador.

2018a. "Central American Refugees Reveal the Crisis of the State." In *The Handbook of Migration Crises*, edited by Cecilia Menjívar, Marie Ruiz, and Immanuel Ness, 213–28. Oxford: Oxford University Press.

2018b. "Renewed Optimism and Spatial Mobility: Legal Consciousness of Latino Deferred Action for Childhood Arrivals Recipients and Their Families in Los Angeles." *Ethnicities* 18(2): 192–207.

Abrego, Leisy J., and Ester Hernández. 2021. "#FamiliesBelongTogether: Central American Family Separations From the 1980s to 2019." In *Critical Diálogos in Latinx/a/o Studies*, edited by Ana Ramos-Zayas and Mérida Rúa, 173–85. New York: New York University Press.

Abrego, Leisy, and Alejandro Villalpando. 2021. "Racialization of Central Americans in the United States." In *Precarity and Belonging: Labor, Migration, and Noncitizenship*, edited by Sylvanna Falcón, Steve McKay, Juan Poblete, Catherine S. Ramírez, and Felicity Amaya Schaeffer, 51–66. New Brunswick, NJ: Rutgers University Press.

Carbado, Devon W., and Daria Roithmayr. 2014. "Critical Race Theory Meets Social Science." *Annual Review of Law and Social Science* 10: 149–67.

Collins, Patricia Hill. 1989. "The Social Construction of Black Feminist Thought." *Signs* 14(4): 745–73.

Fisher, Celia B., and Andrea E. Anushko. 2008. "Research Ethics in Social Science." In *The SAGE Handbook of Social Research Methods*, edited by Pertti Alasuutari, Leonard Bickman, and Julia Brannen, 95–110. London: Sage Publications.

Gilmore, Ruth Wilson. 1993. "Public Enemies and Private Intellectuals: Apartheid USA." *Race & Class* 35(1): 69–78.

González-López, Gloria. 2010. "Ethnographic Lessons: Researching Incest in Mexican Families." *Journal of Contemporary Ethnography* 39: 569–81.

2011. "Mindful Ethics: Comments on Informant-Centered Practices in Sociological Research." *Qualitative Sociology* 34: 447–61.

Gordon, Milton. 1964. *Assimilation in American Life: The Role of Race, Religion, and National Origins*. New York: Oxford University Press.

Gupta, Akhil, and James Ferguson, eds. 1997. *Anthropological Locations: Boundaries and Grounds of a Field Science*. Berkeley: University of California Press.

Hale, Charles R., ed. 2008. *Engaging Contradictions: Theory, Politics, and Methods of Activist Scholarship*. Berkeley: University of California Press.

Luker, Kristin. 2008. *Salsa Dancing into Social Science*. Cambridge, MA: Harvard University Press.

Menjívar, Cecilia, and Leisy Abrego. 2012. "Legal Violence: Immigration Law and the Lives of Central American Immigrants." *American Journal of Sociology* 117(5): 1380–424.

Morgensen, Scott Lauria. 2012. "Destabilizing the Settler Academy: The Decolonial Effects of Indigenous Methodologies." *American Quarterly* 64(4): 805–8.

Negrón-Gonzales, Genevieve. 2014. "The Power of the Pen: Writing Mentorship and Chicana/o M.A. Students." *Journal of Latinos and Education* 13(1): 62–70.

Osuji, Chinyere. 2019. *Boundaries of Love: Interracial Marriage and the Meaning of Race.* New York: New York University Press.

Osuna, Steven. 2017. "Class Suicide: The Black Radical Tradition, Radical Scholarship, and the Neoliberal Turn." In *Futures of Black Radicalism,* edited by Gaye T. Johnson and Alex Lubin, 21–38. London and Brooklyn, NY: Verso.

Park, Robert. 1950. *Race and Culture.* Glencoe, IL: The Free Press.

Sasser, Jade S. 2014. "Giving What to Whom? Thoughts on Feminist Knowledge Production." Research Note. *Journal of Research Practice* 10(2).

Speed, Shannon. 2019. *Incarcerated Stories: Indigenous Women Migrants and Violence in the Settler-Capitalist State.* Chapel Hill: University of North Carolina Press.

Tomlinson, Barbara, and George Lipsitz. 2019. *Insubordinate Spaces: Improvisation and Accompaniment for Social Justice.* Philadelphia, PA: Temple University Press.

CHAPTER THREE

"PRETTY AND YOUNG" IN PLACES WHERE PEOPLE GET KILLED IN BROAD DAYLIGHT

Sindiso Mnisi Weeks

> *You think because you are pretty and young, and people are friendly and smiling toward you, that this is a safe place. . . . People get killed here in broad daylight!*

These were the approximate words delivered by my host, Magogo, when she reprimanded me after I had arrived at her home after dark one evening. It was the first time in almost three years of doing research in the Msinga area – located in KwaZulu-Natal, South Africa – that I had seen or heard my usually extremely loving and friendly host so angry. I knew she must have been very worried about my colleague and me.

This interaction with my host was the first in a series of experiences that would lead me to seriously consider for the first time the relevance and impact of my psychological and emotional well-being, as well as physical safety and health, on my research and findings. From this place, I wrestled with the balance of dealing with the difficulties and responsibilities of fieldwork alongside personal (and professional) challenges. This journey is what has formed me as a scholar-activist, teacher, mentor, and, more generally, as a compassionate human being.

The brief but sobering exchange I had with my host that night brings out some of the important lessons I gradually learned about being an "out-of-place" researcher during my time of conducting research in Msinga. Here, I use out-of-place researcher in the more comprehensive sense of bearing a marginalized mix of identities in *both* the academy

57

and the field site, and thus being an insider-outsider wherever one goes.[1]

This crossover representation of the out-of-place researcher is legitimate because, even in the field, study participants recognize the Black, African woman PhD holder that I am as an anomaly and observe that, of those who have come to study the subject or the area before, few if any looked like me. That is not too surprising. The more daring claim I might make about the crossover significance of this out-of-place researcher persona is that the overlap that exists between my identities and those of the people I study in the field sometimes lowers my credibility in the academy because it is read as meaning that I am less "academic" or identify "too closely" with the study participants. This, as my story shows, has and continues to be a source of deep tension for me.

I am a young, Black, African woman. At least, those are the most salient parts of my identity, as people perceive me, and that very fact has largely shaped the ways in which I am experienced and I myself experience life "in the field." Moreover, the parts of my identity that are less salient (being an Oxford postgraduate student, getting married, becoming a mother, being a Jo'burger by origin and later a Cape Town resident, being a daughter whose family cares for her, and more) have become more or less important to my fieldwork experience – often in ways that I had not anticipated.

Do I identify myself by these labels? With respect to being young: yes. However, I often find it quite entertaining to see how people interact with me when they perceive me as quite a bit younger than I actually am. With respect to being Black: indeed, that is how I would label myself. That is, I identify with the diaspora of melanin-enhanced peoples who have suffered roughly 400 years of systemic oppression under Western "imperialist white supremacist capitalist patriarchy" (hooks 2013, 4). Yet, I have long since learned that that shared identity means many different things in different places – from Johannesburg (the nine million-person-strong economic engine on the northeastern gold reef of South Africa) to Cape Town (the cosmopolitan city of about three million permanent residents in the south west corner of South Africa whose population is doubled by the influx of tourists at the height of the holiday season) to Battle (a storied, historic rural town of about 4,000 people in the south east of the United Kingdom)

---

[1] See Merriam et al. (2001) for a helpful discussion of the complexities of delineating who is an insider versus an outsider.

to Greater Boston (the metropolitan region of New England in the north east of the United States which, as a combined statistical area, boasts a population of over eight million). The same can be said of my self-perception as a woman: as the debates on western feminism, Black feminism, African feminism, womanism and more show, the definition of *woman* cannot be taken for granted.[2] As for "pretty," I would not have used it to describe myself and honestly found Magogo's use of that descriptor jarring.

My primary identification as a young, Black African woman is partly a response to how I am perceived not only in the field in Msinga, but also in the field of law and society. Until the fieldwork experience within which my interaction with Magogo is situated, I had conducted field-based research in sites that might be referred to as somewhat challenging and, as any well-trained ethnographer, I had spent a significant amount of time reflecting on the impact of my identity and positionality[3] as a researcher on my access and acceptance in my field sites as well as the research findings to which these led me. In other words, I had considered what it meant for me to be out of place in the locale where I was conducting my study, where people predominantly spoke a different language – or, at least, a different dialect – from me and were significantly poorer than I had ever experienced being. I was also often out of place in the patriarchal power centers in those communities where men mostly made decisions concerning legal matters.

Before this moment of confrontation with a side of Msinga I had mostly suppressed in my mind until then, I had grappled with questions of what it meant to be an interdisciplinary socio-legal scholar who is a minority in an academy in which the default representative is a white, middle-aged, European and/or American male locked in a single discipline. In other words, I had spent much time considering how best to position myself and my work studying legal power – especially

---

[2] For a taste of what I mean, see hooks (1981) and Oyěwùmí (1997).

[3] There is some debate in the literature about whether identity is an analytically useful lens as contrasted with location and positionality. (See the discussion of this in Anthias 2002.) I use both concepts here because I believe they bring different things to the discussion, in the ways that I use them, with the former, identity, perhaps emphasizing how one is perceived by others while the latter primarily emphasizes the vantage point from which a person engages with those others that they are studying and how that impacts how they see the "other." See England (1994) for more discussion.

considering the fact that I am out of place in the professoriate. This concern was particularly relevant because of how legal power in the formal corridors of executive, legislative and judicial power is substantially informed by, and sometimes mutually constitutive with the power of, voice that comes with being a white male in the academy. A simple example of this can be seen in the fact that, for centuries, the formal law's understanding of the customary law of Black, African people has been based on articulations of such by white, male anthropologists of European or American nationality or ancestry. This is still meaningfully the case.

The exchange I base this chapter on represents some of the heuristic tensions presented by my intersectional identities and how they mutually interacted – within me and with others – in the field site during the course of my research on law and society in remote rural areas of South Africa. As I share in concluding this chapter, my fieldwork has taught me several sobering lessons. Ignorance – by which I mean wilful blindness – is not bliss. Faced with serious risks in the field, instead of thinking carefully and realistically, the strategy that I adopted was to downplay the risks so as to build up my courage to venture into that field site. Relatedly, many lessons that I emerged from the field with center on the researcher's determination and how that impacts one's work for better and for worse. One consequence of working in such a challenging field site as mine was the vicarious trauma that I experienced – especially when I analyzed the data I had collected and wrote up my mostly devastating findings. This lesson was accompanied by the enhanced empathy that I emerged with, which challenged so much of what I had thought I had learned about placing critical distance between myself and my subjects in empirical socio-legal research.[4]

As pertains to legal power, I learned that the same dynamics that make *identity* matters (especially those of race and gender) *power* matters in how they manifest in law often express themselves very similarly in field research because intersectionality *always* matters (Crenshaw 1990; Collins 2019). This is partly a function of the fact that social and legal injustice go together. I sometimes had trouble finding legal power given that it is so diffuse. Due to the plurality of social and other institutions, legal power was both inside and outside

---

[4] See the ground-breaking critique by England (1994).

"courts," often out of sight. Pursuing it also meant that I found myself embroiled in the tensions presented by my subject of choice because the subject (and my authority on it) was always impacted by my own positionality and intersectionality – raising questions such as whether I was too close to my subjects, not objective enough, or not academic at all.[5] In essence, intersectionality presents itself as a proverbial double-edged sword: with many benefits and drawbacks at once.

RESEARCH BACKGROUND

I study law in informal places: that is, outside of state courts. In particular, I study law in traditional justice forums and ordinary rural people's day-to-day lives. In other words, I study law's interaction with society in often modest or dilapidated buildings established or funded by the government – like traditional council offices, schools with long drops (outhouses) for toilet facilities, small but often oversubscribed clinics, and chiefs' homes, as well as police stations. I also study the relationship between law and society in wholly unofficial places such as under headmen's trees, in their homes, in ordinary men and women's day-to-day encounters with law (in the broadest possible sense) wherever those take them: whether that be to dirt roads, grassy trails, and thoroughfares; cornfields, irrigation scheme farm plots, or marijuana harvest fields; cattle kraals, wide open plains where sheep and goats graze, rivers by which women collect water or fresh tree branches, or cliffs where people might work to build a road for small change (in both meanings of money and transformation).

The experience I am sharing in this chapter is primarily based on empirical research that formed the basis of a study published as a book, *Access to Justice and Human Security: Cultural Contradictions in Rural South Africa* (Mnisi Weeks 2018). I originally completed the ethnographic research for the Rural Women's Action-Research project while I was a Senior Researcher in the Centre for Law and Society at the University of Cape Town. At the time of the project's inception, a controversial piece of legislation, the Traditional Courts Bill (B15–2008), was being considered in parliament. The object of the study was to document how traditional courts operate in contemporary rural South Africa and also what traditional leaders (particularly

---

[5] As observed by Zuberi and Bonilla-Silva (2008): "Ah, whiteness grants the gift of *eternal objectivity* to its grantees!" (emphasis in original).

headmen) do as their work on a day-to-day basis. This research could then inform policy discussions about how to regulate traditional courts through legislation under the Constitution of South Africa, 1996. It was, in that sense, aimed at being a kind of "critical ethnography" (Simon and Dippo 1986, 199).

The study was conducted between October 2009 and June 2015 with the bulk of data collected between March 2011 and January 2012 in the form of daily recording of headmen's activities and day-to-day work, observation of traditional dispute management processes such as hearings for the disputes that the headmen participated in managing, follow-up interviews with parties to the disputes and traditional authorities, including traditional council support staff, and focus groups with the members of the traditional councils and groups of local men and women.

Preliminary interviews and observations were conducted from October 2009 to February 2011, and follow-up interviews, focus groups, and report back sessions were conducted from February 2012 to June 2015. During the most concentrated data collection period of March 2011 to January 2012, local fieldworkers and I recorded 183 instances of the informal process named *izikhalo* (cries/pleas), as contrasted with seventy-one formal hearings across the six wards in two traditional communities (what were formerly referred to as "tribes") that were the sites of our research.

Msinga, KwaZulu-Natal, was chosen as the site for this study because, firstly, it is well known to be a very deeply rural and traditional area; therefore, if there was any place in South Africa where traditional courts could be expected to function optimally, Msinga was it. Secondly, the Centre for Law and Society has strong relationships with a nongovernmental organization that was long-established in Msinga as well as another researcher whose work was based there. These relationships served as lubricants for the relationships on which access and acceptance in the turbulent area would depend.

In brief, the findings of the research were that, indeed, for most people in rural South Africa, traditional justice mechanisms provide the only feasible means to legal solutions to conflict (Mnisi Weeks 2018). Yet, while these mechanisms are popularly associated with restorative justice, reconciliation and harmony, the political economy of rural South Africa in which the study was based reveals how historical conditions and contemporary pressures have resulted in a degree of human insecurity that has strained these mechanisms' ability to deliver the high normative ideals with which they are notionally linked.

The book shines a spotlight on the ways in which the South African government – under colonialism, apartheid, and democracy today – has failed to take truly seriously the volatile human conditions of ordinary people and traditional authorities alike, such as poverty, gendered social relations, delicate social trust, and plausibility of violent self-help. The book therefore provides a vision for access to justice in rural South Africa that attempts to address that failure by proposing a more practicable set of solutions to access to justice in rural South Africa. The proposal is of a cooperative governance model that maximizes the resources and capacity of both traditional and state justice apparatus for delivering legal and social justice that meets rural people's basic human needs.

As I will detail below, Msinga has a high propensity of guns as a result of the exploitative political economic arrangements established under prior governments. It experiences police brutality in the name of putting an end to crime and ridding the community of guns and the violence that comes with them. Children there are exposed to high levels of multiple forms of violence – largely grounded in multigenerational poverty and the destruction of the social fabric that were both produced by the political economy of the imperialist and racist regimes of colonialism and apartheid – but the state focuses primarily (really, rhetorically) on the interpersonal and mostly neglects to address the structural.

Furthermore, there is contestation over large swathes of the land (as well as their borders) in terms of who owns it, which law (amidst the plurality that exists) will govern it, and what the content of that law is, and what powers and limits it assigns. The state's role as protector is blurred as often enough the state also acts as violator of people's rights by exercising undue and excessive force against people there or, if not that, simply neglect. Also, there is no bright line between social and legal injustice as the two seem to flow into each other and come very much hand-in-hand. The setting is further complicated by the fact that cooperation between traditional justice mechanisms and the criminal and social justice mechanisms the state purports to make available is woefully inadequate while both institutional structures also compete with the pervasive reality of vigilantism in South Africa (Smith 2019). The above composition of political, economic, and social factors provides a much stronger explanation for the extent and kinds of violence in Msinga than does the standard appeal to cultural explanations. It is in this context that the words of Magogo, my Msinga host, must be understood.

BEING OUT OF PLACE

It had been a lovely afternoon and, on arriving in Msinga from Cape Town after a two-hour flight followed by a three-hour drive to reach our research site, my junior colleague and I had been faced with the decision whether to try to squeeze in one set of interviews before turning in. As the one who had to make the call, I had decided to give it a try. I opted to go to the home of the interlocutor who lived nearest to the place where we would be staying the night.

I was being optimistic – as it turned out, unrealistically so. Firstly, everywhere you go in Msinga is far. The distances between most locations are vast and mostly span dirt roads varying in their car-friendliness. Secondly, having failed to factor east–west variation, I had poorly estimated when it would become dark. Given that South Africa is all on a single time-zone, my expectation of when the sun would set based on living in Cape Town, which is on the southwest coast, was vastly out of sync with the reality in KwaZulu-Natal, which is on the east coast. Consequently, I was taken by surprise at the rapidity with which the sun was setting while we were trying to maneuver our miniature rental car over giant-sized boulders that stood in for a road to the home of the woman we were attempting to reach on the other side of the small mountain.

I shall not lie: It was a scary scene. As I tried to drive us up the mountain pass without damaging the vehicle, getting a flat tire, or ending up stuck there with little to no cellphone signal, and saw the sun setting, I had become quite nervous. Yet, we were so far into the journey that there seemed nothing to be gained by panicking, and turning back seemed like no better an option than proceeding forward. After all, it would be no easier to get our car off the rocks in order to turn around than it was proving to be to move it sideways to reach the then-closer apex. So, I tried my best to keep my cool while I prayed desperately (additionally struck by the weight of having my younger female colleague's life in my hands) and did my best to get us out of there. Thankfully, my prayers were answered.

Once we had reached the home of our intended interlocutor, the interview was so helpful as to feel like a justification of the risk we had taken to secure it. Yet it was becoming dark quite quickly. I tried my best to expedite our departure without appearing rude and then, rather than impose on the grace of an impoverished woman we hardly knew by staying the night, I allowed optimism to lead me to take one final risk that evening. So, my colleague and I got back into our miniature rental and made our way – slowly sliding and rock-jumping – down the mountain pass. Yet again, I was praying like my life depended on it. Because, frankly, it did.

Thankfully, we made it to our accommodation without event. It was our arriving after dark that made our host in the deep rural village of Msinga livid. Magogo chastised us about how dangerous Msinga is for *all* people, but especially two young women driving on their own in what is (by Msinga standards) a flashy car. She went through a litany of scenarios of what could have happened: We could have gotten stuck in that mountain pass and been sitting ducks; on our drive back, we could have found a makeshift roadblock of giant-sized boulders set up by young men who saw us and the car we were in as an opportunity. Simply put, we could have been sexually assaulted, maimed, and/or killed. She ended by making it clear that the risk we had taken had been unbelievably stupid.

It seemed our host was determined to drive home to us in a way she had not done before just how dangerous a place Msinga is for young women like us. So, for added emphasis, Magogo told us of a young, white, female researcher who had been driving near the town center – and thus a presumably much safer part of Msinga than where we had been – while doing research on local beadwork several years ago. She had been shot and killed at 2 p.m. That is how indiscriminately violent Msinga is, Magogo concluded.

Because this was the first such conversation Magogo had had with me directly about my own personal safety in Msinga, I was compelled to think very seriously about it, which raised the daunting question of whether the risks of doing research there were too great for my family and me to bear. When I had told my mother that I would be doing research in Msinga, she had sounded the alarm. Msinga, she said, is extremely dangerous. Her statement was not entirely news to me. Growing up in the late 1980s and early 1990s, I had heard of Msinga as being particularly violent. This was during the height of the anti-apartheid struggle and the tumultuous time of fighting (nearing civil war) in the lead-up to the first democratic elections in South Africa, which had been most intense in KwaZulu-Natal where the Zulu-led

Inkatha Freedom Party had clashed with the Xhosa-led African National Congress.

However, I was determined to believe that Msinga was much safer now and folklore about this place was somewhat misplaced. Nor was I alone. In one of my final focus groups, local headmen were at pains to remind me that Msinga was much better than it had been; they wanted my book to let people know that they had made great strides toward ensuring peace. This is absolutely true. Yet Msinga is still very dangerous, with a history of large-scale violence taking place cyclically.

Through research, I learned that Msinga's history has a very heavy presence of firearms – predominantly illegal ones. According to Creina Alcock (Cousins et al. 2011), in 1868 men walked more than 600 km to work as diamond miners in Kimberley and were there reimbursed with guns as part of their wages. Alcock observes that at the time there was already a rumor that Zulu men possessed thousands of firearms, which rumor was borne out by 1932 when guns were coming to replace spears in local fighting as proven by the propensity of bullet wounds. Suffice it to say that firearms form a significant part of the comprehensively violent conflict landscape in Msinga and are therefore one of the dimensions of disputing that local forums I was setting out to study are required to manage on an ongoing basis.

Louise Meintjes (2017, 288) observes:

> Consider what it might mean to be a gun trade center in a gun-ridden nation. At the millennium's turn, there were 4.2 million licensed firearms in South Africa (Cock 2001, 48). This figure is high for a country of about forty million people, giving some indication of the density of weapon ownership in a hotspot like Msinga. Such easy availability of guns ups the opportunities and perhaps the felt necessities of gun ownership as well as the potential for serious injury (Cock 2001), while the display of weaponry, as well as its use, is a product of years of opposition to apartheid (Xaba 2001).

Needless to say, conducting research in such a setting is probably dangerous – whether one confronts this probability or tends to mostly ignore it as I did. Nonetheless, being young and naïvely optimistic, to be honest, I had thought little of my mother's concerns. If anything, I now realize that I must have subconsciously worn Msinga's dangerous reputation as an article of some pride because doing research in the area then surely meant that I was somewhat of a "bad ass."

That sentiment in itself shows just how out of place I was because it was probably borne more out of privilege than I care to admit. Msinga is a very poor, rural, Zulu-speaking area, and I am a person of Swati heritage who grew up in an urban township (Soweto) but attended private school virtually all my life. From six years of age, I attended what was referred to colloquially in those days as a "white school," located in the Northern suburbs of Johannesburg. I was one of the lucky ones; as my family liked to say, I was "born with a silver teaspoon in my mouth." For reasons that are obviously related to my uncanny privilege considering the circumstances of my birth, I hold the highest attainable degree of education from a very well-known university abroad: Oxford.

The areas I have researched have always been very poor and, while I experienced poverty at times while growing up, it was nothing like the severity of poverty and isolation that many of the (especially female) people I study have and continue to experience. While I was born under apartheid like most who I engage with in my research, I was fortunate enough to grow up in its sunset decade and come of age when it officially ended so that, being as fortuitously positioned as I was, I benefited from many of the opportunities offered by the dawn of democracy.

Areas such as Msinga are very harsh places for (especially young) women; for men too, of course, but in different ways. While the socio-legal institutions I study are male-dominated, sometimes even exclusively male, I rarely felt unsafe or at risk. As far as I could tell, the idea that "ignorance is bliss" had so far proven true for me. In reality, in my personal life, I knew nothing of the overlapping forms of structural and interpersonal violence suffered by the people I often engaged with in my research. The truth, then, is that I probably did not know how to respond when presented with as real a risk as conducting research in Msinga for the first time.

RESPONDING TO BEING OUT OF PLACE

I have generally responded to my being out of place in the areas where I conduct fieldwork by trying to fit in. For instance, I have sought to dress in ways that are considered respectable and respectful in those places, and I have changed my comportment to appear more suitably acculturated. As a Black woman going into spaces that emphasize such external appearances and personal conduct, I have honestly felt that I had no choice.

Invariably, I have misjudged situations at times – perhaps by over-compensating for my foreignness or not modulating my behaviors enough. The anecdote that opens this chapter is a challenging example of the latter fault, while I worry that my first marriage proposal was a product of the former error. The worst that had come of that was disruption of my PhD field research when I ultimately had to change site because of the persistence of one senior traditional leader's pursuits and determination to coddle and woo me,[6] thus denying me access to the places I wanted to study critically (using participant observation).[7] But that was doing research in Swati-speaking communities in Mpumalanga that were vastly different from Msinga.

Some practical challenges have been posed by my identities since the beginning of my empirical research journey; for instance, being a woman who is identifiable with the communities but also clearly an outsider has presented limitations such as the fact that women cannot enter certain spaces in which men have the important conversations. But my mix of identities has also offered a lot of opportunities simply because I am treated differently than other (that is, local) women. For example, because I am a highly educated woman, I have been permitted to visit places that I would not be allowed to if I was a local woman and have been permitted to ask questions that I might not otherwise have been allowed to ask.

These are the same ways in which my personal identity characteristics relate to or may even challenge the power of the colonially legislated and enforced patriarchy of law in my research sites, potentially reshaping my study through my identity, history, and background. Put differently, because of my identity, history, and background, I am able to straddle what (at least, preliminarily) presents as a deep patriarchal divide between men and women as inhabitants of the physical places and legal spaces in their rural lives. Aside from the aforementioned practical challenges, I have been unbelievably fortunate never to encounter severe forms of harassment (or discrimination other than

[6] I have previously written about this (Mnisi Weeks 2014).
[7] By participant observation, I mean that my primary method of information gathering was actively engaging in the daily routine of community members, their events, rituals, and culture, and also being generally vigilant in case opportunities for passive involvement or pure observation of family relations as well as corporate dispute settlement and law enforcement in the local courts would arise. This immersion in the community was complemented by interviews with its members. See Dewalt and Dewalt (2002 at 1, 19); Nader (1997); Marks (2005).

that already mentioned on the basis of access as a woman) in my research. One might even say I was somewhat spoiled.

My determinedly naïve attitude – what one might reasonably label "wilful blindness" (Heffernan 2011) – to Msinga changed quite significantly with the conversation with Magogo that I have recounted previously. From having regarded the personal and professional accounts I was collecting from study participants as mere anomalies (the exceptions that prove the rule of goodwill and safety even in Msinga), I shifted to seeing them for what they were: a patchwork of experiences of severe human insecurity among a near-forgotten people in remote parts of what is often found to be the most unequal country in the world.

As it turned out, the visit was followed by my first real deep dive into the data I had collected in Msinga to analyze it, and this data bore out what I was coming to believe about Msinga as crystallized by that conversation with my host: that Msinga is a comprehensively dangerous place. Confronting this truth led me to a challenging place psychologically and emotionally. Fortunately, this all happened toward the end of my extended data collection period because, frankly, it became very difficult for me to return to Msinga after that. On the one occasion when I returned for fieldwork, I asked a colleague to accompany me. A few months after, I experienced a debilitating case of extreme fatigue – otherwise known as burnout (Chen and Gorski 2015). My doctor placed me on medical leave. While I did not recognize it as such at the time, and did not fully confront until years later while writing this chapter, I was experiencing secondary trauma from delving so deeply into the narratives of struggle and violence that I was collecting through my research.

"Vicarious traumatization" was first named such by Lisa McCann and Laurie Ann Pearlman (1990) who defined it as the symptoms (or "enduring psychological consequences") suffered by therapists who are exposed to traumatic events in and through the support they provide victims of said traumatic experiences. These "cardinal signs and symptoms of the aftermath of a serious victimization" include "nightmares, fearful thoughts, intrusive images, and suspicion of other people's motives," which commonly occur among people who have suffered victimization. What distinguished the study participants McCann and Pearlman were describing as experiencing these symptoms was that they were therapists who had not themselves "directly experienced a victimization or catastrophe" (132). What had brought them these symptoms was their service in the role of "mental health professionals who spend a significant proportion of their professional time doing therapy with or studying persons who have been victimized" (132).

As McCann and Pearlman summarize the phenomenon: "Persons who work with victims may experience profound psychological effects, effects that can be disruptive and painful for the helper and can persist for months or years after work with traumatized persons. We term this process 'vicarious traumatization'" (133). Since McCann and Pearlman's 1990 publication, the phenomenon I describe has become widely identified in the literature under names including "vicarious trauma" and "secondary traumatic stress" (Newell and MacNeil 2010). It has also been closely associated with "compassion fatigue" and "burnout" (Ibid.). Yet, in its crispest definition, according to Dana Branson, "vicarious trauma" refers to "the unique, negative, and accumulative changes that can occur to clinicians who engage in an empathetic relationship with clients" (Branson 2019, 2). As Branson describes, vicarious trauma develops in direct relationship "to client disclosures of trauma, often detailed and graphic" (2), and results in changes that can be mental, emotional, physical and spiritual (2–3).

While I was obviously not serving in the role of therapist, through my research, I was witnessing – over and over again – the suffering of people who lived in deeply vulnerable circumstances and were regularly confronted with serious risks, if not the reality, of harm and helplessness in their locale. Studying the phenomena of access to justice in the context of profound human insecurity (lack of "freedom of want" and "freedom of fear" [Alkire 2003]), was causing me deep suffering that I sought to simply brush aside as "not that serious." After all, I was not the one living with the trauma that faced my interlocutors day in and day out – and being a law and society scholar can hardly be equated with being a therapist, counselor, or social worker. Nonetheless, in hindsight, it is difficult for me not to relate the following summary by Branson (2019, 3) to my experience:

> Engaging in an empathic relationship with a client and understanding trauma from the client's person-in-environment point of view is an essential part of a clinician's skill-set and therapeutic rapport (Chang, Scott, & Decker, 2013). This necessitates the clinician being open to the subjective disclosures of the client, suspending personal values and

judgments, and adopting the client's worldview. Additionally, it entails comprehending what the traumatic events mean intrinsically to the client and corresponding dysfunction(s). This level of therapeutic intimacy creates a vulnerability for the clinician to be "infected" with the cognitive and affective aspects of the client's trauma (Aparicio et al. 2013; Van Hook & Rothenberg 2009).

Much of what a therapist is trained to do is what I, as an ethnographer, sought to do. The sheer empathetic (or, as we anthropologists call it, "emic") exposure to intimate narratives of the terrible insecurity with which people lived on a regular basis was enough on its own to trigger vicarious trauma for me but, as it turned out, it was compounded by my own personal identity's interplay with the truth of that reality in which people in Msinga live.

When the identity lines between insider and outsider are so blurry as they were between my interlocutors in Msinga and myself – and the moral weight of our comparative experiences as great as it was and remains for me – it is difficult for me to see how I could not empathize at such a deep level as to become "vulnerable" to "infection" by their trauma. Thus, because of all the differentiating factors I have named between my study participants and myself, I feel like the main challenges posed by my identity were internal. They began with the impostor syndrome that many people attest to feeling when it comes to being a scholar or being in the ivory tower – especially when a woman, person of color or bearing other "minority" identities in these spaces.

For me, this impostor syndrome has wrapped into it a related "survivor guilt" of sorts (Hutson et al. 2015): that is, "guilt at having survived when others who seem to be equally, if not more, deserving" – as in the case of many of my very own immediate family members – did not (Piorkowski 1983). I have therefore spent a lot of time thinking about – and really struggling with – the fact that, *but for* a number of random events and immense fortune on my part, the positions of the people I study and myself could easily have been wholly reversed. In terms of my being Black, African, and female as are much of the world's poorest and most disenfranchised, I could easily have been just as poor as the vast majority of my race and gender. Hence, my position and that of my study subjects could have been exactly the same; I could have been just as poor, marginalized, and insecure as they. Yet, what an unspeakable privilege to be in my position as opposed to theirs – literally unspeakable, so much so that I could not even tell of the dehumanizing impact of the fundamentally racist separation between their daily worlds and my own that I was suffering to myself.[8]

Working with our local nongovernmental organization partners in Msinga, we had settled on ways to compensate people for their time and participation in the study (some limits were placed on this by our NGO partners' concerns about raising the costs and expectations associated with surveying local residents, as the NGO had to do in order to provide effective services to the local community). We gave the headmen blankets and cellphones as gifts for their extended participation. We gave stipends to the local fieldworkers who assisted us with recording data. We provided transportation to carry people over the vast distances and catered generous meals for focus group participants. We brought small gifts of material necessities to interviewees and, whenever I stopped to spend some time getting to know people and asking them about their lives, they expressed deep appreciation for my doing so – as if it was the first time that they had felt "seen." To me, none of this felt adequate; only relief of their endemic insecurity would do.

Consequently, I sometimes (often?) struggle with entering the intimate spaces of people's lives for brief moments in order to excavate the legally relevant elements therein for the purposes of developing deeper understanding of the tensions between ordinary rural people's legal consciousness and practices, on the one hand, and the legal culture of formal institutions charged with making and enforcing the law, on the other. bell hooks's (1990, 151–2) words deafeningly resound in my mind:

> Often this speech about the 'Other' annihilates, erases: 'no need to hear your voice when I can talk about you better than you can speak about yourself. No need to hear your voice. Only tell me about your pain. I want to know your story. And then I will tell it back to you in a new way. Tell it back to you in such a way that it has become mine, my own. Re-writing you, I write myself anew. I am still author, authority. I am still the colonizer, the speaking subject, and you are now at the center of my talk.

---

[8] Here, I draw on and extend the literature arguing that experiences of racism themselves can be trauma-inducing. See, for example, Bryant-Davis and Ocampo (2005).

How is what I am doing different – not just "black skin" with "white mask" (Fanon 2008)? Yes, I think I have got the "why we speak" that hooks (1990, 151) emphasizes in order. Yet, to what end?

Especially knowing that any positive benefits or consequences of my scholarly contribution will not be immediate for study participants and will probably not be seen directly impacting the lives of those who shared their stories with me, I struggle with justifying to myself why I should dare to ask them to take time out of their daily attempts to merely survive in order to help me understand better the circumstances in which they make those efforts to survive and maybe one day thrive. Those are the inner challenges I grapple with. On the other hand, there are potentially openings presented by my identities too in that I am granted access to those spaces in ways that allow me to hopefully (at best) shed light on aspects of life and law on which others may not have been able. And I have to remind myself that the work I do will hopefully positively impact the lives of my study participants' progeny, even if only indirectly.

In practical terms, how these challenges and opportunities all played out with respect to the ultimate completion of my Msinga project is that I had to step back from it for a long period – to take time to get well again. The first draft of my book was more of a therapeutic writing exercise than a research account of scholarly findings. As colleagues with whom I shared that draft for feedback responded, they understood that this was my attempt at making sense of some extremely dark elements of the human experience. It was an early part of my healing process. In essence, their feedback was to take a break and come back to it anew. Following that feedback, I found I could not really bring myself to revisit my draft again and finish the manuscript for a long time. Instead, I focused on other parts of my professional and personal life. I read. I taught. I wrote other products on mostly unrelated subjects. I attended therapy. I had twins.

It was toward the end of my parental leave that I very cautiously started revisiting my draft manuscript. The conviction that came from my learning of the brutal killing of one of the headmen who had partnered with us on the research largely returned me to the completion of the work. He was shot in broad daylight on February 13, 2016, by young men who were heard shouting, "Babulaleni bonke, bayizinja!" or "Kill them all, they are dogs!" According to our NGO partner's annual report (which I received at the end of that year), "He was the third [Nakudala] induna to be killed in six months, a tally that makes it difficult to find a replacement for the job." Even though he had been one of the more difficult headmen to work with and to understand, I felt a sense of debt toward him. I had the distinct sense that I owed it to him – and to his daughters who I had gotten to know briefly – to tell his story.

My sense of conviction was also aided by my parental leave during Fall 2016 which I found refreshed me at a soul level (due to the sheer relief of safely bringing these two precious, tiny human beings into the world) rather than at a physical level (because it goes without saying that I was not getting much sleep or time to do anything solely for myself during that period). This, even as my high-risk pregnancy and emergency birth experience as a very educated and privileged but nonetheless *Black* woman in America (and the long journey I was beginning of recovery from it), had brought me fresh determination to better understand the very nature of trauma and, later, the best avenues for healing.

LESSON(S)

The lessons I have learned are challenging to talk and write about, as they are still very much unresolved. Everything still feels raw to this day. Even as I wrote this chapter, I found that my recall of events was patchy; elements of a story would return in uncoordinated waves that were difficult for me to confront. As I have tried to understand what it is about the experience that still haunts me, I settle on one main thing: I remain challenged by the privilege of even describing the psychological challenges I encountered due to my fieldwork experience as "trauma." As someone very dear once told me: "you can say that you are suffering because you can [afford to] go to a psychologist." In other words, in a world in which the visibility and validity of human suffering depends on its legitimation by scientific and professional knowledge processes, it is my privileged access to the latter that permits me to say that I have "suffered trauma." Even today, I feel that my "vicarious trauma" was a distinct marker of privilege: the equivalent of "white fragility"[9] or #firstworldproblems. What right then do I have to whine about it, even here, and what lessons do I really have the right to draw from it, as it were?

---

[9] Particularly in the sense of entitlement to comfort in this area of life being challenged. See DiAngelo (2018).

Yet, perhaps two lessons emerge. Firstly, clearly, ignorance during fieldwork is *not* bliss. Rather it can conceal a naïveté and youthful arrogance that is quite dangerous as is wilful blindness; or, perhaps, under a more charitable interpretation, it can conceal a sense of purpose and determination that may not always serve one. Whatever the case, it is important for researchers to think carefully – and realistically – about what risks they are prepared to take to gather their data and how their feelings or assessments of such might shift with time. Concerning my own physical safety, part of me worries that I silenced my own fears because I doubted that, if I faced them, I would have enough courage to persist in conducting the study. Nonetheless, one thing I had not sufficiently pondered in advance was the reality and potency of vicarious trauma. Had I done so, I might have counselled myself to engage in more active self-care in the radical sense in which Audre Lorde used that term (2017), ensuring that I treated it as being just as important to plan for and incorporate as other elements of my research plan and instruments.

Again, I do not wish to suggest that being an ethnographer in places "where people get killed in broad daylight" is equivalent to being a clinician. However, there are parallels as I have pointed out before. These parallels necessitate particular preparation. Branson (2019) writes of this need:

> As a result of the client–clinician relationship, some researchers see VT as an inevitability, natural, and normal response to the therapeutic relationship (Barrington & Shakespeare-Finch, 2013; Sansbury et al., 2015) and therefore should be considered a hazard of the work and a catalyst for prevention development, training initiatives, and supports for practitioners (Branson et al., 2014; Ilesanmi & Eboiyehi, 2012; Iqbal, 2015; Shannon, Simmelink-McCleary, Im, Becher, & Crook-Lyon, 2014).

I know that I would have benefited from having strategic preparation and continued support in managing the psychosocial impacts and emotional aspects of my study to complement all the technical tools and assistance to which I had access. Just having planned on therapy throughout the study could have significantly changed things.

Secondly, I take away from my experience the lesson that identification with and empathy for one's subjects can provide very helpful impetus to do justice to the project. What that looked like for me is that I knew I would rather not publish the findings than to tell a story that amounted to "the natives are killing each other"; yet, at the same time, as I have shared, I also felt real conviction about telling the stories of those who suffered and those who had died. By foregrounding the social and political economy of Msinga and similarly placed communities, as well as taking an asset-based approach (Yosso 2005) (a variation on appreciative inquiry [Reed 2006]) and emphasizing potential solutions in the conclusion that are grounded (Charmaz and Mitchell 2001) in the wealth, strengths, and resilience of the local people as well as "interest convergence" (Bell 1980), the final draft of the book tried to reconcile those goals.

In hindsight, recalling that Msinga had been chosen as a field site because "if there was any place in South Africa where traditional courts could be expected to function optimally, Msinga was it," so devastated was I by what I had found that by the end my narrative aspirations were not very ambitious: They were framed more negatively (in terms of what I wanted to *avoid*) than positively (in terms of the future to which I wanted to contribute). That was also partly an expression of the shame I carry from what I was taught in law school and graduate school *is* and *is not* "good" legal and anthropological scholarship. hooks captures this (mis)education (Woodson 1933; Goodman 1964) poetically when she writes:

> This language that enabled me to attend graduate school, to write a dissertation, to speak at job interviews, carries the scent of oppression. ... Dare I speak to oppressed and oppressor in the same voice? Dare I speak to you in a language that will move beyond the boundaries of domination – a language that will not bind you, fence you in ...? Language is also a place of struggle. The oppressed struggle in language to recover ourselves, to reconcile, to reunite, to renew. Our words are not without meaning, they are an action, a resistance.
>
> (hooks 1990, 146–7)

I realize that I need to write about law and society in places like Msinga in a different language – literally. Hence, the book project that helped get me the utmost privilege in an "imperialist white supremacist capitalist patriarchy" (hooks 2013, 4) – that is, the permanency of employment and income security characterized by "tenure" at an academic institution – has left me with the challenge of clarifying for myself and others what it is about my identification and empathy with my subjects that brings greater insights to the findings of research and how I can use that more effectively in my future work. Indeed, I have found the question that might be summarized as "what does effectiveness even mean?" plague me more than ever.

The implications of this second lesson feel risky to own – let alone profess – if for no other reason than the fact that they push me further out of the mainstream (or "whitestream" [Grande 2003]) of academia than I already was, being as precariously positioned as I have always felt. As Sandy Grande (2016) explains: "The notion of precarity has emerged as a way of describing the effects of neoliberal policy on the human condition" (135–6). As an African raised under the dominance of "settler colonialism" and thus subject (even in my scholarship) to "white logic(s)" and "white methods" (Zuberi and Bonilla-Silva 2008), my existence has always felt like a "nervous condition" (Dangarembga 1988). The assumptions from which I have been taught to depart in looking for social and legal power have always been outside of those that came naturally for me as someone outside of the dominant intersectional identities of "whiteness," "maleness," or "Euro-Americanness."

Again, the prescient hooks (1990) narrates my experience when she writes: "Often when the radical voice speaks about domination we are speaking to those who dominate. Their presence changes the nature and direction of our words. Language is also a place of struggle" (p. 146). The disciplines from which I was methodologically departing in my study were and are imbued with an imperialist agenda and settler colonialist ideals (Mafeje 1976), despite repeated calls and efforts to "decolonize" (Harrison 1997), and, most recently, to embrace "an 'abolitionist anthropology' that unapologetically recasts anthropology as a 'genre of Black study' that troubles the tendency of anthropologists to refuse complicity in the structures of dispossession taken up as topics of research" (Jobson 2020, quoting Shange 2019; also see Ndebele 1994).

Perhaps then the primary way in which the persistent reality of my being "out of place" – in the field, in the academy, and ultimately in my very soul – has affected my study of law and society and shaped my knowledge production is by leading me to despair over the potential of the dominant logics and methods to bring about real understanding and true liberation. While I have always been drawn to applied anthropology and been, at least, intrigued by "ethnography as politics" (Harrison 1997), I have not been able to summon up the courage to really pursue it outside the bounds of what the dominant voices in the field (which, even in South Africa, are overwhelmingly white) say is "good legal scholarship."

The idea of "critical participatory action research" (Torre et al. 2012) as part of rigorous scholarship has seemed lacking for its over-investment in worldly application through justice outcomes. The possibility of making better sense of the tensions of law's pluralism simultaneously with making better sense of the tensions of producing scholarly research on law and society – both from *within* the "hyphen," "interstices," or "third space" (Bhabha 1996) – through methods such as autoethnography has been rejected as being far from credible (Ellis, Adams, and Bochner 2011; Jones 2008).

In a country such as South Africa, where the Constitution was for a long time hailed as being the "most progressive" in the world and having helped to prevent civil war, it is a sacred cow: above questioning or doubt for fear of "opening the floodgates" and ushering in "anarchy" (Ramose 2018). Yet, whether one refers to the extreme and overlapping forms of structural and interpersonal violence prevalent in Msinga or my insider-outsider ethnographer's vicarious trauma, the costs of this kind of silencing are real – an inevitable consequence of the nervous conditions brought about by colonialism. These costs are born of the schisms (cognitive dissonance) (Maté and Maté 2022; Santos 2015) of always being told to silence (or, at least, temper) your inner "rebel" who rages against the violations of your linguistic autonomy (Wa Thiong'o 1992), relational integrity (with each other and with the land) (Okoth-Ogendo 2008), and "temporal sovereignty" (Rifkin 2017) because your arguments are too radical (King 2015; Biko 2002; X 1992).

That said, I draw courage from communities of scholars who have become increasingly vocal and refused to remain silent (for example, see, Sibanda 2013; Madlingozi 2017; Modiri 2017), who have consequently challenged my own work and the analytical lenses I apply to it. With the help of these voices, I am *un*learning law and society – decolonizing my mind and its application to the subjects I study. Therefore, the biggest shift that has resulted from my "out of place" experiences is in who my supposedly "pretty and young" self wants to be "when I grow up." That is not another figure in the law and society canon, as deeply as I appreciate the insights brought by the people who make up that illustrious body.[10] I am striving for a new socio-legal

---

[10] Laura Nader, Martin Chanock, Sally Engle Merry, Peter Delius, and Susan Silbey's work – among that of others too numerous to name – continues to inform my work; and I am very grateful for the mentorship of scholars such as Heinz Klug, Thandabantu Nhlapo, Penelope Andrews, John Comaroff, Dee Smythe, Aninka

scholarship that is grounded in hidden pasts, forgotten futures, and rejected ways of being, seeing, and knowing.[11]

References

Alkire, Sabina. 2003. "A Conceptual Framework for Human Security" [Working Paper]. *Centre for Research on Inequality, Human Security and Ethnicity, CRISE.* Oxford: Queen Elizabeth House, University of Oxford.

Anthias, Floya. 2002. "Where Do I Belong?: Narrating Collective Identity and Translocational Positionality." *Ethnicities* 2(4): 491–514.

Bell, Derrick A., Jr. 1980. "Brown v. Board of Education and the Interest-Convergence Dilemma." *Harvard Law Review* 93(3): 518–33.

Bhabha, Homi K. 1996. "Culture's In-Between." In *Questions of Cultural Identity*, edited by Stuart Hall and Paul du Gay, 53–60. Thousand Oaks, CA: Sage.

Biko, Steve. 2002. *I Write What I Like: Selected Writings.* Chicago: University of Chicago Press.

Branson, Dana C. 2019. "Vicarious Trauma, Themes in Research, and Terminology: A Review of Literature." *Traumatology* 25(1): 2–10.

Bryant-Davis, Thema, and Carlota Ocampo. 2005. "Racist Incident-Based Trauma." *The Counseling Psychologist* 33(4): 479–500.

Bushe, Gervase R. 2007. "Appreciative Inquiry is Not About the Positive." *OD Practitioner* 39(4): 33–8.

Charmaz, Kathy, and Richard G. Mitchell. 2001. "Grounded Theory in Ethnography." In *Handbook of Ethnography*, edited by Paul Atkinson, Amanda Coffey, Sara Delamont, John Lofland, and Lyn Lofland, 160–74. Thousand Oaks, CA: Sage.

Chen, Cher Weixia, and Paul C. Gorski. 2015. "Burnout in Social Justice and Human Rights Activists: Symptoms, Causes and Implications." *Journal of Human Rights Practice* 7(3): 366–90.

Collins, Patricia Hill. 2019. *Intersectionality as Critical Social Theory.* Durham, NC: Duke University Press.

Cousins, Ben, Rauri Alcock, Ngididi Dladla, Donna Hornby, Mphethethi Masondo, Gugulethu Mbatha, Makhosi Mweli, and Creina Alcock. 2011. Imithetho yomhlaba yaseMsinga: The Living Law of Land in Msinga, KwaZulu-Natal. Available at: http://repository.uwc.ac.za/xmlui/handle/10566/390 (accessed: June 10, 2020).

Claassens, Chuma Himonga, Ben Cousins, Mark Fathi Massoud, and many more. However, I removed citations to Comaroff and de Sousa Santos in response to allegations that they had violated women's rights, except in two places where their work and/or mentorship influenced my thinking.

[11] For more, see my forthcoming book, *Alter-Native Constitutionalism: Common-ing 'Common' Law, Transforming Property in South Africa* (Cambridge University Press).

Crenshaw, Kimberle. 1990. "Mapping the Margins: Intersectionality, Identity Politics, and Violence against Women of Color." *Stanford Law Review* 43 (6): 1241–300.

Dangarembga, Tsitsi. 1988. *Nervous Conditions*. Minneapolis, MN: The Women's Press.

Dewalt, Kathleen M., and Billie R. Dewalt. 2002. *Participant Observation: A Guide for Fieldworkers*. Oxford: AltaMira Press.

DiAngelo, Robin. 2018. *White Fragility: Why It's So Hard for White People to Talk About Racism*. Boston, MA: Beacon Press.

Ellis, Carolyn, Tony E. Adams, and Arthur P. Bochner. 2011. "Autoethnography: An Overview." *Historical Social Research/Historische Sozialforschung* 12(1): 273–90.

England, Kim V. L. 1994. "Getting Personal: Reflexivity, Positionality, and Feminist Research." *Professional Geographer* 46(1): 80.

Fanon, Frantz. 2008. *Black Skin, White Masks*. New York: Grove Press.

Goodman, Paul. 1964. *Compulsory Miseducation*. New York: Horizon Press.

Grande, Sandy. 2003. "Whitestream Feminism and the Colonialist Project: A Review of Contemporary Feminist Pedagogy and Praxis." *Educational Theory* 53(3): 329–46.

2016. *Red Pedagogy: Native American Social and Political Thought*. Lanham, MD: Rowman & Littlefield Publishers.

Harrison, Faye V. 1997. *Decolonizing Anthropology: Moving Further toward an Anthropology for Liberation*. Arlington, VA: American Anthropological Association.

Heffernan, Margaret. 2011. *Willful Blindness: Why We Ignore the Obvious*. New York: Simon and Schuster.

hooks, bell. 1981. *Ain't I a Woman: Black Women and Feminism*. Boston, MA: South End Press.

1990. *Yearning: Race, Gender, and Cultural Politics*. Boston, MA: South End Press.

2013. *Writing Beyond Race: Living Theory and Practice*. New York: Routledge.

Hutson, Sadie P., Joanne M. Hall, and Frankie L. Pack. 2015. "Survivor Guilt: Analyzing the Concept and its Contexts." *Advances in Nursing Science* 38 (1): 20–33.

Jobson, Ryan Cecil. 2020. "The Case for Letting Anthropology Burn: Sociocultural Anthropology in 2019." *American Anthropologist* 122(2): 259–71.

Jones, Stacy Holman. 2008. Autoethnography – Making the Personal Political. In *Collecting and Interpreting Qualitative Materials*, edited by Norman K. Denzin and Yvonna S. Lincoln, 205–46. Thousand Oaks, CA: Sage Publications.

King, Martin Luther, Jr. 2015. "Letter from a Birmingham Jail." In *The Radical King*, edited by Cornell West, 127–46. Boston, MA: Beacon Press.
Lorde, Audre. 2017. *A Burst of Light: And Other Essays*. Garden City, NY: Courier Dover Publications.
Madlingozi, Tshepo. 2017. "Social Justice in a Time of Neo-Apartheid Constitutionalism: Critiquing the Anti-Black Economy of Recognition, Incorporation and Distribution." *Stellenbosch Law Review* 28(1): 123–47.
Mafeje, Archie. 1976. "The Problem of Anthropology in Historical Perspective: An Inquiry into the Growth of the Social Sciences." *Canadian Journal of African Studies/La Revue Canadienne Des Études Africaines* 10(2): 307–33.
Marks, Monique. 2005. *Transforming the Robocops: Changing Police in South Africa*. Durban: University of Kwazulu-Natal Press.
Maté, Gabor, and Daniel Maté. 2022. *The Myth of Normal: Trauma, Illness, and Healing in a Toxic Culture*. New York City: Avery/Penguin Random House.
McCann, I. Lisa, and Laurie A. Pearlman. 1990. "Vicarious Traumatization: A Framework for Understanding the Psychological Effects of Working with Victims." *Journal of Traumatic Stress* 3(1): 131–49.
Meintjes, Louise. 2017. *Dust of the Zulu: Ngoma Aesthetics after Apartheid*. Durham, NC: Duke University Press.
Merriam, Sharan B., Juanita Johnson-Bailey, Ming-Yeh Lee, Youngwha Kee, Gabo Ntseane, and Mazanah Muhamad. 2001. "Power and Positionality: Negotiating Insider/Outsider Status Within and Across Cultures." *International Journal of Lifelong Education* 20(5): 405–16.
Mnisi Weeks, S. 2014. "Ethical Quandaries in Empirical, Socio-legal Research." In *Ethical Quandaries in Social Research*, edited by Deborah Posel and Fiona Ross, 140–52. Cape Town: HSRC Press.
———. 2018. *Access to Justice and Human Security: Cultural Contradictions in Rural South Africa*. New York: Routledge.
Modiri, Joel Malesela. 2017. "The Jurisprudence of Steve Biko: A Study in Race Law and Power in the 'Afterlife' of Colonial-Apartheid." DPhil Thesis, University of Pretoria.
Nader, Laura, ed. 1997. *Law in Culture and Society*. Berkeley: University of California Press.
Ndebele, Njabulo S. 1994. *South African Literature and Culture: Rediscovery of the Ordinary*. Manchester: Manchester University Press.
Newell, Jason M., and Gordon A. MacNeil. 2010. "Professional Burnout, Vicarious Trauma, Secondary Traumatic Stress, and Compassion Fatigue: A Review of Theoretical Terms, Risk Factors, and Preventive Methods for Clinicians and Researchers." *Best Practice in Mental Health* 6(2): 57–68.

Okoth-Ogendo, Hastings W. 2008. "The Nature of Land Rights under Indigenous Law in Africa." In *Land, Power and Custom: Controversies Generated by South Africa's Communal Land Rights Act*, edited by Aninka Claassens and Ben Cousins, 95–108. Athens, OH: Ohio University Press.

Oyěwùmí, Oyèrónkẹ́. 1997. *The Invention of Women: Making an African Sense of Western Gender Discourses*. Minneapolis: University of Minnesota Press.

Piorkowski, Geraldine K. 1983. "Survivor Guilt in the University Setting." *Personnel & Guidance Journal* 61(10): 620.

Ramose, Mogobe Bernard. 2018. "Towards a Post-Conquest South Africa: Beyond the Constitution of 1996." *South African Journal on Human Rights* 34(3), 326–41.

Reed, Jan. 2006. *Appreciative Inquiry: Research for Change*. Thousand Oaks, CA: Sage.

Rifkin, Mark. 2017. *Beyond Settler Time: Temporal Sovereignty and Indigenous Self-Determination*. Durham, NC: Duke University Press.

Santos, Boaventura de Sousa. 2015. *Epistemologies of the South: Justice Against Epistemicide*. New York: Routledge.

Shange, Savannah. 2019. *Progressive Dystopia: Abolition, Antiblackness, and Schooling in San Francisco*. Durham, NC: Duke University Press.

Sibanda, Sanele. 2013. "Not Quite a Rejoinder: Some Thoughts and Reflections on Michelman's 'Liberal Constitutionalism, Property Rights and the Assault on Poverty.'" *Stellenbosch Law Review = Stellenbosch Regstydskrif* 24(2): 329–41.

Simon, Roger I., and Donald Dippo. 1986. "On Critical Ethnographic Work." *Anthropology & Education Quarterly* 17: 195.

Smith, Nicholas Rush. 2019. *Contradictions of Democracy: Vigilantism and Rights in Post-Apartheid South Africa*. Oxford: Oxford University Press.

Smythe, Dee. 2015. *Rape Unresolved: Policing Sexual Offences in South Africa*. Cape Town: University of Cape Town Press.

Torre, Maria Elena, Michelle Fine, Brett G. Stoudt, and Madeline Fox. 2012. "Critical Participatory Action Research as Public Science." In *APA Handbook of Research Methods in Psychology, Vol 2: Research Designs: Quantitative, Qualitative, Neuropsychological, and Biological*, edited by Harris Cooper, Paul M. Camic, Debra L. Long, A. T. Panter, David Rindskopf, and Kenneth J. Sher, 171–84. Washington DC: American Psychological Association.

Wa Thiong'o, Ngũgĩ. 1992. *Decolonising the Mind: The Politics of Language in African Literature*. Nairobi: East African Publishers.

Woodson, Carter G. 1933. *The Mis-education of the Negro*. San Diego, CA: Book Tree.

X, Malcolm, and Alex Haley. 1992. *The Autobiography of Malcolm X: As Told to Alex Haley*, Reissue edition. New York City: Ballantine Books.

Yosso, Tara J. 2005. "Whose Culture Has Capital? A Critical Race Theory Discussion of Community Cultural Wealth." *Race Ethnicity and Education* 8(1): 69–91.

Zuberi, Tukufu, and Eduardo Bonilla-Silva, eds. 2008. *White Logic, White Methods: Racism and Methodology*. Lanham, MD: Rowman & Littlefield Publishers.

CHAPTER FOUR

OUT OF PLACE WHEN STUDYING CHINA'S SEX INDUSTRY

Margaret L. Boittin

In the summer of 2006, I was in St. Petersburg, Russia, carrying out preliminary dissertation fieldwork. At the time, my PhD research was going to be a comparative study of the regulation of prostitution in China and Russia. In St. Petersburg, I volunteered with a sex worker outreach organization, and in the early evenings, we would hop into their community outreach van to drive around various neighborhoods where streetwalkers would solicit clients. The social workers would introduce themselves to new women in the area, reconnect with those they knew, give them condoms, and let them know about the various health and other support services that the organization provided.

One such day, we were parked along a large avenue on the outskirts of St. Petersburg, talking to a sex worker who regularly solicited there. As we were checking in with her, someone parked their car a few meters in front of us. A man – visibly drunk – got out of the driver's side, walked over to us, grabbed the sex worker by the arm, and tried to pull her into his car. She resisted, and as the social worker pleaded with him to let her go, he turned towards us, asking who we were. The social worker instructed me to get back into the van, introduced herself and her organization, and told him that I was a visiting researcher from the United States. As I watched from the window, I saw the man pull out a gun, punch the sex worker in the stomach so that she keeled over in pain, try unsuccessfully once again to drag her into the car, and then drive off. As I exited the van and assisted the social worker in tending to the sex worker, they told me that he was an off-duty police officer.

I returned to Russia for more research three years later, this time to Vladivostok, in the Far East, and just a short flight away from my temporary home base in Beijing. I had been carrying out fieldwork in China for almost a year at that point, making inroads that were far deeper than what I had imagined might be possible, including ethnographic observation in brothels and red-light districts, shadowing the police, and setting up surveys of sex workers and law enforcement officers. A week into the Vladivostok trip, whose goal was to lay the groundwork to create similar access in Russia, it became clear that the incident I had previously witnessed in St. Petersburg foreshadowed obstacles that would prevent me from immersing myself in the regulation of the sex industry in Russia to the extent I had in China.

I am a white woman with blond hair and blue eyes. I blend into Russian society. If someone saw me in a brothel or in an area where sex workers solicit, they could assume I was a sex worker. Being a foreigner in Russia in the early 2000s did not bestow privileges: if pimps or organized crime networks were displeased with my presence, they would do what they wanted with me. Not so in China, a country where I cannot conceal my outsider status, and which is often more protective of foreigners than Chinese citizens. In practice, this meant that I encountered fewer obstacles when immersing myself in China's sex industry – I did not have to worry about attracting the unwanted attention of drunk, gun-wielding off-duty police officers. It is this reality that eventually led me to drop the comparison with Russia and focus my project entirely on prostitution in China.

Ultimately, it is precisely because I was so out of place in China's sex industry that I was granted the space to immerse myself in it. In fact, while I was carrying out my fieldwork, I sought to embrace my outsider status, rather than tiptoe around it, in my efforts to connect with respondents in ways that would provide me with the richest possible insights into prostitution. This observation leads me to a broader claim. In all sorts of ways, being out of place closes doors to the creation of scholarship and the halls of academia more generally, and is associated with experiences of marginalization, weakness, and challenges that must be overcome. Yet it can also be a source of strength. When it provides access to realms that are usually impenetrable, it allows researchers to bring to light substantive areas of inquiry that are more often hidden from view. In so doing, it can expand scholarly boundaries, to carve out space for both topics and methodological approaches that are traditionally considered peripheral to one's chosen disciplines.

In my case, I delved into the study of China's sex industry as a political scientist and a legal scholar. This is a topic more often explored by sociologists and anthropologists, and, regardless of the disciplinary approach adopted, it is generally studied through the lens of gender and feminist theory. By situating my approach in other literatures, I show how prostitution is a topic that lies at the heart of central questions in politics and law, and that qualitative research methods were an essential tool for me to pursue my inquiries. In the process, I saw how being out of place allows scholars to push disciplinary boundaries. For instance, I learned about the different ways in which sex workers – all of whom are participating in an illegal activity in China – experience the law depending on the type of prostitution in which they engage. I also discovered how individuals upon whom legal power is bestowed – mainly police officers and public health agents – frequently find themselves in positions of surprising precarity and weakness as they navigate their professional responsibilities to implement prostitution policies.

Putting myself in situations where I felt out of place was a deliberate choice. It was my decision to carry out fieldwork in China, study prostitution, and approach the topic ethnographically. While I did not always anticipate all the implications of doing so, or the extent to which I would feel that I did not belong, I was conscious that I would not fit in. From my roots in the academic realm of law and politics in China, I was committed to a research project that would allow me to shed light on individuals whose experiences of injustice are overlooked. Sex workers fall squarely into that category. This is not happenstance: each additional layer of out-of-placeness described in this chapter provides one more reason for a researcher to direct their attention elsewhere – in a place that is a bit less unfamiliar and uncomfortable. Yet that is precisely where I was committed to be. In short, by studying how sex workers in China experience law and politics, I had put myself in exactly the right place for my own research goals and values.

As pertains to studying the regulation of China's sex industry, my out-of-placeness is threefold. First, I am a foreigner in China. Second, I am an outsider to the regulation of the sex industry: I do not engage in prostitution, nor do I regulate it. Third, the ethnographic study of prostitution in China lies at the methodological and substantive periphery of my academic disciplines – law and political science. In the pages that follow, this chapter elaborates on these three dimensions. In so doing, it highlights four characteristics of being out of place. First, it can help to think of the concept as one that is fluid, rather than fixed, over the course of fieldwork, the life of a research project, and one's academic career more generally. Second, this fluidity is tied to a distinction that exists between the researcher's internal feelings that they are out of place, versus outsiders' perceptions that they do not belong. And of course, these two angles can be mutually constitutive. Third, there are at least two different communities in relation to whom scholars must navigate being out of place – their research subjects, who provide them with the data that defines the content of their scholarship, and the academic communities that evaluate the work produced based on that content. Finally, being out of place is draining to the core. In my case, it took me years to feel excited about returning to China and think of other similarly immersive projects that I might conduct. While the exact nature of the intensity of being out of place might differ across individuals and projects, I have seen that the same out of placeness that can result in boundary-pushing scholarship also takes an emotional toll on the person carrying it out.

THE PROJECT AND THE FIELDWORK

My experiences of being out of place are rooted in a study I conducted on law, society and the state in an authoritarian regime. As pertains to society, it explores how the law shapes the everyday lives of citizens who are engaged in behavior that is illegal. With respect to the state, it delves into the experiences of government officials on the frontlines who are responsible for implementing the policies that regulate the lives of those individuals who are breaking the law. I explore these issues in China, with a focus on the regulation of prostitution.

The project began as a doctoral dissertation. I conducted most of the fieldwork in 2008 and 2009, along with shorter trips in 2005, 2011, and 2014. The study focused on the regulation of female commercial sex work in urban areas. I carried out the bulk of data collection in Beijing, Shenzhen, Guangzhou, Dongguan, Shanghai, Harbin, Shenyang, Changsha, and some smaller cities in Hebei and Hubei provinces. Throughout that time, I used three methodologies: interviews, surveys, and ethnographic observation. The interviews were with actors from both society and the state. They included sex workers, madams, pimps, clients, staff of both domestic and international nongovernmental organizations, and local and central-government officials working in policing, health, and other state agencies. I also conducted two surveys – one of sex workers in a Beijing red-light district, and another of police officers in southern China.

The heart of this project rested in ethnographic observation. In Beijing, I spent my days in the lounge area of a sex worker grassroots organization that was in the center of a red-light district in the city.[1] Women would come by throughout the day on their way to and from the venues where they worked, or during breaks. They would pick up condoms, seek out medical advice from the on-site doctor, surf the web on one of the center's computers, or just sink into a seat on one of the couches in the lounge area, striking up conversation with other sex workers or staff members. I spent a lot of time on that couch, listening to the conversations of women around me, engaging them myself, and observing their interactions with each other. In a red-light district in Shenzhen, Mei Jie, a madam who ran a brothel out of her apartment, took me under her wing.[2] She shared one of the rooms with her husband and, on weekends and holidays when he was back from his boarding school, their seven-year-old son. The second room was rented to a businessman from Hong Kong who spent most weekdays in Shenzhen and who appeared to have unlimited access to Mei Jie's sex workers. These women used the third bedroom for sexual transactions with other clients. The sex workers' own living space was in the apartment's common room. They slept in one corner of the room in a large bed that was surrounded by a makeshift curtain, and they would sit on the couch or at the computer table in between visits from clients. When these men arrived, I would hide behind the curtain – Mei Jie would have had to explain the presence of a foreign woman if they saw me, and she worried that they might decide not to purchase sex if they knew a researcher was in their midst, or suspected that I was a journalist. I would also stroll around the neighborhood with Mei Jie, observe her interactions with members of the community, soak up as much as possible from those exchanges, and follow up individually with people to whom she introduced me. She would link arms with me, to visually signal the closeness of our relationship to anyone who saw us. Association with a foreigner generally elevates one's social status in China, all the more so when the Chinese person in question has low standing, as is the case for a madam such as Mei Jie.

---

[1] I use the term "red-light district" to refer to an area with a high concentration of prostitution.

[2] I use pseudonyms to protect confidentiality.

The ethnographic research for this project also involved shadowing public health workers and police officers. I gave out condoms and educational pamphlets to sex workers alongside public health officials in several cities, and I observed how these state actors interacted with managers of entertainment venues to access the sex workers harbored within those spaces. For example, in one red-light district, as I was chatting with a local health official in a public park, a pimp from a neighborhood brothel wandered over, and the two started debating the merits of legalizing prostitution in the context of contemporary politics, economics, and society in China. In another city, I went karaoke singing with police officers, watching them select hostesses to entertain them throughout the evening. I also observed their daily routines in police stations, listening to them banter amongst themselves. In yet another town, where I was spending time with sex workers in the community and had no connection with local law enforcement, I witnessed police officers arrest several women suspected of engaging in prostitution.

In all these spaces, it was at least partly because I was out of place that someone in the community chose to welcome me into their life. Most often, the person doing so was a madam, a sex worker, a client, a police officer, or a public health official. Their motivations were likely manifold. Some might be self-serving. Mei Jie, for instance, momentarily improved her standing in the community when she showed that a respectable foreign researcher was interested in her. When a former police officer brought me back to his hometown and introduced me to his law enforcement colleagues from his policing years, he was showing them that in his new line of work, his professional success was attracting the attention of foreigners. My contacts also called upon me to tutor their children, nephews, and nieces in English. Other motivations for welcoming me as a foreign researcher were rooted in intellectual and advocacy commitments and, more specifically, a belief in the importance of the issues I was investigating. Curiosity, tied to both my outsider status and interest in their lives, usually played a role in their initial willingness to hear me out, and establishing a personal connection helped sustain our relationship over time. Across the board, these were individuals willing to incur the risks associated with welcoming me into a place where I did not fit in, and whose roles were necessary for me to overcome the obstacles that being out of place presented in the field.

OUT OF PLACE IN CHINA

As a foreigner, I do not belong in China. This observation holds regardless of whether I am there as a researcher, in another professional capacity, or as a tourist. It also remains constant irrespective of the specific topic of academic inquiry in which I engage in China. Like all foreigners who are not ethnically Chinese, it does not matter how many years I live in China, or how well I speak and read Mandarin: most Chinese citizens will always consider me to be an outsider because I do not look Chinese.[3] Throughout my fieldwork, two characteristics of Chinese politics and society served as a constant reminder of my outsider status. First, China is an authoritarian country. Second, it is a society that both views itself as conservative, and, in contrast, perceives the Western world to be more open.[4]

As a foreigner carrying out research in an authoritarian regime, I knew that at any time, I could get into trouble with the state. More importantly, I knew that anyone who spoke with me could suffer retribution from the state. The stakes for me were, in the grand scheme of things, relatively low – the most likely worst-case scenario would be expulsion from China, and blacklisting that would prevent me from returning in the future.[5] At the time, contemplating such an outcome felt incredibly consequential: I was paralyzed at the thought of being unable to complete my dissertation for lack of data, and having to abandon my professional aspirations as a scholar of contemporary China, after ten years devoted to living there and studying the country. The stakes for my informants, however, were much greater. There are

---

[3] More seasoned China hands concur. The writer Ian Johnson (2020), who had lived in China for twenty years and had to leave the country when his journalist visa was canceled in early 2020, noted the following: "China wasn't an easy country to call home. It is the original land of genetic determinism; you cannot really become Chinese unless you look a certain way. You can be a sixth-generation Chinese American, speak only 'ni hao ma' [*which means hello*] and know little more about the place than General Tso's Chicken, but to China (and to many Americans in the United States) you are Chinese."

[4] In general, my informants would view "the West" and "Westerners" as a unified category with which to contrast China, without considering variation that might exist within this unit.

[5] I carried out my research when Hu Jintao was in power. The stakes might be higher had I been carrying out this research under Xi Jinping, an era marked both by increased repression within China and greater tension between China and other countries.

no limits to the atrocities the state in China will commit when it comes to individuals whom it perceives are threatening its stronghold on power.[6] These realities provided me with powerful and anxiety-producing reminders that I was out of place in China. The democratic states that I have at various times considered home (France, the United States, and Canada), and where I generally feel a sense of belonging, are also guilty of outrageous violations of the rights of individuals living both within their borders, and beyond them. Yet a variety of checks and balances exist in those places that can serve as sources of possible redress. In China, I have no viable recourse against state interventions into my life or that of participants in my research.[7]

The likelihood that I would actually attract unwanted attention from the state was low, and in fact, to my knowledge it did not occur. Prostitution is a sensitive topic in the sense that it is against the law, but it does not raise alarm bells to the extent that occurs with respect to research on China's most politically charged issues.[8] Yet, the fear I sometimes felt on the ground was real, and at times overpowering. I remember during one particularly stressful period realizing that the watch I had left on the bedside table of my Beijing apartment had stopped working, and being surprised that the battery had not lasted longer. I convinced myself that a state agent had entered my apartment and tinkered with my watch in order to mess with my mind and send a signal that I was being observed. Lest this anecdote be interpreted

---

[6] Human Rights Watch (2021, 8) notes that "[t]his has been the darkest period for human rights in China since the 1989 massacre that ended the Tiananmen Square democracy movement."

[7] While I can reach out to my embassies in the event that I encounter a problem, they are limited with respect to the assistance they can provide. As a prominent example, two Canadian citizens – Michael Kovrig and Michael Spavor – were detained in China from December 2018 to September 2021 on dubious charges. The situation was widely viewed as retaliation against Canada for arresting Meng Wanzhou, a Chinese business executive facing fraud and conspiracy charges in New York, at the request of the United States. In this situation, the Canadian embassy in Beijing was very limited in its ability to assist Kovrig and Spavor.

[8] Examples of the latter include protests, which raise questions about the long-term stability of the CCP, and internment camps in Xinjiang, which lie at the heart of human rights concerns that have garnered significant attention abroad. China is the world's most populated and fourth largest country, and it has finite amounts of state capacity. It cannot keep track of what all foreign researchers are doing on its territory, and I made many inroads by simply staying under the radar of the state. And when I was interacting with officials, it likely helped that prostitution was not at the very top of their list of hot-button issues.

solely as providing insight into my own idiosyncrasies, other foreign China researchers have shared similar types of reactions. I once had a house guest who was staying with me because he feared that the authorities were trying to kidnap him, and he did not want to be alone. One morning a tile fell from the bathroom ceiling while he was brushing his teeth, and he rushed out, convinced that someone from the security bureau had loosened the tiles and rigged them to fall as a warning sign. These types of reactions provide vivid illustrations of how overpowering feelings of being "out of place" can be in an authoritarian regime.

This first characteristic of China – that it is an authoritarian country – creates an out-of-placeness that has the potential to affect foreign researchers regardless of their substantive area of investigation. In fact, it can play a powerful agenda-setting role as scholars try to ascertain not only the feasibility of a particular topic, but also the likelihood that it might lead to sanctions that could cut short one's professional aspirations. By reminding us that we are out of place, the Chinese state, and the fear it induces, shape knowledge production about many aspects of the country.

I turn now to an observation that is specific to the study of prostitution in China, as well as other similarly situated topics, but that is not necessarily shared across all substantive areas of inquiry. Specifically, the predominant perception in mainland China is that it is a socially conservative society, and that, in contrast, the West is more open. As pertains to prostitution, this view translated into two related assumptions that I encountered repeatedly over the course of my fieldwork: first, that Westerners are more sexually permissive than the Chinese and, second, that prostitution is legal throughout the West. These were views that a variety of individuals expressed, including sex workers, clients, police officers, other local officials, and members of the general population without particular ties to the sex industry. These assumptions shaped the interactions I had with people in China in countless situations, and regularly made me feel not only out of place, but also, at times, quite uncomfortable.

Two of the most vivid experiences I had with these assumptions in fact took place years before I was carrying out the fieldwork for this project. The first occurred in 2001, when I was teaching English in a Chinese primary school in the city of Ningbo. A few months into the job, I took a four-hour bus ride to Shanghai for the weekend. At the time, I spoke hardly any Chinese, and the man who took the seat next to me struck up a conversation in English. When I asked him why he was headed to Shanghai, he nonchalantly explained that he lived in Ningbo with his wife and child, but that he was going to Shanghai to visit his mistress. He then explained to me that while such an arrangement was considered inappropriate in China, he felt comfortable telling me about it because I was from the West, a place he noted was much more open about such relationships. This is a misconception on at least two levels. First, there is no evidence that extramarital relations are more common in the West than in China. Second, regardless of relative prevalence, during my fieldwork I saw men in mainland China who were quite comfortable being public with their extramarital affairs. They discussed their sexual affairs not just with harmless-seeming foreigners like me, but also with their friends and colleagues. The Chinese women with whom I discussed male marital infidelity were generally resigned to such behavior, rather than outraged or prepared to leave their marriage on account of it. The exchange on the bus has remained ingrained in my memory; it was my first window into an aspect of Chinese society that would eventually become my academic area of inquiry.

Another particularly indelible encounter pertaining to Chinese perceptions of Western sexual permissiveness occurred a few years later. I was in Beijing for the summer as an intern for a prominent women's rights nongovernmental organization (NGO). I headed to work one hot and humid morning, dressed in a tank top and ankle-length skirt, like many of the other female commuters heading to work that day. A man grabbed my chest as he walked past me in the opposite direction on the sidewalk. When I arrived at the office a few minutes later and told my female colleagues what had just happened, one of the staff lawyers told me that I brought this upon myself because my shirt was, to her, too revealing. What has stuck with me over the years is not so much the man's behavior, unpleasant as it was. Rather, it was the realization that a lawyer with one of the country's most progressive women's rights NGOs blamed me for the assault. Both this experience, as well as the bus conversation, occurred because as a visible foreigner I was seen as "out of place" from mainstream views of gender, sexuality, and morality in mainland China.

Likewise, assumptions about sexual permissiveness in the West shaped the opening tone of many exchanges I had in China over the course of my fieldwork. Police officers assumed I was an advocate for legalizing prostitution. I learned to phrase my research in a way that highlighted similarities between US and Chinese prostitution policies, noting that sex work is criminalized in most places in the United States. I was also careful to note that in Singapore, much closer to China, the exchange of sex for money is not an offense, even though activities such as pimping and public solicitation are against the law. As pertains to clients, I was careful to not disabuse them of their perceptions: like my bus companion, they would share freely with me, feeling safe and comfortable in their views that, as a Westerner, I endorsed and understood their behavior. They would actually go out of their way to interact with me, rather than hide from me. At Mei Jie's apartment, a client's gaze once landed upon me when he entered the apartment before I had the chance to hide behind the living room curtain. After Mei Jie clarified my status as a researcher rather than a sex worker, he made himself comfortable and opened up about his life, family, and experiences as a client. He did not, however, actually stay to have sex, instead telling Mei Jie that he would return another time. Another time, an informant introduced me to his friend, Tang Ming, who had recently been released after six months of incarceration for purchasing sex. Tang Ming was outraged by his sentence – he claimed that the state obscures the possible sanctions to which a client can be subject, and that while everyone knows sex workers can be incarcerated for prostitution, the state does not clearly communicate the fact that clients can also be institutionalized, instead only emphasizing that they can be subject to fines. In both of these encounters, clients seemed interested in engaging with me precisely because I was a foreigner – as though they assumed that I was a sympathetic ear who understood how China's policies and culture around sexuality unfairly stifled their daily lives. Sex workers similarly were quick to open up to me: their misconceptions that prostitution is not stigmatized in the West led them to share freely with me the personal pathways that led them to sell sex, and their experiences as sex workers, in ways that would have been more difficult if I had been a Chinese national.

OUT OF PLACE IN THE SEX INDUSTRY

In addition to feeling and looking out of place studying prostitution in China because I am a foreigner, I am out of place because I am neither an actor in nor a regulator of the sex industry. This aspect of my outsider status would apply in any country in which I might study prostitution. Yet it is more pronounced when combined with my status as a visible foreigner, which led most people, upon seeing me, to immediately identify me as neither a participant in the sex industry nor a state actor. There were occasional exceptions to this observation. In some situations, people asked me if I was a Russian sex worker, as there are entertainment venues in various cities throughout China that cater to the demand for non-Chinese sex workers, and that draw from neighboring Russia, amongst other countries. A woman who solicited in a Shenzhen brothel asked me if I was a sex worker from Xinjiang – she realized that I was not Han Chinese, but thought I bore a resemblance to her image of Uyghurs. In another instance, a sex worker wary of my presence thought that the state had sent me in as an informant, musing out loud about the length to which the government would go to crack down on illegal activities such as prostitution, going so far as to hire foreigners to investigate the criminal behavior of its citizens. Yet by and large, most respondents assumed I was neither a sex worker nor a state regulator of prostitution, regardless of whether they were societal or state actors.

My position as an obvious outsider to the sex industry served me in ways that were similar to my status as a foreigner in China: respondents who opened up to me tended to do so precisely because I had no connections to their daily lived experiences. The societal and state actors with whom I spoke all knew that I personally had no stake in their experiences with the regulation of prostitution. As such, they were at liberty to reveal themselves in ways that were much less guarded than would occur if they felt that I was somehow part of their community.

Sex workers, for example, are frequently in situations where they are in competition with each other. If they related to me as a colleague, they would thus be unlikely to share their vulnerabilities, or even provide me with basic information such as the amount they earn per sexual transaction, or the number of clients they have on any given day or week. If I had been a man doing this research, and if they had perceived of me as a potential client, they would have presented me with a narrative aimed at seducing me and eliciting pity, in order to earn as much as possible. This might involve stories about their personal struggles, and a decision to sell sex tied to victimhood, rather than agency. If over the course of my research clients had viewed me as a sex worker, the substance of our conversations would likely have been very different. For instance, they would likely tell a different narrative about their family life, other experiences with the purchase of sex, and attitudes towards prostitution. Finally, had state actors viewed me as a participant in the sex industry, our interactions would have revolved around their regulatory responsibilities, which would have resulted in a very different type of research experience: police officers would have arrested me, and public health workers would have carried out various outreach and testing activities with me.[9]

OUT OF PLACE IN ACADEMIA

I now turn away from the field and the feelings of not belonging that emerge from the researcher's interactions with research subjects, to instead examine experiences of being out of place that emerge from my engagement with the academic environment, particularly because the object of my scholarly inquiry is sex work.

The study of prostitution is generally perceived as peripheral to mainstream questions in legal and political science scholarship. Authors of such research tend to approach it through lenses of feminist legal theory and gender politics (e.g., Kotiswaran 2011; Outshoorn 2004), which are subfields that are not viewed as part of the canons of law and political science. And even as they explicitly connect their projects to issues that are understood as central to the study of law and politics, they continue to be relegated to the sidelines.[10] In addition, ethnography is a methodology that is not central to either of these disciplines. When it comes to empirical research, quantitative and experimental methods are held up as the gold standard. Law also

---

[9] To be clear, I am not suggesting that being a visibly foreign woman who is external to the sex industry and its regulation are all prerequisites for gaining in-depth access to this world for academic study. I aim simply to reflect upon the elements of being out of place that I personally experienced in this substantive area of inquiry. For instance, the author Tiantian Zheng (2009), was a Chinese PhD student in anthropology at an American university when she carried out an ethnography of the sex industry in the northern city of Dalian, during which time she lived with hostesses and worked alongside them. In the opening paragraphs of her book, she describes hiding from the police along with twenty-five hostesses in one of the entertainment venues where she was carrying out her fieldwork.

[10] Remick's (2014) work on the regulation of prostitution in Chinese history and Majic's (2013) research on sex worker health-service organizations are both examples of political science research that convincingly ties the issue of sex work to mainstream disciplinary issues: state-building and social movements. For further discussion on the marginalization of the study of prostitution in political science, see Ferguson (2015).

privileges doctrinal studies of legal codes, rules, and case judgments. Over the course of this research project, I have often been told that I am out of place (in a political science department, in a law school), and then instructed upon where my place actually is (sociology, anthropology, gender studies). These attempts by gatekeepers to the profession to put me in my place have serious implications for knowledge production: they impoverish our understanding of law and politics by placing artificial barriers around the types of issues and research methodologies that are considered acceptable in the discipline.

A second issue tied to being out of place in academia also plagues women who carry out research on female sex workers: while scholars frequently immerse themselves in topics in which they have no personal experience as participants, when it comes to sex work, one of the questions that often lurks not very far beneath the surface is whether the researcher engaged in prostitution as part of their project. The question that is being asked, in this context, is the extent to which the researcher was actually "out of place," or whether they were instead fully immersing themselves in the lived experiences of their research subjects.

I have not personally been on the receiving end of this inquiry, most likely for two reasons. First, this question comes up less often in my disciplines of political science and law than in sociology and anthropology, simply because scholars of politics and law spend less time thinking about both ethnography and prostitution. Second, other China experts would be well aware that, unless mine was a study that was specifically about relationships between foreign sex workers and Chinese clients in China, my own engagement in prostitution would not be particularly informative with respect to the experiences of Chinese sex workers. That said, it is an important question to address from the perspective of principle. First, it includes salacious undertones, reserved for researchers working on the subject of prostitution, as opposed to topics that are not socially stigmatized and morally controversial. Second, it is gendered, and racialized: as pertains to my area of research, it is much more likely to be asked of a woman who is ethnically Asian than a white man. Another way of phrasing this point is that it is directed at researchers who are considered "out of place" in academia more generally. As Hoang (2015), a Vietnamese American, notes, in relation to her study of the sex industry in Vietnam, she "always wondered if male urban ethnographers were regularly asked if they partook in acts of violence, engaged in drug activity, or participated in sex work with and around their research participants" (20). She notes, furthermore, that:

> [c]ertain close relationships developed in the field are subject to greater scrutiny than others, depending on the gender, race, and class background of the research subjects and the researcher herself. The types of relationships that I had to develop in the field receive far more scrutiny than the types of relationships that other ethnographers develop, because of my gender and racial-ethnic background as well as those of my research subjects.
>
> (20)

A certain type of researcher engaging in "cowboy ethnography" – male, and most often white – is often heralded as a hero for studying "dangerous or hard-to-reach pool populations," and for enabling "readers to go on voyeuristic journeys with them as they detail their heroic efforts to break into dangerous field sites" (21–2). Yet researchers who are marginalized in academia instead face higher levels of scrutiny for engaging in such substantive areas of inquiry.

CONCLUSION

In this chapter, I have examined being out of place in the field, as a foreigner in China and an outsider to the sex industry and its regulation. I have also reflected upon my experiences of not belonging in my academic disciplines for this project, specifically connected to my methodological approach and substantive area of inquiry. I conclude here with some broader reflections on these two aspects of out of placeness.

First, it is worth thinking about being out of place as a concept that is relative, and in flux, rather than an immutable characteristic of a researcher's relationship to their object of study and their academic communities. For instance, my own experiences of being out of place were much more pronounced towards the beginning of my fieldwork. The more time I spent in China talking to sex workers and police officers, the less uncomfortable I felt, and the more comfortable others seemed to be around me. My most vivid recollection of this transformation occurred one day when I was in Mei Jie's brothel, about eighteen months into my fieldwork. A client walked out of the room where he had been having sex, wrapped in nothing but a towel, strolled past me, and hopped into the bathroom to take a shower. When I wrote up my field notes that evening, I almost forgot to discuss that moment. And then I remembered how many pages of notes I wrote the first time I spoke at length with a sex worker, and how overwhelming it felt to just spend a few hours in a karaoke bar with her. The differences as reflected in my field notes, and my emotional recollections of the two events today, are stark. More generally, the difficult stories I observed and heard about over the course of my fieldwork weighed on me much more towards the beginning of my research than the end. This realization was disconcerting – I worried at times that I was becoming numb to the human suffering to which I was exposed. One of my dissertation advisers told me that I would know when I was done with my fieldwork because I was no longer getting any new or surprising information from my informants. Yet perhaps another way of answering this question is instead to say that our fieldwork is complete when we no longer feel out of place. The concept of fluidity can also help understand being out of place in academia. Disciplinary proclivities change over time, even in part tied to the work that some of its misfits carry out and that sometimes succeeds in convincing others of how certain marginalized methodologies and topics should in fact be considered central to the discipline. This observation opens the possibility that a project initially considered peripheral could be viewed as more mainstream over the years, thus changing definitions of what is considered out of place.

Second, and relatedly, from whose vantage point should we be thinking about whether we belong? This question touches on the difference between our own feelings of being out of place, and the perceptions others have of what our place is. These two perspectives can influence each other: we can act in ways that make others think we do, or do not, belong; and others can similarly engage with us in ways that make us feel in or out of place. At the same time, it is important to keep in mind that our personal feelings and the perceptions of outsiders might not be aligned. I sometimes forgot, in Mei Jie's brothel, or in the Beijing outreach center, that a newcomer would likely be startled by my presence. And while I have always felt that anyone who is training to be a lawyer needs to learn about how China might shape both the world and their own practice experience, the small number of law schools who have faculty members specialized in Chinese law are a constant reminder of how in that view, I am a minority. Similarly, it seems obvious to me that ethnography brings immense value to the study of politics and law, and that the study of prostitution lies at the heart of mainstream questions in those disciplines: I do not feel like

I should be out of place asking these questions, in these ways. Yet academia relentlessly reminds me that it does not agree.

As pertains specifically to my fieldwork, it is not always possible to identify whether feelings and perceptions of not belonging were driven by the fact that I am out of place in China, out of place in the sex industry, or out of place in any other number of ways that I have not even addressed in these pages. And while I have provided separate examples of being out of place in China versus in the sex industry, many of them would likely belong in both categories. When it came to my own feelings about a specific situation, I often felt it was the combination of these two characteristics of my identity that were coming in to play. I imagine my informants would also experience a similar thought process and would not necessarily be able to identify whether they were opening up to me because I was foreign to China, or because I was external to the sex industry.

Yet regardless of why respondents perceived me to be out of place, I believe that the reason I was able to get in-depth access to actors within the sex industry and the state was because I embraced these outside identities. For example, regardless of whether I was reaching out to a sex worker or a police officer, I would tell them that I wanted to learn about their lives precisely because they are so different from mine. That type of framing would often open the door to all sorts of information about their daily experiences and opinions. What I sought to do was to accept these two characteristics of my identity as an outsider as a given, and then use them as strengths. Of course, it did not always work. I was not welcome everywhere. I had interviews that lasted only a few minutes, with informants who had no desire to be forthcoming. It took many months to develop strong enough ties in a sufficient number of communities to get the access I needed. Yet it paid off, in the sense that on a regular basis, I felt I was establishing meaningful connections with the individuals who shared their stories with me. More often than not, after I thanked respondents for talking with me and letting me into their lives, they thanked me. They noted how refreshing it felt for someone to ask about their lives, thoughts, and feelings – not only sex workers and clients, but also local police and health officials. They repeatedly mentioned how the questions I asked allowed them to reflect on aspects of their lives that they did not feel they could talk about with members of their own professional and personal communities. It was precisely *because* I was such an outsider that they felt comfortable sharing these experiences and thoughts with me.

The last point I want to make is to highlight the exhaustion that accompanies feeling out of place in one's fieldwork and scholarship. Living and conducting research in China, I was stressed, depressed, and deeply unsettled on a daily basis. I spent a lot of time in dingy, dark, and loud brothels. Sometimes, only a thin wall separated me from a sexual transaction that was occurring. I witnessed clients, madams, police officers, and health workers abuse sex workers emotionally, verbally, and physically, and also witnessed sex workers mistreat one another. I heard stories of sadness, violence, and harm. I also saw interactions characterized by warmth, care, and empowerment. But the dark ones wore me down.

When I left China after nineteen months of fieldwork, it took me several years to feel excited at the idea of returning and carrying out other, similarly immersive projects. And while I can remedy my feelings of being out of place in the field by returning to places where I may feel more at home, it is harder to escape feelings of academic displacement. The years I have spent contending with my data and, in particular, trying to show its relevance to disciplines that may not see value in it, have been tiring in other ways. In fact, while it was hardly a conscious decision, the project in which I embarked following this study protects me from many of the feelings of displacement that emerged in my work on prostitution in China. While substantively, the issue area is similar (human trafficking), it is centered around large-scale quantitative data collection. Instead of being the individual who interacts with research subjects on the ground, I have outsourced that experience to survey firms. And since this second project uses survey and field experimental methods, it fits squarely within the confines of mainstream political science and empirical legal research. There are significant tradeoffs that come with such a project, when compared to the qualitative, immersive research that is the focus of this volume. Yet I highlight what might be my own unconscious coping mechanism here so that other individual researchers who experience the toll of being out of place might consider ways in which they can similarly protect themselves from some of its most draining aspects while still engaging intellectually with issues they care about. The alternatives, including writer's block and burn out, might prevent their findings from ever seeing the light of day, and deprive academic discourse of voices that struggle the most to be heard.

References

Ferguson, Michaele L. 2015. "Beyond Gender Politics? Mainstreaming the Study of Sex Work." *Perspectives on Politics* 13(2): 437–45.

Hoang, Kimberly Kay. 2015. *Dealing in Desire: Asian Ascendancy, Western Decline, and the Hidden Currencies of Global Sex Work.* Berkeley: University of California Press.

Human Rights Watch. 2021. "World Report 2021," www.hrw.org/world-report/2021.

Johnson, Ian. 2020. "Opinion | Kicked Out of China, and Other Real-Life Costs of a Geopolitical Meltdown." *The New York Times.* July 16, 2020. www.nytimes.com/2020/07/16/opinion/sunday/china-us-cold-war.html.

Kotiswaran, Prabha. 2011. *Dangerous Sex, Invisible Labor: Sex Work and the Law in India.* Princeton, NJ: Princeton University Press.

Majic, Samantha. 2013. *Sex Work Politics: From Protest to Service Provision.* Philadelphia: University of Pennsylvania Press.

Outshoorn, Joyce, ed. 2004. *The Politics of Prostitution: Women's Movements, Democratic States, and the Globalisation of Sex Commerce.* Cambridge: Cambridge University Press.

Remick, Elizabeth. 2014. *Regulating Prostitution in China: Gender and Local Statebuilding, 1900–1937.* Stanford, CA: Stanford University Press.

Zheng, Tiantian. 2009. *Red Lights: The Lives of Sex Workers in Postsocialist China.* Minneapolis: University of Minnesota Press.

CHAPTER FIVE

FEELING AT HOME OUTSIDE

Embracing Out-of-Placeness in the Study of Law and Resistance

Lynette J. Chua

床前明月光
疑是地上霜
舉頭望明月
低頭思故鄉

Bright moonlight before my bed
Seems like frost on the ground
I lift my head to gaze at the moon
As I lower my head, I yearn for home
静夜思 Jing Ye Si (Thoughts on a Quiet Night)
李白 Li Bai

Jing Ye Si is probably one of the first poems that any child learning Mandarin Chinese will chant and one that they can recite by heart for the rest of their life. The verses are easy to read and roll off the tongue, one after another, in melodic cadence. English translations do disservice to the twenty words that elegantly capture the melancholy of the great Chinese poet Li Bai, his feeling of being out of place.[1]

---

[1] I could not find a satisfactory translation and cobbled together parts of other translations, particularly one that several websites credit to a "Christopher Evan," with my own modifications. Translating classical Chinese poems to English is a thorny task (or even to vernacular, contemporary Chinese), because single words or phrases in classical Chinese often embody complicated concepts or refer to entire historical events. It is also challenging to decide whether to translate the poem's most superficial layer of meaning or its deeper layers. The former, a literal translation, leaves behind the embedded figurative meanings, which might contain political

My first exposure to *Jing Ye Si*, learning to recite it, and now (re) interpreting its beautiful verses and my initial encounter with it evoke many aspects of out of place – not feeling that I belong to a social group, or not being regarded as belonging, whether it was due to my ideas, or whom or what I might seem to represent. My being out of place is not a condition of being on one side of a binary vis-à-vis being in place. It slides in scales and shades, and shifts according to my relationships to things, locations, and people. Its one constant is that it is ever changing.

I have always been drawn to being, and have always been, out of place. As a child, I was educated as an outsider, grappling with unfamiliar languages as I moved through different school systems. In my teenage years at a Chinese independent school in Malaysia, I realized I was an ethnic minority living in a country with explicitly discriminatory racial policies. In graduate school, I was a "first generation" student, the first in my family to have attended college, and what's more a PhD program. At home, constant rejection of my parents' hopes and wishes pitched me against the traditional authority of the parent. I felt incredibly lonely, growing up with parents who love but do not know how to love me, and the expectation of convention to behave a certain way toward them.

My wariness of coercive state power as well as unquestioned, unquestionable authority of traditions and customs were intuitive, active long before I learned about structure, domination, or hegemony in university. From the struggles with language, ethnic identity, class, and parental authority, I also taught myself to embrace the ambiguities and contradictions of who I was becoming and would be. Looking back, I think these external and internal struggles also made me empathetic toward out-of-placeness and human agency in the face of power. With that empathy came a curiosity about resistance. I tried out different aspects of my out-of-placeness, and sometimes reshaped it, making choices and following my intuition that paved my own journey into academia.

Thus, choosing to *live* out-of-placeness, not simply manage it as a condition, inspires my scholarship and informs my study of law.

criticism or social commentary, whereas the latter approach may fail to convey the beauty of the superficial layer, which shows off the poet's talent with words and rhythm, and skill at embedding the figurative in the literal. For this homemade translation, I settled for a superficial, literal translation.

I investigate law out of places – from the ground up, through fieldwork and empirical data – and try to understand people who are marginalized, seek belonging, and resist powers that try to put them in places that demean them. I have conducted ethnography on rights activism under and against authoritarian conditions in Singapore (Chua 2014) and Myanmar (Chua 2019), and I have recently begun to explore aging and the authority of family and state law. In Singapore, I found pragmatic resistance, nuanced challenges against legal power that sometimes play with, and other times play against, law itself. In Myanmar, I felt the intimate role of emotions in the manner by which activists made sense of human rights and used them to rally, organize, and claim for recognition and redress. Of late, I am poring over the love as well as hurt and manipulations in the intimate relationship between parent and child, and parsing through the power of family and state that purports to govern them as the parent ages and the child turns adult.

ROOTS OF OUT-OF-PLACENESS

I knew nothing of Li Bai's *Jing Ye Si* until I was seven and attended Primary One in my birthplace of Kuching on the Malaysian side of the world's third largest island, Borneo. This was where my out-of-place journey began. Unable to string together a sentence in Mandarin Chinese, much less a poem, I was immediately assigned to the "slow group." Unlike other children in the class who would have attended kindergarten in Mandarin Chinese before attending a public primary school that used Mandarin Chinese as the medium of instruction, I was an interloper from an English-speaking kindergarten, where I had also been out of place.

With a little luck, my parents had enrolled me in the kindergarten that catered to British expatriates, securing one of the few precious slots left for locals. They had worked hard to afford the high cost of tuition because they believed an early mastery of English would help me get ahead. But I could neither utter nor comprehend a word of English and started out, of course, as the dim-witted kid. At home, for the first four years of my life, I had conversed in Hokkien, a version slightly removed from other Hokkien diasporas, approximating the Minnanese in Taiwan and other variants across the South China Sea in Singapore and Penang. My father's ancestors had migrated from Fujian (Hokkien) province, China, and settled across Southeast Asia, at one point fleeing anti-Chinese purges on Sumatra Island. My mother's family, also laying

105

claim to Hokkien ancestry, were the sort of ethnically ambiguous folks who checked "Chinese" in the census box. Really, they were ethnic Chinese who had settled in Southeast Asia several generations ago and had a history of intermarriages with Malays and Europeans.

At the English-speaking kindergarten and the Mandarin Chinese primary school, even after picking up their dominant language, I could not stay in place. My parents did not win the ballot that gave locals the scarce opportunity to send their children to the English-speaking primary school affiliated with the kindergarten. That was how I ended up in the Mandarin Chinese public primary school. Six years later, they sent me to a Chinese independent secondary school (獨中), part of a network of community secondary schools set up by ethnic Chinese across Malaysia. Most of my primary school friends transitioned to public secondary schools where they took classes in Malay, the only language of instruction in the public system from Form One onward. I entered a new phase of life, the out-of-place girl, once again.[2]

Over the next six years, even though I made friends and found my footing, being an independent Chinese school student in Malaysia was to be out of place and to enact resistance by simply being so. The curriculum exuded almost an ethnocentric pride and adulation for an imagined cultural motherland. But it also heightened my sense of discrimination and marginalization. Probably from that time onward, I developed an acute awareness of overt and subtle forms of power and resistance. They were everywhere. The teachers spoke of racialized policies of the government, including university admissions, property, and employment, and we were urged to learn "our" "history" and "culture," lest they perish quietly one day, their vitality slowly strangled, day by day, generation after generation. Looking back, I realized that students like me were steeped in everyday politics (Kerkvliet 2009) and asked to live out-of-placeness with resistance, not in open protest but in its everyday forms.

[2] In Malaysia, three kinds of primary schools in the public system, Primary One through Six, offer the same curriculum in three different languages: Malay, Mandarin Chinese, and Tamil. At the secondary school level, Form One to Form Six, all public schools teach in Malay only. Chinese independent schools offer six years of alternative secondary school education taught in Mandarin Chinese, culminating in a diploma that Malaysian public universities and government sectors refuse to recognize but universities elsewhere, including Singapore, the United States, United Kingdom, Australia, and New Zealand, have accepted as admissions qualifications.

At home, I was a child furiously insisting on stepping out of pace with her parents' hopes and aspirations. My parents had no opportunity to go to college. Their ambition was for my younger brother and me to earn college degrees that would help us advance economically in a world that they could only view as stacked against those who lacked the right paper qualifications, skin pigmentation, and spiritual persuasions. In me, they found an offspring who excelled academically but had little desire for a "practical" profession such as law, medicine, engineering, or accountancy. As I grew older, I saw the contradictions of our ambitions with sharpening clarity. I grew increasingly frustrated with the realization that they could never fathom my fears and desires, whereas I not only appreciated theirs but also understood their reasons and thoroughly disagreed with them. So, I lived in resistance against their suffocating love and incompatible dreams, their bundle of disappointment, squander, and might-have-been.

MOBILIZING GAY SINGAPORE: STEPPING OUT AS A SOCIO-LEGAL SCHOLAR

Contrary to *Jing Ye Si*'s nostalgia, I wanted to yank myself from my birthplace. After finishing six years of secondary school, I left and did not look back to Kuching as my home. I studied journalism in the United States. I chose journalism probably because I love getting to know people and trying to understand their worlds and their worldviews. But then the deadlines got to be too much. I had little time to sit down and think.

Eventually tired of chasing news stories, I decided to return to Southeast Asia to study law at the National University of Singapore. But I had no intention of practicing law, much to my parents' dismay. I saw no reason why I had to take up the profession for which I was supposedly trained, just because that was what most of my peers did. The more I read judicial opinions, scrutinized statutes, and thought about their implications, the more I wanted to expose myself to the workings and power of law.

In 2005, I wound up at the Jurisprudence & Social Policy (JSP) program at the University of California, Berkeley. I had no grand plan for an academic career. The choice was intuitive. JSP's approach to law stood out from other PhD law programs, such as Cambridge, Oxford, Harvard, and Yale, which many of my colleagues attended. At JSP,

I would learn to study law in a way that enabled me to investigate power and empathize with oppression and resistance.

At the same time, I also felt out of place at JSP. I assumed that most of my peers came from pedigree schools and had parents or family members who were academics or held advanced degrees. This was probably a wrong assumption. Surely, some of my peers felt just as out of place as I did. Nevertheless, I somehow formed the impression early in the first semester that everyone in my classes knew a lot more about our field of study and the whole business of being an academic, probably based on the confident way they critiqued the readings and discussed the authors. I was that doltish kid again.

Yet Berkeley was where I started to embrace being out of place. My reading of the giants in my field and newer works was unfiltered by preconceived ideas of what research ought to look like or how an academic career ought to develop. Passing remarks from two mentors were formative. "You know more than you think," said Catherine Albiston when I expressed anxiety about my seminar paper during the first semester of graduate school. "Lynette, you are in the zeitgeist," said Kristin Luker in her usual reassuring tone (I had no clue what she meant, but she made me feel great). These words helped me realize that being out of place was a gift.

Outside JSP, I was busily reshaping my appearance. After getting my first tattoo, I decided that I wanted more. I enjoyed the process, the sometimes painful, sometimes invigorating, sessions and the messy, inconvenient healing and scabbing of wounds. So, the tattoos came, one after another. Soon enough, I literally did not look like the same person who had entered Berkeley. When my parents saw me, they immediately worried that I would be rejected by respectable circles, let alone academia, despite their ongoing belief that I had thrown away the chance to be a lawyer to become "just a teacher." Whereas my parents reacted from a place of fear, I did what intuitively felt right to me. Soon, tattoos would become a significant part of conducting out-of-place fieldwork.

My ideas, unfiltered by how others think and how others think they ought to think about being a PhD student and a successful academic, made me fearless or, more likely, naïve. I picked a dissertation project that any savvy PhD student would shun for being too marginal – the gay rights movement in Singapore, a state known for its strict controls over activism, tight restrictions on civil-political freedoms, and conservative attitude toward homosexuality. I wanted to study how these movement activists organize themselves, make claims under tough constraints, and whether and how rights matter to their efforts.

The project's inquiry makes it a classic law and society study, one that asks whether and how people make use of rights to achieve progressive social change. Nonetheless, the project was frequently treated as oddball. It focused on a society in which scholars might not expect a social movement around a tabooed issue. The typical response would be that there is little rights mobilization in Singapore, and there is nothing much to see, since the obvious answer is that rights and mobilization are suppressed. If you were to look for court litigation, a common site for the study of rights mobilization in the United States, you would agree. At the time of my study, the late 2000s, there was no constitutional challenge for gay rights, and, to date, no victory in the courts.[3]

The apparent absence of rights excited me. Rights mobilization and gay rights activism are out of place in Singapore. I did not start nor end at the courthouse. I searched for rights where they would have been experienced or put into action – by the very people struggling for belonging in their society. Intuitively, I was studying law out of place, doing what a socio-legal scholar should.

I interviewed 100 past and present activists and allies of the movement, some of them multiple times, observed their activities, and analyzed movement paraphernalia, media reports, and legal documents. I was not part of the movement, and I was not Singaporean. However, because I was Malaysian and had lived and studied in Singapore, neither was I a total stranger, a "Westerner." I perceived that people were willing to go into detail about the Singaporean political context when they explained their actions or views, not because I was less of a threat, but because they thought I would better appreciate the political ins and outs. Few bothered to ask me about my sexuality (or gender, for that matter). I do not know why. Perhaps they presumed they already knew the answer. With my Berkeley credentials and tattoos, I probably looked safe enough not to be a right-wing infiltrator.[4]

---

[3] Several court challenges against the constitutionality of the law that criminalized same-sex relations between men have been filed since 2011, after my fieldwork for *Mobilizing Gay Singapore*. None of them has succeeded, and the highest court has upheld the law. I conducted a smaller ethnographic study and published an analysis on the first set of litigation: Chua (2017).

[4] For more details, see the appendix in Chua (2014).

Embracing the ambiguities and assumptions that stemmed from my being out of place, I welcomed whatever my interviewees were willing to share. I also paid attention to what might be missing or left out of their conversation. I watched and listened, and let my intuition about power and resistance guide me along with my formal training from Berkeley.

Although these activists did not always espouse rights openly, I noticed that rights formed an integral part of their motivation, hopes, and dreams. Rights emerged from and embodied their activism and responses to the authoritarian constraints. By toeing the line – written state law and its unofficial norms – and pushing the same boundaries, Singapore's gay rights activists engaged in a strategy of pragmatic resistance that enabled them to steer clear of state retaliation, carry out rights mobilization, and nudge forward their claims for gay rights. Having to come up with creative tactics just so that they could organize, gather, and speak out, that is, exercise basic civil-political freedoms to make substantive claims, suggests that rights remain largely aspirational. Rights mattered not as courtroom vindications, for those were yet to be attained. Rather, I found that rights lived in their movement as quiet motivation, pushing these activists to strive for the ultimate aims of rights – dignity, freedom, and equality.

Hence, rights mattered by producing snowballing, everyday effects for the movement. While socio-legal scholars had written about the individual, self-transformative aspect of rights, I showed that even in hard places, rights mobilization could bear collective implications. Singapore's gay rights activists imagined a brighter future as they turned to the aspirations behind rights to learn to accept themselves and reinterpret their relationships. Although they did not demand rights out loud, rights empowered them to take action, to question prevailing social institutions, and to band together. Drawn to an out-of-place movement, the out-of-place researcher in me identified the power of rights and the strength of human agency to forge resistance against the odds.

THE POLITICS OF LOVE IN MYANMAR: FINDING MY OWN PRACTICE OF SOCIO-LEGAL SCHOLARSHIP

Rereading the final chapter of *Mobilizing Gay Singapore*, I realized that my next project picked up a salient thread running through the former. *The Politics of Love* continues my exploration of law, power, and resistance, but focuses much more intently on the intimate relationship between rights and the self, and its cumulative consequences for collective action.

The Politics of Love did not start out the way it ended up in final book form, an experience that many socio-legal scholars probably share. Being and desiring out of place can become wearisome. Trying to secure a university press for *Mobilizing Gay Singapore* was exhausting, not the least because some editors saw it as a book about an obscure movement in a tiny Asian country (i.e., not China). Moreover, my story about vibrant human agency was an unfamiliar one about Singapore, whose dominant Western narrative was that of an oppressive place with a strong economy and compliant population – Said's Orientalism by another name.[5] Finally, Temple University Press's Janet Francendese and series editors Janice Irvine and Regina Kunzel recognized the manuscript's potential and took me on.

Fresh from signing the contract in 2012, the last thing I wanted to do was to pursue another out-of-place project. Around the same time, Myanmar's transition from military to semi-civilian government was all over the news. I gave the ensuing academic chatter little heed because I could not imagine myself conducting research on anything related to Myanmar, an even more out-of-place proposition for me. I also did not plan on a second project on LGBT rights. I was fed up with queries from local reporters and the university's corporate communications office on any legal issue that contained the word "sex," such as sexual violence, sex work, and incest.

Then one day, I came across a news report about a celebration of International Day Against Homophobia (IDAHO) across five Burmese cities and towns.[6] The report mentioned that the organizers spoke about the violations of human rights of lesbian, gay, bisexual, and transgender (LGBT) people. My out-of-place intuition was tingled. Given the suppression of human rights and activism in Myanmar for decades, I was curious about how these organizers came into contact with and understood human rights. My training as a socio-legal scholar told me that their interpretations might not be the same as that of a legal scholar or international human rights activist from the Global

---

[5] Besides, other researchers have provided accounts of the use of law to achieve political control and social order in Singapore (see, e.g., Rajah 2012).

[6] Now this globally commemorated event on May 17 is known as International Day Against Homophobia, Transphobia, and Biphobia.

North. The IDAHO event looked coordinated and could not have popped up overnight simply because the country had supposedly liberalized. I suspected that something more far reaching was afoot.

As a self-described LGBT rights movement, this was a group of out-of-place people fighting to belong in a society that ranked heterosexual, cisgender men at the top of its hierarchy. Their efforts were also out of place in scholarship. Scholars of Myanmar mostly tended to study its constitutional law, civil-political liberties, (heterosexual, cisgender) women's rights, ethnic or religious minorities, land rights, or corporate and financial reforms. Sexual and gender minorities, and mobilization around their issues, received scant attention. Only a few scholars had written about *apwint*, often described as transgender women in Western parlance, or "spirit dancers" often mistakenly conflated with the former, and hardly anyone worked on rights mobilization by any sexual or gender minority group. In fact, this topic was considered to be so out of place that an old guard of Burmese legal studies lambasted my presentation in the early stages of my fieldwork. He opined that scholars should study "important" issues such as detention and forced labor, implying that sexual and gender minorities' concerns were insignificant.

The brusque retort startled but empowered me. With *The Politics of Love*, I would show that out-of-place, "insignificant" people can teach a lot about the ingenuities of human agency, and the strengths and deficiencies of rights mobilization. For nearly five years, I plunged headlong into fieldwork. Supported by two research assistants, I interviewed 125 former and current movement activists and allies, examined their movement documents, photographs, and videos, reviewed legal documents, and attended their workshops, meetings, and public events.

Even though *The Politics of Love*, too, focuses on rights and sexual and gender minorities, it is distinctive from *Mobilizing Gay Singapore*. The main plot in the Singapore text focuses on how activists overcame the repression of civil-political rights to mobilize and make claims, and, consequently, demonstrates how rights mattered in quiet, unobtrusive ways. The repression of rights activism is certainly a key element of *The Politics of Love*, but its storyline tracks how activists learned about human rights, adapted them, and cleverly used them to build a movement and make claims, in other words, how they practiced human rights.

The driving forces behind this group's human rights practice were emotions and relationships. People from far-flung locations connected with the movement and one another through ties of suffering and political disaffection. They understood the meanings of human rights by feeling what it was like to endure the opposite: indignity and fear. Recasting their painful experiences as human rights violations, they transformed their self-identities, from feeling ashamed and afraid to feeling empowered and responsible for improving their circumstances. They cultivated an emotional fealty to human rights as they joined the movement and bonded as a community of solidarity known as LGBT rights activists. Through these emotions and affective bonds, a group of out-of-place people built a home in their hearts for what would have been an out-of-place discourse.

While conducting the fieldwork for *The Politics of Love*, I was even more aware of out-of-placeness, compared to my time spent with Singapore's gay rights movement. In the appendix to *The Politics of Love*, I reflected on my positionality, which most would describe as an "outsider" to Myanmar and the movement. However, the parameters of who is an outsider or an insider – like who is "out of place" in this book – are never entirely clear and always in relation to time, place, and other people. Usually, I was the outsider, clearly out of place in relation to Myanmar and the movement. Other times, maybe I was less out of place with the movement than Burmese who rejected sexual and gender minorities, or misunderstood their world. The activists spoke to me at length and shared their photographs and stories with me. I gave presentations on Singapore's gay rights movement, which the activists welcomed as useful information and lessons for their own endeavors. Maybe they also made assumptions about me based on my earlier research and my tattoos, just like their Singaporean counterparts had.[7] I also reflected on what it meant to be an insider. My two research assistants, a Karen Christian cisgender woman and a Burmese Chinese cisgender woman, live in a predominantly Burman Buddhist society. Does "insider" connote the same "in placeness" for a man who is

---

[7] One incident, however, vexed me for a while. After his interview, an ally of the movement repeatedly asked if he could come over to my lodgings to photograph my tattoos. After politely declining his self-invitation twice, I decided that this was definitely not a case of language or cross-cultural miscommunication. I flatly told him that I was unavailable, but tossed and turned for weeks. This interviewee was a highly connected person among human rights activists in Myanmar, and I worried that he would make the rest of the fieldwork difficult for me. Fortunately, that concern did not come to pass, and I continued to meet and talk to other people in the field.

cisgender and Burman – the dominant ethnic group – as it does for a woman, or an ethnic or religious minority?[8]

Being out of place but feeling comfortable with LGBT rights activists, I asked questions whose answers might have seemed obvious to an insider to the movement, such as the meanings of certain Burmese terms. The frank responses revealed why people who joined the movement could enthusiastically adopt "LGBT" identities – which human rights critics warned could sideline local cultures – while maintaining Burmese references to their sexual or gender subjectivities. The answer lay in the different feelings that they had for the different words, those associated with the human rights-based movement and those with social networks that they had maintained long before the movement. They moved fluidly in and out of these worlds with different emotional attachments.

Of course, these activists and their rights practices are fraught with human fallibilities. My out-of-place research assistants and I noticed that their movement was principally made up of Burmans and Buddhists, and dominated by those assigned the male gender at birth, whether they would identify as cisgender gay men, transgender women, or *apwint*. In spite of, and perhaps because of, the way they adapted human rights to gain emotional fealty and social belonging, they could not overcome and even perpetuated the faults and fault lines of sexuality, gender, and racism in Myanmar. Such findings would lend support to criticisms of human rights, but they also showed that human rights were far from achieving any hegemonic status. Instead, human rights were an additional discourse that Burmese LGBT rights activists had managed to inject with limited success into their political context.

When I was developing the book manuscript, self-doubt crept in every now and then. I was writing about out-of-place people, again, and compounding the challenges by daring to take emotions center stage. Legal scholars, sociologists, and anthropologists have studied emotions, but the segregation and denigration of emotions as irrational and difficult to study, compared to thoughts and actions, linger.[9] Nonetheless, reviewing my notes and data, I realized that the only story

---

[8] For more details on my fieldwork and reflections on my positionality, see the Appendix to *The Politics of Love*, and my responses to a series of commentaries on the book, Chua (2020).

[9] For more extensive discussion of the study of emotions in law and in social movements, see chapter 1 of *The Politics of Love*.

I wanted to tell with conviction was one where emotions belonged in the heart of rights mobilization. So, I took a deep breath and stepped out there.

FILIAL RESPONSIBILITY, AGING, AND LAW

The Politics of Love transformed me. The fieldwork was draining, and it fueled me with boldness and passion in my research and writing. Writing *The Politics of Love* gave me the courage to confront the most intimate types of power and resistance, within the family and between parent and child.

For my third major project, currently ongoing, my starting point is parental maintenance laws enacted by governments in Taiwan, China, Singapore, and Vietnam. These laws require adult children to provide financial support, and, in some instances, emotional care, to their elderly parents. I want to find out whether and how parents would use these laws to sue their children.

At first, this project does not appear to be out of place, as it could be considered a rather conventional study of legal mobilization around a widely accepted concern for elderly care, a far cry from *Mobilizing Gay Singapore* and *The Politics of Love*. But I trusted my intuition, remembered my belief in studying law out of place, and let the fieldwork take me. And it did – to plural sources of power. What I call family power – patriarchal, filial responsibility norms in the guise of moral virtues – sometimes colluded with and sometimes contradicted state power in the arena of official law. The young and old, parent and child, participate in the everyday politics of family, living, resisting, and making what it means to be a parent and a child. These personhoods arise in relation to each other and to others, such as grandparents, grandchildren, siblings, and spouses, who are in enmeshed relationships with one another (Ingold 2011). Although scholars from a broad range of disciplines have explored aging, kinship, and filial responsibility, and legal scholars have considered parental maintenance laws, neither has approached the two together undergirded by questions of plural sources of power, everyday politics, and resistance.

The taken-for-granted, self-evident expectations of filial responsibility come to light in the hundreds of interviews I conducted with people from southeastern China, Taiwan, Vietnam, and Singapore, including judges, social workers, lawyers, village heads, and ordinary folks with little knowledge about parental maintenance laws. Children who defy the overwhelming structures of family power are behaving in a manner that takes them out of place, deviants who have committed a great act of immorality. The norm to look after one's parents is so deeply rooted that interviewees often had difficulty explaining why it was critical or why they were adhering to it, and thought it was silly of me to even ask such a question. With parental maintenance laws, the state seeks to regulate out-of-place behavior. Meanwhile, like many other social orders, filial responsibility varies and changes with the relationships among people, and between them and things, creatures, and locations, notably, family structures, economies, governments, and population flows.

Journeying across seven cities and their surrounding areas for this project, I found that the sensation of being out of place was more nuanced than my previous experiences. The weight of filial responsibility could be so heavy that some interviewees started out cautious about what they really thought of their relationships with their parents or children. Maybe they worried about deviating from stereotypically exalted views, seeing that I was someone highly educated and thus supposedly possessing higher "moral" standards for filial responsibility. On my part, I held back my views of filial responsibility, careful not to fall out of place in the eyes of judges, elderly parents, and other guardians of "morality." For good measure, I wore long sleeves to cover up my tattoos. Between the interviewee and me, I detected passing moments of sussing each other out, before settling into a comfort zone of sharing the pain and joy of what it meant for them to be a parent or child or both.

The fieldwork is still unfolding, so I do not know exactly what kind of story I will tell in the end.[10] What I now know is that my out-of-placeness as a child seeded this intellectual curiosity. In the interviews and writings that I have collected, where others might see love, I see authority; what they might identify as morality, I discern as power; whom they might describe as immoral or disorderly, I feel for the differences in construction of personhood and empathize with resistant agency.

* * *

---

[10] I have published an article inspired by the fieldwork thus far, "Interregna: Time, Law, and Resistance" (Chua 2021), but I am not sure where it fits in the overall, larger book project yet.

In *Jing Ye Si*, Li Bai was feeling out of place, because he longed for his hometown. Whenever I did visit Kuching, where I was born and raised, I would feel out of place. Or, maybe the provincial city seemed out of place in my present. The air tasted heavier, the buildings looked wearier, and my old schoolmates familiar strangers.

Growing up with out-of-placeness, I learned to recognize the human condition of feeling out of place, to embrace it when I encountered it, and to be curious about the power and resistance involved in its making. The desire to uncover oppression and to appreciate how people deal with coercion, from the most blatant to the most insidious, elusive forms, led me to socio-legal scholarship. Empathy and curiosity molded my approach to studying law, and I followed my intuition as I walked into the field, to understand law out of many places and human agency that rejoin and counter the out of place. Out-of-placeness threads through my research, the past, the present, and the unknown. Throughout this journey, I change as I travel to new lands and meet new people, and thus my out-of-placeness keeps on shifting its meanings and implications.

Maybe we are never fully in nor out of place, but always moving. Even as I continued to work on the filial responsibility project in 2020, the SARS-CoV-2 virus loomed, and would soon kill hundreds of thousands and fling billions of lives into disarray. Unable to travel for fieldwork, and, during two months of strict lockdown, forbidden from meeting anybody in person, I felt disjointed *and* stuck. Then a former colleague asked me to write a paper on law and the pandemic. Although I was initially reluctant because it seemed like an endeavor outside of my interests, I accepted the invitation. I was worried about the virus. But I was also terrified by the force of law and deployment of surveillance technologies to control its spread, and saddened by the disparities and inequalities, and by seeing how marginalized communities were disproportionately affected by the pandemic as well as its control measures. I started a new project, "Governing through Contagion," to explore the patterns of out-of-placeness that both contagion and the strategies of control would reveal and exacerbate.[11]

Maybe our scholarship and its place in our lives will never be the same after the pandemic. Contagions have upended and continue to

---

[11] "Governing through Contagion" is still in the early stages of development, but I have since written a paper with a coauthor setting out the preliminary theoretical framework (Chua and Lee 2021).

upend human lives. Even as vaccines against SARS-CoV-2 became available at the time of writing this chapter, far more contagious strands were making their ways from continent to continent. What I do know is that I will continue to be an out-of-place scholar, to understand what it means to live law out of place and to give those who are out of place their own rooms in our writings.[12]

References

Chua, Lynette J. 2014. *Mobilizing Gay Singapore: Rights and Resistance in an Authoritarian State*. Philadelphia, PA: Temple University Press.

2017. "Collective Litigation and Constitutional Challenges to Decriminalize Homosexuality in Singapore." *Journal of Law & Society* 44(3): 433–55.

2019. *The Politics of Love in Myanmar: LGBT Mobilization and Human Rights As a Way of Life*. Palo Alto, CA: Stanford University Press.

2020. "Response to Commentaries" (to "Book Discussion on *The Politics of Love in Myanmar*"). *Asian Journal of Law & Society* 6(3): 607–12.

2021. "Interregna: Time, Law, and Resistance." *Law & Social Inquiry* 46(1): 268–91.

Chua, Lynette J., and Jack Jin Gary Lee. 2021. "Governing through Contagion." In *COVID-19 in Asia: Law & Policy Contexts*, edited by Victor V. Ramraj, 116–32. New York: Oxford University Press.

Galanter, Marc. 1981. "Justice in Many Rooms: Courts, Private Ordering, and Indigenous Law." *The Journal of Legal Pluralism and Unofficial Law* 19:1–47.

Ingold, Tim. 2011. *Being Alive: Essays on Movement, Knowledge and Description*. London: Routledge.

Kerkvliet, Benedict J. Tria. 2009. "Everyday Politics in Peasant Societies (and Ours)." *Journal of Peasant Studies* 36(1): 227–43.

Rajah, Jothie. 2012. *Authoritarian Rule of Law: Legislation, Discourse, and Legitimacy in Singapore*. New York: Cambridge University Press.

---

[12] Marc Galanter wrote an article entitled, "Justice in Many Rooms" (1981).

CHAPTER SIX

OUT OF PLACE IN AN INDIAN COURT

Notes on Researching Rape in a District Court in Gujarat (1996–8)

*Pratiksha Baxi**

In this chapter, I reflect on the experience of conducting fieldwork on rape trials in the rural District and Sessions Court in Ahmedabad (Gujarat) over eighteen months between 1996 and 1998. The experience of inhabiting the field illustrated how judicial hierarchy and social discourses make rape survivors, complainants, experts, women lawyers, or women generally feel out of place in a court. This out-of-placeness which is productive for male judicial hierarchy, has a thin threshold of tolerance for difference. The vignettes that follow describe how the performance of shame and decency were critical to the *doing* of the fieldwork. I describe the sensory and emotional out-of-placeness of the field that acquired different intensities over time for me.

I am unlettered in law, not having formally studied at a law school. Not having a law degree produced a specific kind of out-of-placeness, for neither did I have the kind of access to a court that wearing a black gown might provide nor did the practice of criminal law always resemble what was written in law books. I learnt criminal procedural and evidentiary law in conversation with lawyers, reading paper books, observing trials, and spending time reading law digests in the court library. I gained proficiency in Gujarati and criminal law

* This essay is a revised and expanded version of excerpts from *Public Secrets of Law: Rape Trials in India* (Baxi 2014). Thanks to Lynette J. Chua, Mark Fathi Massoud, and all the contributors to this volume for their engaging and thoughtful comments. Thanks also to Mouykh Chatterjee, Ghazala Jamil, and Janaki Abraham for very helpful feedback.

simultaneously. Medico-legal and forensic vocabularies used in court-room speech required a working familiarity with how evidence is analyzed and recorded in hospitals and laboratories. I learnt that what one may learn in a law school or by memorizing a legal digest was out of place in a courtroom, for it was the socio-legal practice of law that taught me how precisely illegality sits at the heart of state law. Illegality was not out of place – rather it was folded into legal discourse in specific ways (Baxi 2014).

I had to learn how to inhabit the court, for the monumentalization of judicial hierarchy itself produces an out-of-placeness. Doing ethnography in a court was more complex negotiation than a question of certification or expertise, or whether I was adopted as an insider or treated as an outsider. It meant embodying judicial hierarchy in an everyday sense. Judicial hierarchy was foundationally sexist, barely tolerant of women in law. Doing fieldwork in court meant wearing the color of law. Fieldwork meant learning how to walk purposively, who to speak to and who to avoid, where to sit and where to converse. It meant refusing certain kinds of access to victims where power was indifferent to causing further trauma to survivors. It meant recognizing the directions in which male desire was inserted in the place of law.

Feeling "out of place" was borne by the encounter with moral discourses about how women should speak about sex, sexuality, and sexual violence in public. It indexed how texts recording violence are consumed voyeuristically and move into the realm of the pornographic that sanctions rape. It signals towards the unspoken and unwritten that shadows the ethnographic text – the nightmares that followed writing; the frozen memories of certain scenes in the courtroom; attachments with children I met briefly; and the memory of the trials as these shaped my affective life long after formal closures to fieldwork and writing up. The life of the field as it persists, after the publication of the ethnographic text, after two decades, presents a peculiar challenge, especially in times of the lockdown and the pandemic. For the sensorium of law marks ethnographic imagination long after fieldwork is over.

FINDING THE COURT

I reached the city of Ahmedabad to begin my fieldwork on rape trials during the hot summer of July 1996. I began my research with feminist frameworks, and in conversations with feminist activists and journalists. I got in touch with women's groups in Ahmedabad and Baroda.

Within a couple of days, I had travelled to another small town to participate in an anti-rape protest. I met activists, journalists, and lawyers to get a sense of the debates and interventions on violence against women in the state. In Ahmedabad, I tried to get permission to work on the cases of rape that went through one of the oldest women's organizations in the state and interviewed key activists there. However, I had to abandon this plan as the organization's leadership was not too keen on this idea.

I was fortunate to meet younger lawyers, who were excited about my research project and introduced me to senior lawyers of the Gujarat High Court. A well-known human rights lawyer introduced me to an eminent judge at the Gujarat High Court known for pro-poor and human rights friendly judgments. He gave me permission to work in the record room of the court. I was introduced to Mr. B who then helped me sift through case files, to find rape cases filed along with cases of bootlegging, anti-social activities, riots, and murders.

Over a few months, I made a list of 150 cases dating back to the 1980s, an archive that I thought might be useful to reflect on the legal history of rape in Gujarat. Beginning fieldwork in a record room seemed like the first step, since the world of law is a world of files (Latour 2009/ 2002; Riles 2006; Holden 2008; Taneja 2017; Ghosh 2019). Today, one can read many judgments synchronically and diachronically through a web search, even for trial courts. Not only are orders and judgments available online, but also the legal file itself is thought of as a hypertext (Suresh 2016, 2019). In the 1990s, computers were only recently introduced and the digitization of judgments an unimaginable possibility. Yet the smell of legal power in the record room was dusty, and afflictions with allergies and fevers followed me through different courts.

The Gujarat High Court was then located in a building that was said to be a hospital building; it has since moved to a new multi-story building further away from the city center. It was a congested court. Women often dodged male bodies. To reach the courts and offices of the court, one had to walk past a corridor which opened into male bathrooms which were always in use. The strong stink of the male urinals inscribed the maleness of the space in olfactory normalcy. It felt like masculine sensory gatekeeping that had to be endured to access the life of the court.

The court was not built with separate stairways and passages to allow a separate movement for judges between courtrooms. I was taken aback when the *sheristadar*, a court official in a ceremonial costume who escorts judges, made way for a judge in the crowded corridor of the court, swinging a baton in the air as lawyers and litigants flattened themselves on the wall to make way for the judge (see Baxi 2014, also see Khorakiwala 2020). I almost caught the baton aimed at me by reflex but avoided contempt of court by imitating the lawyers who made way for the judge. Legal ethnography is done in the shadow of contempt of court (see Dembowski and Korff 2011). Out-of-placeness is in aware-ness of law's violence.

This was not the only court where I worked. I also visited the two district courts in the city. Eventually, I was to research the district court which had jurisdiction over the rural district of Ahmedabad. Although I got permission from the Commissioner of Police, Ahmedabad City, I was unceremoniously thrown out of a couple of local police stations, whereas a few police offices, such as in the Crime Branch, consented to give me interviews. I managed to spend a day in the Forensic Science Laboratory in Ahmedabad, conduct interviews with forensic experts and doctors in the Civil Hospital. A single day could be busy going from a court to a hospital, police station, or a lawyer's chamber on public transport up and down the city in hot sweltering summers.

PERMISSION

A senior lawyer in the High Court of Gujarat told me that a law student would not find anything of interest in studying the rape trials and surmised that I was perhaps interested in following rape trials because I was a sociologist. When I told him that law students do research rape trials in other jurisdictions, he wondered out loud: *What would they possibly say?* Similarly, lawyers in the trial courts often told me that I should research appellate courts, since most rape cases were "compromised" in trial courts. It is not legal to compromise rape cases, however pressure, terror, settlement, or an offer to marry the woman causes witnesses and victims to routinely turn hostile to the prosecu-tion's case. Such cases were seen as "garbage" cases without any doctri-nal or precedential value. And hence, even as a site of research the trial court was not considered worthy of legal research by lawyers. "Compromise" cases were out of place in serious legal research. Locating the research project in a trial court was out of place for law students.

In 1996, as I began my fieldwork, High Court lawyers were animated by conversations about an allegation of rape against the Inspector General of Prisons by a woman student of sociology. It was alleged that the nineteen-year-old woman, daughter of a retired mill worker, was given permission by the Inspector General (IG) Prisons to enter the Sabarmati Jail as part of a conspiracy to organize a prison break of "notorious criminals" who included alleged "Pakistani spies" and "Anti-Nationals."[1] The allegation was that the young woman conversant with "martial arts etiquette and arts of conversation" acted as a "courier" to help the incarcerated "spies" escape from the prison. The Addl. Inspector General (Prison) was accused of rape and abuse of office, as well as conspiracy. The court order noted that the woman "revealed the conspiracy only when she was given full protection by the Anti-Terrorist Squad (A.T.S.)," and charges were brought against twelve accused. In February 1997, the case was handed over to the Central Bureau of Investigation, as the Addl. Inspector General (Prison) denied these charges as politically motivated. During my fieldwork, the coverage of this case folded into everyday conversations in the court. The lawyers felt that the accused was being framed due to political considerations, and the rape allegation was politically instrumentalized, or that the woman was a victim of blackmail by antisocial elements to malign the accused by levying a false accusation. At the same time, this framing of sexual violence within the context of state security produced suspicion of all women researchers.

In the High Court, I was repeatedly told I would not get permission to sit in on rape trials that were normally held in camera, because this case proved that it was unsafe to allow women (ostensibly trained in the "art of conversation") to research courts or prisons. I approached a High Court judge, a friend of my jurist father, who put in a word for me with the presiding judge in the District and Sessions Court. The District and Sessions judge granted me permission to research in camera trials, but he advised me not to reveal that I was a student of sociology. I was asked to maintain the fiction of being a law student, to gain more legitimacy in the court, in this discursive context where a rape allegation was exceptionalized.

---

[1] Bijal Revashanker Joshi *vs.* State of Gujarat (1997) 2 GLR 1147, https://indiankanoon.org/doc/466263/.

SCOLDING AS A PEDAGOGY

I was often scolded for researching rape. It was also out of place for the woman clerk in the Gujarat High Court's administrative wing to talk about rape trials: "women should not do work like this. It is only when you have misconceived ideas of bringing change that you do work like this. It simply means inviting trouble. It is partly women's fault that they are raped. I have learnt a lot from practical life. Women are helpless. We have no power. I can tell you all of this." The clerk believed that it was dangerous for women to reveal such public secrets. For her, researching rape meant refusing to know "what not to know" (Taussig 1999, 3). The stigma and danger attached to a rape survivor's public revelation of sexual violence was given the quality of contagion: it attached a certain kind of gaze on the researcher. This framing of my research was iterated during my fieldwork in different ways, and inflected discussions after the work was published.

The very project of researching rape trials typically produces social anxiety or even excitability that marks the production of public secrecy. Such forms of anxiety surfaced repeatedly when I mentioned my research topic, whether hostile or laudatory. Typically, I would be asked "but why did you take up this topic? Why could you not research 306 (IPC provision on abetting suicide) or something else? It is difficult to talk about it." When I asked why talking about rape was so problematic, I was repeatedly told that it was difficult, especially for male lawyers, to talk to me since I was an "unmarried" woman – male lawyers often said, "I cannot be free with you." Not surprisingly, I was expected to script shame and embarrassment in my interviews. This motif of shame was accompanied by the idea that the act of witnessing rape trials wounds women. One lawyer advised me not to document the circulation, witnessing and recitation of narratives of sexual violence. He said, "you see, your work will affect you. You see varieties of men in the court. You have already seen a lot. It will have a psychological effect on you." For him talking about rape did not offer the possibilities of transformation or that "meanings, in as much as it is established in a chain of signifiers, can always slide, producing new meanings" (Aretxaga 1997, 20). Rather, he meant that my inner life would be so wounded that I would be repulsed by marriage.

I do not wish to suggest that lawyers do not know that the testimony of rape survivors, who are silenced or on whose behalf men speak, is more than a confession or merely coming out. They know that testimony "works as an act, a reclaiming of history, and does so in a particular manner which asserts the fragility of the silence which counters it. In this way, testimony is a coming to voice, an insistence on speaking and not being silenced or spoken for" (Feldman 1993, 17; also see Herman 1992). Every lawyer knows that women's testimonies are distorted, disciplined, and misrepresented in rape trials. Defense lawyers talk, sometimes boastfully, about how courtroom speech routinely converts the testimony to rape into a confession of consensual sex. Judges know that courtroom talk in rape trials typically titillates, excites, and provokes. We know that legal records freeze this drama of sexualizing the raped body in stylized ways. Even when a trial results in a conviction, the law addresses a phallocentric notion of society, or deploys male standards of injury, thereby causing injury to survivors testifying against rape.

Researching rape offers many provocations to the social and legal mechanisms of silencing women from speaking out against rape. Talking to male lawyers as an expert (and even as an equal) meant transgressing social boundaries, wherein transgression itself is an experience of alterity. Transgression is not alterity in the sense of being a subversion of that which it violates (Jervis 1999). Instead, it implies the interrogation of the mechanisms of power and authority that articulates the limit, while at the same time engaging with its complicity in that which it prohibits. Marcus suggests that we must move away from thinking of complicity as a "partnership in evil," rather links complicity to the sense of being "complex, or involved" (1997: 100). In this sense, the very process of conducting ethnographies of rape trials, to an extent, is complicit in the making of the public secret. Such ethnography of rape trials offers pictures of the social and political process that script research as shameful, shape out of court negotiations, traffic in inducements, bargain with terror, and purchase dignity. Equally the process of research brought an uncanny awareness of out-of-placeness of feminism (also see Basu 2012, 2015) .

THE NYAYA MANDIR

The district court, at the time still under construction, was set apart from the street that led into a bustling market in the walled city, by a large court compound and an imposing flight of stairs. The Indian flag and a signboard marked out the court building as the Nyaya Mandir, which literally means temple of justice, in Gujarati and Hindi. The noisy court compound comprised a parking lot where police vans of prisoners were a common sight, and usually was crowded with typists, touts, and litigants. The building had eight floors, with the ground floor comprising spaces for lawyers to work. Scores of lawyers worked on chairs and tables, placed close to each other, and tied to each other with iron chains to secure each workstation. The court canteen was located at the other end. The first floor opened into the District and Sessions judge's courtroom at one end, and the Additional District and Sessions judge's courtroom on the other. The second floor housed the Assistant District and Sessions judges' courtrooms. The public prosecutor's office was located here. The upper floors were allocated to the magistrates of various ranks, the rank decreasing in the hierarchy, from the lower floors to the upper floors.

Goodrich (1990) points out that the ritual character of legal proceedings is marked by the ceremonial dress donned by the legal actors or the features of address and procedure, which are highly systemized. On my first day in the courtroom, I remembered Peter Goodrich's words:

> The day in court is likely to be experienced in terms of confusion, ambiguity, incomprehension, panic and frustration, and if justice is seen to be done it is so seen by outsiders to the process. Nor is justice likely to be heard to be done by the participants in the trial. The visual metaphor of justice as something that must be visible and seen enacted has a striking poignance in that it captures the paramount symbolic presence of law as a façade, a drama played out before the eyes of those subject to it.
>
> (1990: 191)

The noisy, busy, and sweaty courtroom with simultaneous hearings was unfathomable. On that unforgettable first day in a courtroom, I made many mistakes. The court was yet to begin its session. I looked around and sat down on a comfortable chair reserved for lawyers and was at once chastised. Abashed, I walked to a bench, which was reserved for the accused. Yet again I was scolded. Then I walked to the first row of chairs, to be told again that this row was reserved for witnesses. As days passed by, I managed to mark a chair with a broken armrest nearest to the witness box as my place in the court. Sometimes when I was lucky, I could secure permission from the court to sit at the lawyer's table from where I could hear the proceedings better.

Even from the first chair (towards the witness box) reserved for the public, it was difficult for me to hear what was being said. The accused separated spatially cannot hear most of what is being said but views the proceedings from a distance. I agree with Goodrich that the court is an auditory space organized on the principle of "visibility of justice rather than its audibility" (1990: 191). I noted that the greater the audibility the closer is an individual to privilege. More often than not, depending on the viewing and listening positions of the actors in a courtroom, the courtroom is experienced as "theatrical autism with all actors speaking past each other" (Carlen cited in Goodrich 1990, 193). This sense of speaking past each other, and not being able to hear legal proceedings, kept legal order in place.

FOLLOWING THE PROSECUTOR

After a few days of sitting in the courtroom, a middle-aged male lawyer who knew about my work, gestured to me to follow him. Hesitantly, I followed him to his chamber not knowing he was one of the five Additional Public Prosecutors (hereafter, APP). The APP, whom I call Hirabhai,[2] asked me many questions about my research and social background. Soon I was incorporated as a researcher amongst his juniors, mostly women. Two APPs allowed me access, but I worked predominantly in Hirabhai's office.

Hirabhai's office was a small room with a desk and two chairs, separated from other offices by a wooden partition. Hirabhai was named my "guide" by one of the judges whose courts I used to observe. Over time, I was situated like one of the juniors, as if I too had to be trained in the art of prosecution yet learn to observe judicial hierarchy. When I left the field, the presiding judge in whose courts I sat regularly wished me luck and remarked that I had become a part of their "family."

One of Hirabhai's junior lawyers, Beenaben, became a confidante and defended the validity of my research, which was keenly contested by lawyers (both men and women) in the court. In the chamber, my research was characterized as courageous. Hirabhai's journalist friend wanted to do a story on my courage. When a woman clerk said that I was shameless to do research like this, Beenaben stoutly defended me and refused to talk to her. Later she added, "do not be discouraged. These people are very narrow-minded. They do not know how

---

[2] In all these cases, I have fictionalized the identities of the victims and their families, witnesses, accused, prosecutors, lawyers, police officers, and medical experts in order to protect the identity of the rape survivor or the complainant.

courageous you are. Women, like you and me, are very few. We are different." The support by the prosecutor's office in pursuing the research, although the topic was considered shameful, was built on friendships with women lawyers especially. These friendships were forged through confidences and secrets about work and life. Beenaben drove me to court through an eerie curfew in the old city following a local riot on her scooty so we could be in time for a hearing; and another time, I skipped an important hearing to attend her marriage to her partner in the face of familial disapproval of an inter-caste marriage of a Rajput woman with a Brahmin man. Without this support and friendship, I would have probably not been able to do my fieldwork.

In the trial court, each case had to be photocopied, compiled, and indexed by sifting through dusty bundles of miscellaneous judgments, wrapped in red cloth. The record room yielded some information about ongoing cases, however I was entirely dependent on each prosecutor's office to help me enumerate how many rape cases were listed during the fieldwork. I could barely read the illegible handwritten cause lists announcing the daily roster of cases pasted on the board outside the courtrooms.

Twenty cases of rape, abduction and/or kidnapping were assigned to Hirabhai. Not all twenty cases were heard during this period. I could not choose which rape trials to follow. I followed six cases over a period of one and a half years, over a hundred hearings. I followed five cases prosecuted by Hirabhai. I followed one case with the assistance of another APP, Mr. Rajput. These cases concerned complaints of statutory rape (involving children below sixteen years), and rape, abduction and kidnapping of minors (applicable to girls below eighteen years). In the book, I chose to write about four case studies of the six trials. Two of these trials went on appeal to the Gujarat High Court. Sufficient time had elapsed, between the trials and the appeals, for these cases to be written about.

I combined my notes on what was spoken in the court with the court record of what was dictated to show how courtroom speech was not transliterated in court records. Rather, the court record of the testimony by the victim or the witness was translated and standardized by the judge or other actors in the trial such as the prosecutor or the police officer. The juxtaposition of courtroom speech and court records, alongside interviews in each case, made for the ethnographic retelling of each case.

OUT-OF-PLACE INTERVIEWS

This was tedious and painstaking work, just as sitting in the courtroom over 100 hearings had been. Makhija (2019) describes the experience of litigants as marked with boredom as "waiting for something to happen." Often complainants, victims, and witnesses would complain of the sheer discomfort of squatting in the court lobby or sitting on broken chairs with nothing happening in court. The sense of time weighing heavily on litigants, victims, and witnesses along with the heat of the summer produced a soporific sense of time. Lawyers and even judges caught a catnap during the proceedings, at times. I sat in the prosecutor's office waiting for trials to be heard in the courtroom, and when the prosecutor was busy, I loitered in court corridors, sat in the courtrooms, or read in the lawyer's library. I met experts, police officers, victims and their families in the prosecutors' office or the court lobby. Although I had permission to follow trials, and over time, I was incorporated in the chambers of the prosecutor, I negotiated feeling out of place in the court building on an everyday basis.

Although the District and Sessions Judge had granted me permission to document in camera trials, I secured consent from the complainant in each case to follow the proceedings. Trials could take a long time to complete, and it was very difficult to follow all hearings in one case even over a period of eighteen months. Many cases that came to court were filed by parents who opposed their daughters' sexual or romantic choices of inter-caste and inter-faith relationships. These cases were usually prosecuted under the rape, abduction, and kidnapping laws. The criminalization of love by using these laws sometimes meant jail terms for both men and women, as undertrials (those who are under investigation or charged with a crime) are routinely incarcerated in India. Love was not seen as out of place in criminal trials of rape, for women's consent to intimate relationships was seen as mediated by paternal authority, caste, and community.

Consent for me did not mean the routine ways of securing informed consent but was based on full disclosure of my own location in the world and my specific work (see Baxi 2014). The interviews were difficult in the absence of support services for victims, or their families. In the case of statutory rape, the anxiety generated by the legal proceedings, and fear of harm to the children precluded the possibility of ethnographic interviews. However, I found that the parents perceived talking to a stranger therapeutic, while revealing that what happened to the extended family was perceived as a source of stigma with long-term deleterious consequences for the child's future. Rapport then was not a measure of the amount of time spent with the person interviewed, nor did it remain a given as the case unfolded over time. I was present in the courtroom during their testimonies, yet we would never meet again or keep in touch.

Most interviews with the complainants and their families happened in court corridors in ongoing cases in the prosecutor's office. The lack of privacy posed a problem as time went by. I was nicknamed 376, after the section on rape in the Indian Penal Code (IPC), by some male lawyers, posing an indexical relationship between my presence and the topic of my research. Once when I was interviewing a father – whose ten-year-old daughter had been raped – four male lawyers who were passing by, stopped. They pointed to his daughter, "this is the one, look at her, so small and she has been raped." I asked the men to leave and stopped the interview. The fact that I was seen in their presence directed a gendered gaze on the child – I struggled with this attention for the court corridors afforded no privacy to the survivors and their family.

Interviews with witnesses, or the families of survivors happened in the court lobby. I remember being scolded by a lawyer for squatting on the floor outside the courtroom next to a *panch* witness: the independent lay witnesses in trials who certify rather mechanically that the police had seized evidence as per procedure. Sitting on the floor with a working-class witness was seen below my status; and as someone who worked in a prosecutor's office, blurring class and gender boundaries. It was out of place in court hierarchy for me to squat on the floor. However, it was not out of place to make a witness, or a victim sit on a dirty floor while waiting for her turn to testify.

I interviewed five sitting judges of the Gujarat High Court, either in their office or at home. The experience of interviewing a judge was unique. While the interviews were not hostile, it seemed to me that they were not used to being asked many questions by a non-expert, and the slight annoyance that crept into their responses was despite the tone of curiosity rather than interrogation. I had many curiosities and less time. I realized that judges have a monopoly over the judicial habit of asking questions rather than being questioned. I learnt how to interview judges differently from lawyers as the protocol of how one speaks to a judge even in an academic setting is seeped with the extension of judicial aura and sacrality. It was better to ask fewer questions slowly while communicating exaggerated deference and respect.

BEING SCHOOLED TO "FIT INTO" THE SCENE OF THE LAW

Researching rape itself was unsafe, attracting the charge of indecency, sexist comments, and even sexual harassment. Conversations about sexual affairs between lawyers marked every other lunch in chambers, while rumors about sexual harassment abounded. I recorded several stories of women lawyers resisting sexist comments, even in open court – in one instance, a woman lawyer slapped a male lawyer during court proceedings. In this predominantly male space, lawyers often swapped stories about rape cases in other courts in Gujarat. One such conversation took place in Mr. Rajput's chamber when his colleague, a defense lawyer, joined our conversation. He had just won an acquittal in a rape case by citing case law on how women with bad character lie about rape. And in another case, he was kicked that the victim was so scared of his cross-examination that she did not return to complete her testimony. Such shared mirth between prosecutors and defense lawyers when humiliating rape victims during a cross-examination was routine and indicative of what some male lawyers in Delhi call a "rape" bar.

Initially no one was willing to speak to me about the ongoing rape trials. I had yet to learn the vocabulary of how to speak about rape in the court. Just as I had begun to despair, Hirabhai introduced me to a young woman, in a statutory rape and kidnapping case that he was to prosecute. He then took me to the courtroom where he made a request to the bench clerk for the case papers. We sat at the lawyer's table, and he turned to the medico–legal aspects of the case. Turning to the accused's medical certificate, in his usual booming voice which echoed in the half empty courtroom, Hirabhai said "you know what a man's primary sexual organs are, do not you?" A little taken aback, I nodded.

Then he turned to the victim's medical certificate. After going over the other details about bodily development and superficial injuries, he asked me, "do you know what a hymen is?" I responded in the affirmative. Rather theatrically, he drew a vagina on small piece of paper to explain the technical terms for injury on the labia minora or labia majora. The discussion carried on in the chamber where he instructed Beenaben to explain "it" to me. After he had left, she said, "Pratiksha, do you know that a man cannot rape a woman by simply touching her, or

131

kissing her." I nodded even more puzzled and curious now. She carried on "well, how do I explain how a man rapes?" I replied, "Beenaben, do you mean partial or complete penetration?" She nodded in relief.

In performing a specific revelation of the public secrets of rape, Hirabhai directed my attention to the vocabulary by which I could research rape. In insisting that medical jurisprudence separates, the social from the clinical, Hirabhai maintained that a "decent" legal practice could coexist with frank discussions on the topic of rape. The route to generating this "frank" space initiating the research, as he put it, was enabled through medico–legal vocabulary. I was taught that I already knew. This pedagogy was out of place.

In so many ways, Hirabhai and his junior Beenaben made it possible for me to undertake this research. Hirabhai, whom I called "Sir," unlike other women juniors who addressed him by fictive kin terms, was like a "teacher" instructing me in the ways of the court. He did not hesitate to reprimand me on many occasions. I was taught what constituted "decent" modes of dress, appearance, gait, posture, and speech. I was instructed who to speak to and told who to avoid. I stopped wearing bright colors to the field, preferring the lawyer's garb of white and black.

More recent ethnographies by women researchers also record how they had to mute the colors they wore, even if the lawyer's gown was worn. Khorakiwala, a lawyer who conducted fieldwork on court archi-tecture and judicial iconography in three High Courts also narrates her experience of feeling out of place in the Calcutta High Court thus:

> On one day I wore a blue and white striped shirt and a black jacket under the gown, and people repeatedly told me that I was incorrectly dressed and must leave the courtroom. A slight change in the white color of my shirt and I was chided by lawyers in court by saying that either I should leave the courtroom or not wear the band and gown. This situation occurred enough times for me to re-check the Bar Council of India Rules, 1975 that prescribe the dresses or robes to be worn by advocates. These rules are written for advocates who intend to appear before the court. As I was not appearing before the judges, the rules being imposed seemed out of place.
>
> (Khorakiwala 2021, 99)

The daily instructions of how to look, walk, and talk, which were linked to access to the court, verged on alterity. The awareness of being on the verge of alterity was acute. As if aware of this, Hirabhai would reassure me without any stated cause for such a reassurance, "Baxi, you are safe here." When I was leaving the field, almost reflexively,

Hirabhai said to me, "I do not know why Baxi, but I never looked at you with that kind of gaze (*nazaar*). I liked you because you work so hard. Do invite me to your wedding." In other words, women were out of place in hyper-masculine and sexualized chambers of prosecutors. This ability to desexualize a woman researcher, who was located outside the framework of kinship, appeared to surprise Hirabhai.

The complicity with adopting medico–legal vocabulary as the modality of talking about rape was deeply problematic. I did not ask sexually explicit questions. For instance, I could not ask direct questions about what lawyers and prosecutors meant when they said that women are habituated to sex. I knew that the determination of whether a woman is a habitué follows a clinical test, which doctors conduct routinely. This test, popularly known as the two-finger test, is used to determine the absence or presence of the hymen, and whether it is distensible or not. If the doctor finds that the hymen is broken and there are old hymeneal tears, s/he may write that the rape survivor was habituated or used to sexual intercourse in the medico–legal certificate (MLC). When a prosecutor or defense lawyer reads a medico–legal certificate, which declares a woman to be a habitué, often they conclude she has lied about being raped. Minimally, a defense lawyer uses such a MLC to establish past sexual history. I wanted to know why prosecutors, who purportedly represent the victim, exploit the category of the habitué.

Towards the last phase of the research, I decided to ask direct questions, which may have been thought of as talking about secrets men do not share with women as equals in a professional setting. These secrets "appear in ethnographic texts as signs of alterity" (Jong 2004, 257). I cite here a discussion with Mr. Rajput who argued that women could not be raped unless there is grievous violence; and women who were habituated to sex without marks of injury frequently lied about rape. This was not an uncommon view in the court. He pursued this question in the privacy of his chamber to explain to me why he thought that 'habituated' women were liars. He asked me to sit in a chair besides him and lowered his voice so that his colleagues could not overhear him, through the wooden partitions that separated the chambers of the public prosecutors. And he spoke in English.

R   : That day you were saying about habituated. I did not say anything because other people were around. A woman cannot really be raped.

PB : Why?

R   : It becomes quite large. The opening in a habituated woman therefore becomes quite large therefore habituated.

PB   : You mean the vaginal canal?

R   : Yes, that's why two fingers go in quite easily.

PB   : But that's what I was discussing with Dr. B (a forensic expert) – that is, the finger test is quite unreliable. What about masturbation?

R   : That is there. But see if two fingers go in easily (mimicking such penetration with his fingers) it means that she is habituated, the entire hole, that's why I say a woman cannot really be raped.

PB   : But that was not my point of view. I was trying to say that why must her past sexual history be linked to her credibility?

R   : But it must.

PB   : Why? Why should it be considered against morality?

R   : Because it is. Because with married women rape is not possible, and in our society sex before marriage is not allowed.

PB   : Why do women have to experience rape as worse than death or shameful that they will kill themselves? I am arguing for another point of view.

R   : But a woman cannot be raped ... how do I explain? Do you know what secondary sexual organs are? Do you know why doctors write secondary sex organs are well developed?

PB   : I mean ...?

R   : The organ develops after a woman has an erection, that's why they are well developed, that's how they find out she is habituated. How do I explain this to you?

R   : The woman becomes wet. The penis cannot go in unless the woman is not willing. She cannot be willing unless she is wet – like a machine – a rod cannot go in without lubrication (and then he demonstrated with his hands how a rod penetrates a machine).

PB   : But what about cases in which there is partial penetration?

R   : I have not found such cases, they all claim complete penetration, that is why I am saying that a woman cannot be raped.

Mr.   Rajput stopped when a colleague walked in. He added:

You see, I am MSc in Biochemistry. We were taught all of this. I have worked in a hospital for one year. Come again we will discuss this.

I did not go again to his chambers.

This lesson in "biochemistry" was a lesson in alterity – of how men experience pleasure while talking about rape and women's bodies. Desire is inserted in the very way prosecution is architected – or in the place of law. It is directed at the victim on the stand and at the researcher in talking about how the prosecution is erected, literally. The prosecutorial body itself becomes a desiring body inserting in talk about rape male passions to possess and objectify. During a trial, a survivor knows that her testimony gives men pleasure and experiences the questions put to her as unbearable humiliation, yet since such talk is staged in a court of law, the process is imbued with the values of objectivity and such talk is classified as evidence. The survivor is then made to feel being out of place when male desire inserts itself in the place of law.

Courtroom research demanded a threshold of toleration of sexism and sexual harassment, while having to calculate how to keep oneself safe. I did not share information about where I lived in the city. I told my uncle who lived in the city about my whereabouts if I was anxious about an interview. The lawyers constantly talked about how to regulate danger and safety in the court. Whether or not this was a discursive way of keeping women in their place, it meant using intuition to judge what felt safe or not. The need to keep oneself safe from physical violence became a part of doing the research. And later I was to tell my doctoral students that it was alright to leave if that field encounter felt unsafe.

Inhabiting academia after fieldwork was written up heightened feelings of isolation or being marked. I was perhaps unreasonably hurt when a colleague told me at a seminar at my university that many people did not come to hear my paper because they assumed that the talk was about sexual violence. Being considerate to what people want to hear was a constant thing for many academics simply did not want to talk about sexual violence because "It's depressing." Another time, I was surprised when a senior professor in Germany told me that I read my paper on the medical jurisprudence clinically as a "weatherman" would. Although the comment was meant to communicate admiration, it made me uncomfortable. Not displaying emotions or vulnerability (which is often wrongly equated with weakness) was perhaps seen as out of place. I was speechless when an eminent German professor in Berlin said to me, "it is not important to ask why men rape women, rather the more important question is why I might not rape you" (also see Baxi 2016). Not only was one's work often essentialized as if sexual violence is not a cultural aspect in the West, but this sexualized and racialized 'question' was meant to put a brown woman back in her place.

CONCLUDING REMARKS

The embodiment of fear, disgust, and anger through frequent episodes of illness were part of the field experience and the writing thereof. The experiences of conducting fieldwork seemed relevant to me only to highlight the narratives of survivors in court and describe courtroom culture. Anger and grief experienced in the field was deferred to writing. I could not talk to anyone after I returned from the field, nor leave my home for days. Once I was able to go to my department, I felt I was not in my own skin. I was out of place in the university and home felt unfamiliar. Images of the sexual humiliation witnessed in court were part of daytime afflictions and nightly nightmares. I got used to these, as I wrote. The pace of writing was slow, and its tone strove for a distant intimacy with the emotional and sensory memories of the field. The immediate aftermath of the fieldwork also meant having to over-come a brief period of repulsion for any intimacy. Law had interpolated the intimate in ways that I was unaware of. To cope with the field was to accept periods of anger, silence, lack of articulation, morbidity, and chronic affliction. But it also meant not losing the ability to love.

This invitation to reflect on the question of how to cope with fieldwork is to acknowledge the work of intellectual and political companionship throughout. Profound gifts of solidarity, kindness, and love made fieldwork and its writing possible. I learnt how to live with the field by recognizing how law's attachment to cruelty marked the self. If law's attachment to cruelty marked the self, then the ability to love and be in solidarity is the necessary condition for living with the field.

References

Aretxaga, Begoña. 1997. *Shattering Silence: Women, Nationalism and Political Subjectivity in Northern Ireland.* Princeton, NJ: Princeton University Press.

Basu, Srimati. 2012. "Judges of Normality: Mediating Marriage in the Family Courts of Kolkata, India." *Signs* 37(2): 469–92.

     2015. *The Trouble with Marriage: Feminists Confront Law and Violence in India.* New Delhi: Orient Blackswan.

Baxi, Pratiksha. 2014. *Public Secrets of Law: Rape Trials in India*. Delhi: Oxford University Press.

2016. Impractical Topics, Practical Fields: Notes on Researching Sexual Violence in India. *Economic and Political Weekly* 51(18): 80–8.

Dembowski, Hans, and Rüdiger Korff. 2011. "Stealth Censorship: How the Calcutta High Court is Suppressing a Sociological Book on Public Interest Litigation." *Socio-Legal Review* 7: 71–86.

Feldman, Hannah J. L. 1993. "More than Confessional and the Subject of Rape." In *The Subject of Rape (ISP Papers)*, edited by Monica Chau, Hannah J. L. Feldman, Hannah Kruse, and Jennifer Kabat. Monograph. New York: Whitney Museum of Art.

Ghosh, Shrimoyee Nandini. 2019. "'Not Worth the Paper It's Written on': Stamp Paper Documents and the Life of Law in India." *Contributions to Indian Sociology* 53(1): 19–45.

Goodrich, Peter. 1990. *Languages of Law: From Logics of Memory to Nomadic Masks*. London: Weidenfeld and Nicolson.

Herman, Judith Lewis. 1992. *Trauma and Recovery*. New York: Basic Books.

Holden, Livia. 2008. *Hindu Divorce: A Legal Anthropology*. Aldershot: Ashgate.

Jervis, John. 1999. *Transgressing the Modern: Explorations in the Western Experience of Otherness*. Oxford: Blackwell.

Jong, Ferdinand de. 2004. The Social Life of Secrets. In *Situating Globality: African Agency in the Appropriation of Global Culture*, edited by Wim Van Binsbergen and Rijk Van Dijk, 248–76. Leiden and Boston: Brill.

Khorakiwala, Rahela. 2020. *From the Colonial to the Contemporary: Images, Iconography, Memories, and Performances of Law in India's High Courts*. London: Hart Publishing.

2021. "The Law, the Visual and Access to Justice in the Colonial Courts of India." In *Invisible Institutionalisms: Collective Reflections on the Shadows of Legal Globalisation*, edited by Swethaa S. Ballakrishnen and Sara Dezalay, 91–106, New Delhi: Hart Publishing India.

Latour, Bruno. 2009/2002. *The Making of Law: An Ethnography of the Conseil d'Etat*. Translated by Marina Brilman and Alain Pottage. Cambridge: Polity Press.

Makhija, Sonal. 2019. "Nothing Happens: Everyday an Ethnographic Study of the Everyday in a Lower Court in Mumbai." PhD Diss., Faculty of Law, University of Helsinki.

Marcus, George E. 1997. "The Uses of Complicity in the Changing Mise-En-Scène of Anthropological Fieldwork." *Representations* 59: 85–108.

Riles, Annelise. 2006. *Documents: Artifacts of Modern Knowledge*. Ann Arbor: University of Michigan Press.

Suresh, Mayur. 2016. "The File as Hypertext: Documents, Files and the Many Worlds of the Paper State." In *Law, Memory, Violence: Uncovering the*

Counter-Archive, edited by Stewart Motha and Honni van Rijswijk, 97–115. Abingdon and New York: Routledge.

2019. "The Social Life of Technicalities: 'Terrorist' Lives in Delhi's Courts." *Contributions to Indian Sociology* 53(1): 72–96.

Taneja, Anand Vivek. 2017. *Jinnealogy: Time, Islam, and Ecological Thought in the Medieval Ruins of Delhi.* Stanford, CA: Stanford University Press.

Taussig, Michael. 1999. *Defacement: Public Secrecy and the Labor of the Negative.* Stanford, CA: Stanford University Press.

Vismann, Cornelia. 2008. *Files: Law and Media Technology.* Translated by Geoffrey Winthrop-Young. Stanford, CA: Stanford University Press.

CHAPTER SEVEN

AT ODDS WITH EVERYTHING AROUND ME

Vulnerability Politics and Its (Out of) Place in the
Socio-legal Academy

*Swethaa S. Ballakrishnen**

At an external workshop discussing my first book, *Accidental Feminism: Gender Parity and Selective Mobility among India's Professional Elite*, a participant, an older white male professor, asked me why I felt the need to bring my identity (a strain that grounds the book's premise) into my research. A generous reading of this question is that it was curious about method: Why do I place myself at the center of my research, what does that perspective of reflexivity offer my writing, what could it have been if I had just relied on my "strong" and "convincing" data instead of personal narrative? The answer that I gave him in the moment was that thinking with identity was simultaneously a personal and political act, and one that I did not have the luxury of theorizing without. And, further, that if I did leave it out, someone else was likely to assume incorrect identity priors on my behalf. After all, as a global south interdisciplinary scholar in the American legal academy, I was marginal in ambiguous and inescapable ways.

In the months since, I have been considering the ways in which my self-reflexivity has evolved alongside my coalescing research agenda. Over the last several years, my scholarship has focused on the lived

---

* The title of this chapter references bell hooks' definition of queerness as beyond sexual choice and instead as a version of the self that is "at odds with everything around it and has to invent and create and find a place to speak and to thrive and to live." *Are You Still a Slave? Liberating the Black Female Body*, May 6, 2014, The New School for Liberal Arts. Full video available at www.youtube.com/watch?v=rJkOhNROvzs.

experience of different kinds of diverse actors within legal organizations and institutions. Particularly, I have been – and remain – interested in critically examining law's commitments to inclusion by investigating how minority actors claim agency, navigate, and excel within its structures. Although the methods (such as ethnography, interviews, surveys, content, and network analysis), sites (such as global law firms, law schools, outsourcing units), and identities of interest (such as gender, immigrant, queer, racial, religious) have varied across my projects, three interrelated strains frame their broader focus. The *first* has been to locate the ways in which legal sites create and dismantle new kinds of structural hierarchies by paying attention to who is being excluded with any policy of inclusion and vice versa. The *second* has been to observe the dissonance between intention and action by tracking both the ways in which inequalities persist despite projections of equity, as well as to notice positive outcomes and progress produced without intention. The *third* strain has been an analytical approach rooted in grounded ethnography and critical race theory that is centered around the experience of minority actors within the contexts of inquiry rather than to study them as additional points of analysis. Across these agendas past and current, the navigation of identity has been key to my research – *how do different laws and market structures legitimate the ways in which "good inclusion" and "problematic deviance" is done? In transforming cultures, what categories of analysis remain fixed and what are more flexible? Particularly, how is the researcher's own identity implicated in the production of these narratives and the mutability of legal categories?*

The more elaborate answer to the prompt at the workshop is perhaps that vulnerable positionality was not just a choice or calling, but something I considered to be an important coordinate in research, especially when writing about legal institutions and processes that are considered "neutral." Central to this idea of neutrality is the illusion of fixed categories, and identity subverts these assumptions by being inherently flexible and layered. I certainly identify as a global south queer marginal within the American legal academy (where few professors receive primary legal training outside the United States), but this identity of being on the periphery sits alongside a range of what I theorize as "local north" advantages (Ballakrishnen 2021, 195) of cosmopolitan class, location, and privilege. For instance, I am the first person in my family to travel to the United States, and it is true that I could not have accessed or completed any of my three post-secondary degrees without complete scholarships and financial assistance. Yet, simultaneously, as a child of educated forward-caste parents in India, who grew up speaking English in a postcolonial urban city, I had inherent privilege and access to these mobility trajectories. Writing about and with identity, especially from these complicated positions of marginality and privilege, can be an ethical choice when writing about the law. Although they might not always be directly in question, identities often help expand *and* expressly constrain one's ability to do research. In pointedly writing about myself and outing my priors, I am allowing readers to receive my findings with more clarity. What appears to be non-neutrality is, instead, what I consider to be the most grounded extraction of the phenomena I am trying to explain or theorize about.

Beyond mutable positionality, different modes of belonging within research sites also change across a range of temporal dimensions. Although some core parts of me might have stayed (or appear to have stayed) the same, my identity is also an interactional and living organism that shape-shifts with environment, exchange, and reception. As a researcher, parts of my identity that might be an "advantage" in some spaces might effectively be the very thing that isolates me from the field in others. Furthermore, these dimensions of proximity and distance are not static or mutually exclusive: a researcher might, for example, be excluded *and* privileged in the same instance, or feel included *and* seen as improper or irrelevant. These notions of belonging and propriety become even more relevant when the research interrogates legal structures and institutions which are encased in logics of normativity, especially for actors on the periphery (however structured) interested in understanding mechanisms of alterity within them.

Thinking about positionality within the coordinates of being out of place offers a new way to think about its politics in research and the usefulness of it as method. Drawing from my experience through two book projects and a line of new research about peripheral actors within legal structures, I approach this call to think about sites and our places within them as socio-legal researchers in four main parts. First, situating my own out-of-placeness, I locate the broad hegemonies that create the outsider, as well as the normative considerations that make a range of less "ideal" researchers feel out of place. Next, using comparative experiences across projects where I have studied "up" and "down", I offer that peripheral identities are nonlinear and shift depending on context and temporality. Third, I use lessons from several projects, and especially my last two major empirical projects – my manuscript *Accidental Feminism* on elite Indian lawyers and a collaborative project *Invisible Institutionalisms* on the constructions of global conversations around law and society – to locate the ways in which methodology and theory are interdependent and recursive praxis that reinforce each other. Finally, I offer ways to think about vulnerability as method in conducting socio-legal research and its possible praxis limitations. I hope that, together, these examples illustrate the ways in which being out of place at different stages (both of the research process and my own trajectory as a scholar), and in these different ways (across projects, sites, and moments in time) has informed my socio-legal research. Altogether, I hope to argue that law, like identity, is predicated on trust, exchange, and power, and each, when moderated with self-reflexive vulnerability, hold within them the capacity to belong, break-open, and build anew.

LOCATING THE HEGEMONIES THAT CREATE THE OUTSIDER

In my first book, *Accidental Feminism: Gender Parity and Selective Mobility among India's Professional Elite*, I studied elite professionals across different kinds of organizations to understand the possibilities and limitations of parity and performance across settings. My findings – which revealed that women in new kinds of domestic law firms had better prospects at parity in their work environments than their colleagues in other sites – are not as relevant for the purposes of this chapter as the actual variation and similarities between these sites from my perspective as a researcher. The organizations which were the main sites of my study were similarly elite to keep the comparisons about their structure theoretically useful, and, across these contexts, their shared hegemonies also had similarities.

Given my central focus on identity, perhaps a note on my own is overdue, at least as relevant for the context of this project: I am an Indian-born dual-trained lawyer with experience in international transactional law. These data – 139 semi-structured interviews conducted between 2011 and 2015 – were collected when I was affiliated with prestigious Western schools in different capacities as scholar, fellow, and graduate student. As other critical scholars have noted (e.g., Gustafson 2011, 189), all of these interactions and capacity for access were symbolically influenced by my own identity and engagement. Although my

social networks were crucial in granting me access to these busy professionals, it is possible that their representations to me were in response to
my then-current professional and academic affiliations.

But these interactions were also simultaneously modified by the ways
in which I was in and out of place within them. For instance, during the
entirety of data collection, I was a doctoral student in Stanford
University's Department of Sociology, a position that made it seem to
my respondents that their time was being lent for a class project. Still,
at different times, I would also prime them that I was a research fellow
at Harvard Law School's Center on the Legal Profession, a title that
allowed me more legitimacy as a scholar even if I continued to be a
student researcher. In other words, I was out of place in these identities
depending on the site, but the nature of this othering was different.
Similarly, being a lawyer meant I knew many of my legal respondents
by professional association – an interdependency that made me less of
an outsider in some sites (but not others). But it also possibly made me
more cautious as an ethnographic witness because what I wrote might
be read by connected networks. In contrast, my training in sociology,
despite being less directly translatable to these professionals, perhaps
felt less threatening because of the distance it offered.

Other ways in which my socio-legal disciplinary training complicated
my belonging were more structural. I went back to graduate school after
years of legal practice and scholarship, and although I felt supported as
a scholar within interdisciplinary clusters, my research alienated me
from the primary discipline that I was being trained in. I highlight in
my book how my immediate surroundings were central to my writing
choices in both agentic and incidental ways (Ballakrishnen 2021,
180–3), but I offer it here to highlight that the position I inhabited
as a sociology graduate student in a US department studying non-
Western elites from a law and society lens was peripheral to the
academy in several independent and interconnected ways.

Crucially, over the past decade, at different stages, I have had to
defend my research and make it compelling to differently placed actors
that I have wanted to be in conversation with. These audiences, while
invigorating, also introduced new kinds of struggles, and as an interdisciplinary scholar, I found myself constantly trying to engage, usually
from a liminal position, their shape-shifting nature. Similarly,
I remained preoccupied about the usefulness and reach of my work.
At the core, what did it mean to be a global south scholar writing about
"one's own" (Altorki and El-Solh 1998) and who would it serve?

Over the course of becoming the scholar who could produce research that I felt intellectually aligned with, I have had to contend with the difficult and frustrating contradictions of relevance dictated by this positionality. I have had to accept that being visible to a global audience, and being able to make interventions in global scholarly debates and questions, necessarily makes a contribution less useful for those on the backs of whom it is written. These complicated relationships about method, usefulness, and service are not much different from the other frustrations about voice and narrative that I anguish over in the preface of my book, but I mention it because this out-of-placeness was experienced as having the real and recurring fear of being a "bleached out" (Wilkins 1998) academic. And for this reason, this disorientation and the "disciplinary agoraphobia"[1] it produced, continue to plague my outsider status, even though in the years since I have been better received within disciplinary communities.

Finally, the heteronormative institutions which situated all my interventions felt persistent in their capacity to the other me. I present as female but have been increasingly identifying with a more gender-fluid identity (and use they/them pronouns when I write now, which I did not when I was in the field). As I explain in *Accidental Feminism*, this located identity as a global south queer was a key reminder of the ways in which I was an outsider, even as I might have passed as an insider. The interiority of this dissonance is crucial – I use the term "queer" here as hooks (2014) does: as a self-identifying category beyond rigid categories of sexuality and within praxes of oddness, alterity, marginality, nonconformity, and deviance. This located me centrally within academic conversations about queer methods in research, but as a researcher not studying queerness per se, and as a person experiencing these connections to queerness differently across communities, I was constantly unsure about how much of it to "bring" to the research site. Or, indeed, whether such bringing was relevant to the subjects I was interested in. Was my personal politics about heteropatriarchy relevant

---

[1] In addition to design determinations, I argue in *Accidental Feminism* (2021, 181) that I was struck by various kinds of what I call the *disciplinary agoraphobia* at different stages of the project. I note that being socialized in a specific kind of department, at a specific moment in time, was central to the research design. But at different stages, exposure to new kinds of thinking and framing offered a way to return to the work and its implications differently, often with feelings of anxiety and a feeling of being overwhelmed.

to my subjects' experiences as professionals? Was I doing the inter-action an injustice by not bringing my "whole self" to the field (and if so, where does one stop when defining this "whole self")? This feeling of out-of-placeness in method – that is, not knowing when one's identity and its alterity is relevant to the most ethical methods of inquiry – adds yet another layer of agoraphobia in research.

Further still, as I suggest in the next section, this complicated connection to identity was simultaneously also juxtaposed with a lot of what I call "local north" advantages. My queerness has both evolved and become more central to my contexts over the years. At the same time, it has also interacted with its surroundings with increasingly less reactionary hostility as I have become more comfortable with the fungibility of my identities.[2] These complex categories of belonging and distancing have, beyond othering, produced a feeling of distance from the field that recursively moderate the import of my research.

Despite the interpretive implications and limitations of these sub-jectivities, I hope these narratives also offers perspective on how pre-sentation of self is moderated when engaged with external expectations and standards. Still, as hegemonies shift, so do identities of the outsider; and it is to this shifting location that I turn to next.

SHIFTING IDENTITIES AND FLEXIBLE OUTS OF PLACES

As I have begun to suggest, despite any personal narrative and identifi-cations I might claim from deviance, my identities have had different interactional privileges depending on their site and possibilities. Being a researcher from Harvard Law School might have been more relevant than my being queer or a sociologist for access to elite law firms in India, but this did not make my interactional vulnerabilities any less important to my experiences within these sites or my perspectives as I wrote from my data. This might be true for different identities, but I highlight some temporal sways of my own here to be able to illumin-ate this shifting positionality as integral to locating an out-of-place researcher.

Key to this is the acknowledgment that alongside my peripheral identities sit several interpersonal and visible advantages.

---

[2] I explore this increasing clarity with identity flexibility in a recent article (Ballakrishnen 2023).

In *Accidental Feminism*, I use the term "local north" to make central these many advantages and "successes," both ascribed and achieved, that have been offered to me. For instance, myriad *Savarna* (forward caste) privileges have culturally and socially lubricated my experiences in the world, even when removed from India. The privileges of caste and class that I enjoy as a cis-presenting Brahmin from an urban Indian city, who was raised by multiple college-educated adults, all of whom communicated in English to them, was central to not only my local socialization and success within private and public educational opportunity, but also to my relatively seamless socialization into American urbanity and academy. These buffers have served me even as they have distanced me from my own vision of presentation.

Still, ideas of privilege shift over time and place. My urban/global/*savarna*/cis positionalities might have lubricated access to elite law firms, but they also meant I was less likely to seamlessly access actors who were on the peripheries of these sites (e.g., attrition actors or those who were actively antagonistic to these firms politically and personally). These positionalities also have had different valences over the course of the research and shifted with time. I embodied advantages but I was also seen, for the most part, as a student completing their research project; a position that made my relative insignificance central to my capacity to collect data.

It is worth reckoning with the difference in this positionality now that I am no longer a student. If I were to collect these same data now, as a published author, perhaps this situation would be felt differently (although given the ways in which academics are perceived across contexts and their relative power within them, perhaps not). But as a student I was seen as both not having enough authority to demand space, and not enough of a threat to restrict access. Some of this counterfactual was revealed as I recently conducted research on law students from my position as a tenured law professor with a distinct difference in the power of that interpersonal exchange.

In her study on elite US law firms, Jennifer Pierce (1995, 97) argues that even though she was seen as having "unacknowledged ethnographic authority" at the start of her research, this very same lack of authority was met with "less angst" over time. Similarly, from a personal perspective, feelings of guilt and anxiety (about, for example, inaccurate or incomplete representation) started to move towards feelings of "frustration, resentment, and anger" in my case as well. As I recollect in

Accidental Feminism, many of my interviews were focused on professionals seeking mobility rather than those with entrenched achievement
(for example, named partners who inherited law firms).[3]

As other qualitative scholars who "study up" (study sites and people
who are structurally more powerful than them) have argued, these
hierarchies are complicated and not always linear (see, e.g., Ortner
2010, studying Hollywood as an anthropologist living in the same city).
The elite professionals I studied were more powerful than me in some
ways, but they were also made vulnerable anew because of how much of
their lives they shared with me during this process and how much more
easily they could be outed in comparison to a more generalizable
population. For many of my respondents the primary model for being
interviewed was the press, and most were pleased (and many required)
that I did not reveal their identities in published research, lest their
clients or peers would recognize them in the data. My interest in culling
representative data from these exchanges had to be balanced against
the recognition that these individuals were harder to anonymize than
other projects I was involved in. Together, these considerations reveal
that the flexibility of identity is not just about site, but can as easily be
also about temporality and interaction within the same site.

Still, variations across sites and the fungibility of identities within
help further refine ideas about out-of-placeness. When I was working
on *Accidental Feminism*, I was also simultaneously engaged with other
projects where I was not "studying up." Being in these spaces helped
recalibrate theories about method beyond an elite site. For example, in
2017, I was conducting ethnographic fieldwork in a remote Kerala
village studying families of migrant laborers and the experience was
instrumental in shaping my understandings of the power inherent in
access and use of data. The very privileges that allowed me access to an
elite site like a large law firm, were what made me decidedly an outsider
that did not fit in in remote Kerala. Although the professionals in my
book were more "elite," access to them was in a sense easier than it was

---

[3] Beyond an interest in mobility, this reluctance to include more set and public actors
was rooted in a worry that it would have been hard to anonymize them within an
already small and high-status population. However, although they were not interviewed, their publicly available ideas and narratives (e.g., content analysis of their
news articles and public interviews before, during, and after these data were collected) were key informant nodes that shaped the main ways in which I analyzed
these findings.

in rural Kerala where people were (legitimately) suspicious of me in their midst. Even though I spoke the language and was, in a sense, "from" there to the outside world (I was born in Kerala, but have not lived there for any length of time), within the village itself, it was evident I was not *from* there.

Further still, these positional coordinates were neither linear nor insular. The fact that I was an outsider made my respondents hesitant to share, but once I established rapport, the fact that I was seen as a foreign professor (I was not, but academic did not really translate in Malayalam to anything else) gave me authority and status. As other critical scholars have argued (Priyadarshini 2003), this crutch of other-ness also shifted to a real sense of power once I *left* the field. Once I started to analyze and write from the data, my respondents' early reluctance was reified. It was clear that fewer people I was writing about were likely to read or rebut my work, making my commitments to their narrative and the protection of their exchanges differently salient than populations that were studied up.

As other scholars who have struggled with "studying their own" have offered, inclusive identity categories can also be the very coordinates that stifle one's capacity to report on the data. It might complicate one's ability to push back against harsh singular narratives while simul-taneously calling upon them to be apologists in ways they do not mean to be.[4] At times, I felt conflicted between wanting to be protective of subjects I had relative power over, and committing to "going where my data was taking me" to be the most reflective scholar I could be about the site. And unlike studying up which might have allowed one the illusion of non-belonging to produce "neutral" knowledge, non-belonging in other sites instead triggered responsibilities in the produc-tion of similar knowledge. Finally, the idea of "studying one's own" also had interactional implications in that "own" was a constantly shifting category depending on the audience. I was certainly not a Malappuram resident to my neighbors in Kerala, but I was attempting to speak on behalf of them with a certain authority and proximity while addressing a reader possibly even further removed from their experience.

None of this is to suggest that the eventual extensions of being "out of place" can modify its very real impact as a lived experience. Identities may shape-shift and have varying interactional power, but

---

[4] See, for example, Altorki and El Solh's (1988) *Arab Women in the Field*, and Abu-Lughod's (2008) *Writing Against Culture*.

they matter, even beyond self, to method and theory. And this is what I turn to next.

USING ODD/IDENTITY TO BUILD LEGAL THEORY: LESSONS ON POWER, VULNERABILITY, AND VISIBILITY

This increasing obsession with methods and positionality across my projects has evolved beyond a way of just data collection, to a more central dynamic of theory building. *Accidental Feminism*, for example, is steeped in this commitment as a way of framing its purpose (see its preface), and, as it expands centrally in its concluding chapters, this non-linear intermingling between method, theory, and possibility runs deep in what I hope becomes its import.

My second book, *Invisible Institutionalisms: Collective Reflections on the Shadows of Legal Globalization* (2021), a long-term collaborative project with Sara Dezalay that brings together scholars and activists from different locations in the Global South, goes even further in cementing this commitment in that it draws from it as the conceptual core. In similar vein, my current projects on legal education and the profession illuminate a range of ways that inform my identity memberships, and these coordinates are central to theory building within these fields. I use these projects across time illustratively to make three extensions – on power, vulnerability, and visibility – to this idea of being *out of place* as well as to further illustrate the argument that identity is temporal and context driven, as is its capacity for building legal theory.

This idea that out-of-placeness is predicated on power has been a central vein of my research orientations. Expressly to deal with this head on, in *Invisible Institutionalisms*, Sara Dezalay and I adapted a version of a communal "long table" format to structure the theoretical and methodological blueprint of our book.[5] In contributing chapters, participants were invited to exchange and share the ways their positionality and method was central to their writing. The hope was to

---

[5] The "long table" was a performance/discussion format stylized and adapted by Lois Weaver first as a performance project (2009–12) and subsequently as a structured stylized open-ended, non-hierarchical format for interactional participation and intellectual political commitment. The idea is to structure conversation as it might be at a long table for a dinner party. There are hosts who invite the community (here, the "editors" of the book), but anyone at the table is a guest and an active performer, with an invitation to stay, share, or leave at will, since conversation is the "only course."

bring to bear the everyday rituals and exchanges that could otherwise be invisible, and to offer them, extending the metaphor even further, a "place at the table."[6] In our view, this place-making for new kinds of knowledge was essential to foster an interactional capacity for reveal, even if at times this process was ambiguous or not "clear" within the definitions of the discourse (Ballakrishnen and Dezalay 2021, 8). In some sense these journeys without agenda were not just an addition to, but, instead, the core of the intervention.

Dezalay and I were interested in the gaps that were produced by the illegible and the deeply personal – trusting the value in the kinds of dissonances that could be produced by these exchanges. We also recognized the cost: that such narratives of the self could make the writing within disciplinary syntax more complex. Each "grouping" brought together two scholars in conversation that might not share disciplinary views or orientations and the book itself was a recording of that recursive exchange alongside personal narrative. We considered that an established TWAIL (Third World Approaches to International Law) theorist might not want to say much about Colombian white-collar crime and regulation. But we hoped that the structure which curated an invested but mutually out-of-place audience could offer "an illustrative exercise in noticing the points of friction and similarity across language."

This idea of speaking across disciplinary and language boundaries with reflexive method but without visible agenda is not unique to our project.[7] Feminist and queer theorists have long approached their communities with this kind of generous and generative curiosity that

---

[6] The long table is a performance structure popularized by New York City's theater company Split Breaches. It borrows from the movie *Antonia's Line*, in which the protagonist continually extends her dinner table to accommodate a growing community of outsiders and eccentrics until, finally, the table must be moved out of doors. The long table brings what might often be seen as "outside" in – to a realm of conviviality – while simultaneously showing how everyday, domestic things which might remain hidden can be brought out, into a realm of public ideas and discourse.

[7] As we suggest in the book (Ballakrishnen and Dezalay 2021, 8–9), it has long been at the core of feminist methodology and praxis. Audre Lorde, for example, uses the logic of feeling and affect as an important method to think about knowledge production, when she talks about the work of poetry as "not being luxury." Feeling, Lorde argues, is not just the other, feeling and affect is a source of knowledge, it is a tool, it is a way of breathing new life into old ideas. What Lorde says about feeling is true about repeated human connection and meaning making that comes from recursive and intentional conversation.

places identity and affect central to the ways in which they theorize. For example, as Sara Ahmed (2014, 218) reminds us, there are cultural politics to emotions, feelings are sticky and attach to objects and theories, not just people. In turn, they can have a stickiness and circulation of their own – accumulating new kinds of affective values. Seen this way, being out of place is not just a thing to "fix" but, rather, a thing to pay attention to as a new way of seeing.

But just as there can be opportunity for renegotiating power with new kinds of sight, there also remains power with/in proximity. Just as being out of place can sometimes offer positions of power in data recollection (as my relationship to the field in rural Kerala did sometimes), recent research on legal education I collected data for as a law professor reminded me how there can also be power in *not* being out of place. For example, after a set of focus groups with Black law students for a project on the precarious performance demanded by "progressive" diversity initiatives in legal spaces, I received an email from one of the respondents thanking me for conducting my study. In relaying its thanks, it read: "*I really feel heard and like I can make a change by sharing my experiences with you. It is nice to be able to identify with you and have similar shared experiences. It made me feel more comfortable to share.*" On the one hand, this capacity to be able to make space with ease and connection is a privilege since rapport is central to "good" data collection, and there is virtue in making research collaborative and identity-forward. Further, because vulnerability is often not expected, especially when interrogating the law, it can create new inroads, especially when engaging with subjects who might need that space of trust to be able to share their own story. Out-of-place subjects within hierarchical legal structures might require – rather than just be advantaged by – such vulnerability.

But on the other hand, upon critical reflection of my own power and place within the field, the rewards to vulnerable and visible identity become a bit more complicated. Normally, this would have been a sweet note to receive – a reminder that I had "made a difference" to a student who felt seen. Instead, in the context of having collected this data as a professor – someone with direct power in relation to my subject – rather than a student researcher, the note of gratitude complicated my sense of commitment to both the data and analysis. As a way of forging connection and making myself more accessible, I had made my identity visible to this group of students and explained my own background as an international student in legal education.

Yet, considering this note, that act of conflating our journeys felt ill-informed in its integrity. If they were sharing because they thought I was "like them" – which I was not, given my current relative position as a professor, but also more generally given our variations in actual life trajectories – how did it change my capacity to elicit this data? If they were sharing because they thought I was going to "make a change," did it actually put pressure on me to read the data in ways that would seem "change making"? Seen another way, would I be tempted to read the data for strains of change and the possibility that I might not have if I was just "following the data" more neutrally? As I mention earlier in this chapter, neutrality has its own complications, but thinking about closeness to subjects as an additional complication allows us to consider the limits to camaraderie, and the relative usefulness to being out of place.

In her book, *Complaint!*, about the harassment claims within the academy and the usefulness of complaints as methods for institutional change and theory, Sara Ahmed (2021) reminds the reader of the limits of asking those in positions of precarity to share for the purposes of our research. Sharing, she reminds us, is not always easy, and it places at stake affective vulnerability politics. In particular, she urges the consideration of the limits in sharing from precarity: "being shattered is not always a place from which we can speak" (14). I highlight this here because it aligns with my own nervousness about the signals I might be offering in being read as proximate to students whose many issues I cannot solve by just offering them another space to file their grievances. I may trust that writing and theorizing will have a life in this world that will benefit the populations I serve, but I also must acknowledge that such an agenda for change is long and fraught with institutional strife, and may not offer the hope one expects.

And then there are the ethics implicated in *forgetting* (or non-remembering) certain kinds or strains of data. Just as what we remember and record impacts theory, what we forget can have specific implications, too, for what we write and what our writing can mean. Something can be familiar but forgotten within a context (e.g., proximity deployed to establish rapport might also have shaped responses), and what this forgetting means can have implications for how it is read and received and replicated in other contexts – especially as one advances in the academy and has power of readership and mentorship.

Proximity, however, is not the only thing that produces this kind of complicated reflexivity between method and theory building. Distance from identities can sometimes produce the same frustration. In setting up the theoretical core of *Accidental Feminism*, I grapple in the preface about the politics of representation and the complexity of claiming categories (Ballakrishnen 2021, 14, fn. 9). For instance, my current self-identification with – and within – queer categories of citizenship could be reflective of a belonging typical of my diasporic identity. But the journey towards this citizenship has made me think more critically about the use and usefulness of claiming identities and the work it can do in different contexts. Words and meaning-making do have power, but non-claiming of positionality could do its own work too. As other queer thinkers have offered (Nelson 2015), perceived choice making and its received visibility among community – or even inter-actional partners – is not always aligned with one's own inherent tendency towards alterity or their urgency in needing to claim it. Specifically, as Gayatri Gopinath (2005) cautions, thinking about categories as direct products of Western (or other hegemonic) move-ments and markers does not do justice to locating people and their praxis and it is particularly unstraightforward for South Asians. Since citizenship itself is fragile, claims to queerness have to be "constructed at the interstices of various strategic negotiations of the state regulatory practices and multiple national spaces" (Fortier 2002, 194, citing Gopinath 1996, 121). Seen this way, it could be that I was no more or less queer twenty years ago while living (or seeking) what might have presented as a cis-straight-heteronormative life.

But this urgent claiming of peripheral citizenship is only one sliver of a much more multifaceted identity matrix. Significantly, as I mention earlier, I also inhabit the caste-determined advantages of someone writing on behalf of women and bodies that do not share in this power. In *Accidental Feminism* (Ballakrishnen 2021, 195–6), I attempt to think through the idea of a "brahmin or *savarna* fragility" – which makes speaking on behalf of caste hard, both when it is done and not done. There is a certain inadequacy and guilt entrenched in the narrative – a summon to use privilege to call the self out on one's own positional advantage *and* a chide to be sure not to let it reek into a counter narrative that has more agency. If *savarna* feminists like me with an access to so much global space and network and resources do not use those spaces to talk about intra-group solitary beyond our own, that feels like one kind of violence. And to find – using those very same privileges – spaces that will take our narratives more seriously or as more "nuanced," "accessible," or "meritorious" because of a set of cultural factors that we have inherited feels just as violent too. Yet, the luxury to debate which is more violent, to ponder and agonize about which is doing more damage and for whom, and to feel entitled to an audience that will empathize or sympathize with what feels like such legitimate – if dramatic – indecision, feels most violent of all. Alongside this hesitation to speak on behalf of another, is the fear of being wrong and of speaking on behalf of spaces one has no business speaking about. These *ethics of fear* also ask how the work of solidarity can be done more quietly (even if that quiet can sometimes be read as a way of *not* doing the work) when one is out of place. In these ways, among others, deliberation across identity categories produce nonlinear and atemporal possibilities for research.

Finally, it requires acknowledging that the task of being vulnerable with one's temporal and interactional deviance, that is, being "odd" with everything around oneself, especially while studying the law, is hardly a straightforward or simple task. Still, there are tools to be unearthed with the *lack* of ease that vulnerability demands. In *Accidental Feminism* (180–2), I make the case that anxiety over how one's research "fits" within a larger system of inquiry (i.e., being "out of place" or odd within the academy) can have important long-term implications and benefits for the writing process. In particular, I argue that even if projects can feel "elliptical" (an early reviewer's honest feedback about the narrative of one submission, which I initially received with horror, but now look back on with gratitude) or under-resourced[8] at different stages, they can offer, especially to scholars who are (or identify as) out of place, important tools to work with.

Early career researchers, for example, may have pressures to conform within known scripts of the academy: but paying attention to affect and anxiety in their journeys could help reveal new kinds of conduits from which to connect to existing literatures. Similarly, the "disciplinary

---

[8] For example, Ahmed reminds us that sometimes decisions made for pragmatic reasons (e.g., space, funds, resources) are often the right reasons from research and ethical points of view as well (2021, 11–12). "I did not experience this situation as a lack, or only as a lack, but as an opportunity to conduct a project on my own terms and in my own way" she argues: the slower self-transcription, for example, meant that she had more time to "consume each work" to take in all that was there to be taken in, to be "immersed in the material." I imagine the many ways in which my research was circumscribed by timing, with logic and pragmatic eventuality shaping my points of view as well (although I cannot admit to feeling that way about it when it was the case).

agoraphobia" that plagues interdisciplinary scholars might eventually make new spaces for research, even if the process to reach there feels disorienting. In short, not knowing where one is going with writing, especially at the start of the project when one is an "outsider," and the horror of feeling unsure and stuck at different stages, can produce more nuanced portrayals of the experiences one is trying to write about. Seen this way, the complicated juxtaposition of discomfort and power inherent in being *out of place* or odd can, like the anxiety in research I mention above, be productive even when (especially if) exhausting.

CONCLUSION

Over the course of this chapter, I have tried to unpack how the lived experiences of oddity, trust, and power in research can frame our understandings of law and its study. To conclude, I go back to where I started: to a deliberation about data and its valorized neutrality in research about the law. It stands that the even longer response to the charge about the usefulness of identity in socio-legal research goes beyond the defensive deflection that I offered at my book workshop.

Identity centrality might still be a protective method to make sure one is understood better, but it also is an inherent theoretical necessity to *understanding* our sites and narratives more clearly. In fact, one could argue, *how* can data be convincing if it does not consider the reflexive limits and attributes of positionality? If anything, what makes findings strong and convincing (rather than biased and lacking in veracity because of its personal construction) *are* their grounding in their circumscriptions. This is especially true when introspecting institutions that have historically been seen as neutral or normative, such as the law. In these sites, questioning neutrality is not just useful, but imperative to unveiling seemingly uncompromised priors that make up our power structures. It also makes space for peripheral actors to take more central narratives in the discussion and description of these normativities, thereby queering their possibilities and reach.

Beyond making the subjects comfortable, positionality might matter for other audiences too. Distinctively, the researchers' place and personal politics as they approach the questions before them offers a way of unpacking that brings the reader into the research with more clarity and care. A related extension lies in questioning the inherent suggestion that anything actually *can* be neutral. It can almost as easily be argued that not being self-reflexive, not putting oneself in the middle of a project, to have identity *not* matter is, in a sense, privilege. A privilege, more specifically, of neutrality, of not needing to locate a sense of place within what is assumed to be normative.

Still, the converse – that is, to do the work of introducing and navigating identity in research – is hardly an easy instruction to follow. The examples in this chapter only start to reveal the ways in which vulnerability is not a static method, just as identity is not an invariable characteristic. Part of the difficulty in executing this vulnerability as socio-legal method is to pay attention to how it shape-shifts depending on power hierarchies in interactional relationships and contexts. In turn, this malleability can impact how we think about the structures we study, and demand our self-reflexivity about their trajectories.

This matters particularly when one identifies within categories that are seen as peripheral. Distance from normativity – however constructed – can have important implications for perspective and writing, especially about structures with institutional sanction that are usually taken for granted as "good" or "humane" or "right." Making space for this deviance also matters because it allows for the structures in question – the normative assumptions about law – to expand in possibility, and for new meaning to be made within it, focusing on actors that might have otherwise been rendered invisible.

Although the work of vulnerability has implications for all research, affective method has an especial role to play in socio-legal inquiry. Given the ways in which research on law and its structures implicates power, there are constant background questions of power that need attention. How subjects trust you and how much power they have in moderating and mitigating that trust, are all imperative to the construction of positionality, and they have important implications for expanding on the ideas of legal power in itself. Acknowledging that identity is inimitably flexible also allows one to approach the rigidity of law and legal structure with less conviction. Once we start with the premise that legal normativity *can* be different, that law would look different if it had different preconceived frameworks, the method allows for a way in which law and legal theory can offer new prospects.

Vulnerable positionality also allows us to operationalize broad categories of identity with more nuance. Law cannot, for example, always deal with the expansive possibilities of identity, but legal research, in paying attention to coordinates of relationships and the power between them, can afford more fleshed-out opportunities for us to make sense of law's opaque structures. Seen this way, the experience of positionality – of paying attention to whether one is out of or *in* place, is crucial through the research process since it can impact the creation and recording of the things we take for granted. It offers a chance to queer subjects that the law deems linear, rigid, white, cis, straight, etc., while terming itself neutral.

Simultaneously, being self-reflexive with our capacities for such deviance (and acknowledging our limits for its resultant vulnerability) can allow researchers to do the important work of self-care while locating themselves in the field. It is here that flexibility becomes a crucial attribute for understanding vulnerability as method: on the one hand, being vulnerable and making connections that do better justice to less observed constituents in our sites is important, but if that focus comes at the cost of depleting the researcher's own capacity to be in the field, the method fails on its own terms. Similarly, if focusing on oddness or homogeneity comes without the capacity to gauge when the interactional power in these relationships has shifted, they do not do the work of inclusion and representation that vulnerability could otherwise offer. Positionality in research, then, is not a state, but a process.

In responding to this call, the kinds of knowledge production that I am committed to flows from – and flourishes within – an alterity that defines my socio-legal scholarship and community. Building alongside other kinds of peripheral actors – as this book project attempts to do – who are willing to traverse spaces beyond disciplinary silos allows us to infuse our conceptual spaces with "everyday utopias" (Cooper 2014). It also offers a chance to immerse ourselves in what Richa Nagar calls "messy terrains" or "radical vulnerability,"[9] or a hope that these spaces we inhabit might probe comrades to be open to non-linear possibilities of knowledge productions. The attraction this could have for other out-of-place actors is, hopefully, obvious.

Yet, even as I make this proposition, its caveat feels even more obvious. Although there certainly might be attraction to build with others in alterity, logics of sanction and visibility never really go away in academia. In turn, even as we look away and try to queer our

---

[9] As Nagar (2014) offers, feminist friendships afford spaces for "radical vulnerability" but they also allow us to create "messy terrains" where meanings might get lost or misunderstood, but where conversations can – and do – produce important kinds of dialog that can trigger different points of continuity and contrast to actors who are implicated in the exchange.

interventions, our spaces might continue to demand a sort of normative performance. This *queer failure* can demand that we be "in place" even as we try and make sense of the rich and ambiguous utopias that vulnerable oddity may offer. For instance, in choosing sites and projects that are attuned to the intricacies of identity, I am necessarily reinforcing these very identities and their positionalities.

But there is also hope in the idea that when paid attention to, the periphery can become a place where, over time, new structures and communities can be built and nourished. In committing to oddity both as a person who inhabits it and as a person who seeks to engage with it, I also have had to redefine its coordinates as one where new ways of seeing are not just accommodated but expected. Altogether, these lines of research and writing have helped me unravel the ways in which identity builds theory – but also how simultaneously theory can recursively build and cement identity too. Still, even as identity shape-shifts, it matters: Like agoraphobia, it can exhaust, but it also is crucial to fueling our creative capacities as critical socio-legal scholars.

References
Abu-Lughod, Lila. 2008. *Writing Against Culture*. London: Routledge.
Ahmed, Sara. 2014. *Cultural Politics of Emotion*. Edinburgh: Edinburgh University Press.
　2021. *Complaint!* Durham, NC: Duke University Press.
Altorki, Soraya, and Camilla Fawzi El-Solh. 1998. *Arab Women in the Field: Studying Your Own Society*. Syracuse: Syracuse University Press.
Ballakrishnen, Swethaa S. 2023. "Aunty/Anti as Critical Method: From Gendered Resistance to Soft Grace." *Journal of South Asian Studies*, DOI: 10.1080/00856401.2023.2141449.
　2021. *Accidental Feminism: Gender Parity and Selective Mobility among India's Professional Elite*. Princeton, NJ: Princeton University Press.
Ballakrishnen, Swethaa, and Sara Dezalay. 2021. *Invisible Institutionalisms: Collective Reflections from the Shadows of Legal Globalization*. London: Hart.
Cooper, Davina. 2014. *Everyday Utopias: The Conceptual Life of Promising Spaces*. Durham, NC: Duke University Press.
Fortier, Anne-Marie. 2002. "Queer Diaspora." In *Handbook of Lesbian and Gay Studies*, edited by Diane Richardson and Steven Seidman, 183–97. London: Sage.
Gopinath, Gayatri. 1996. "Funny Boys and Girls: Notes on a Queer South Asian Planet." In *Asian American Sexualities: Dimensions of the Gay and*

Lesbian Experience, edited by R. Leong, 119–27. New York and London: Routledge.

2005. *Impossible Desires: Queer Diasporas and South Asian Public Cultures*. Durham, NC: Duke University Press.

Gustafson, Kaaryn S. 2011. *Cheating Welfare*. New York: New York University Press.

hooks, bell. 2014. Are You Still a Slave? Liberating the Black Female Body, May 6, The New School for Liberal Arts. Available at: www.youtube .com/watch?v=rJk0hNROvzs.

Nagar, Richa. 2014. *Muddying the Waters: Coauthoring Feminisms across Scholarship and Activism*. Champaign: University of Illinois Press.

Nelson, Maggie. 2015. *Argonauts*. Minneapolis, MN: Greywolf Press.

Ortner, Sherry B. 2010. "Access: Reflections on Studying Up in Hollywood." *Ethnography* 11(2): 211–33.

Pierce, J. 1995. *Gender Trials: Emotional Lives in Contemporary Law Firms*. Berkeley: University of California Press.

Priyadharshini, Esther. 2003. "Coming Unstuck: Thinking Otherwise about 'Studying Up.'" *Anthropology & Education Quarterly* 34(4): 420–37.

Wilkins, David B. 1998. "Fragmenting Professionalism: Racial Identity and the Ideology of Bleached Out Lawyering." *International Journal of the Legal Profession* 5(2/3): 141–73.

CHAPTER EIGHT

TRIGUEÑO INTERNATIONAL LAW

On (Most of) the World Being (Always, Somehow) Out of Place

*Luis Eslava**

> Trigueña *or* trigueño, *depending on whether the person is female or male, is someone identified with three (tri)cultures. Namely, someone of Indigenous, African and Spanish heritage. It has been used in the Latino/Caribbean culture as a term of endearment, a compliment but also as a descriptive word when neither* morena *or* blanca *seem to completely describe the subject.*
>
> Urban Dictionary

Putting oneself "out of place" or "in place" are common methodological strategies in socio-legal research, as in the social sciences more generally. As a socio-legal researcher, you are invited, early on, to leave the library and go to unfamiliar places in order to see the world from new vantage points – with fresh eyes. Having performed this act of displacement – having become "out of place" – you are then asked to "emplace" yourself; to ground yourself in the norms and routines of your new place in order, for example, to find out how the law operates on "the streets" compared to in "the books." These acts of transmutation and reembodiment have characterized socio-legal writing and thinking for a long time. And regardless of how the assumption that "fieldwork" requires you to go to "exotic" places has been dismantled, such

* I must thank Paulo Bacca, Carolina Bejarano, Lina Buchely, Rose Parfitt, and Silvana Tapia for their valuable comments on earlier versions of this text; Jenifer Evans for her editorial support; and Lynette J. Chua and Mark Fathi Massoud for inviting me to reflect on my sense of being out of place. All opinions and shortcomings are entirely mine.

strategies continue to be used to make the familiar, including the familiar law, strange (Shklovsky 2016).

Many charges can be advanced against this dichotomic and static way of approaching the relationship between oneself and the place in which one exists and studies. "In," then "out," then "in" again – it's just too simple! As Queer, Chicana, Mestiza social theorist, Gloria Anzaldúa (2009) would say, it is (destructively) too clean! Our gender identities, racial and ethnic backgrounds, and class positionalities mean we are always, and have always been, out of place somehow.

And if this were not enough, good-old globalization has further complicated things. The fact that multiple global realities cohabit and traverse every place today has also shattered, into a thousand pieces, the claim that we need to "go somewhere (else)" in order to find out something interesting about law or the world. Rosemary Coombe (1995) made this point powerfully back in the mid-1990s. Even if we are not studying explicitly global phenomena like migration or international trade, "the mobility of capital, investments, goods, imagery, and ideas" should compel us "to reconsider the 'sites' of our research" (791). "[E]ven if we remain in one 'place,' it is no longer possible to understand 'place' in static terms or from any singular vantage point" (828). As Eve Darian-Smith (2013) has put it, better than anyone else, today is a moment of "laws and societies in global contexts."

In this text I want to push these reflections on the relationship between being "out of place" and "in place" a bit further. My primary preoccupation is with the disciplining function of such categories, and in particular with the implications of assuming that one can ever be "in place" – a stable "in-placeness" from which an "out-of-placeness" can be then judged. I am particularly concerned with this configuration because of its relation to my field of study, international law, and to my own experience of being always, somehow out of place.

As many international law scholars have pointed out in recent decades, one of the discipline's main tasks, since its inception in the colonial period, has been to organize the world based on a sense of what is, and what should be, the correct place for humans and things. Eurocentric in its orientation and universal in its ambitions, when people or things are considered "out of place," according to international law, it tries to bring them "into place," whatever that place might be according to the cannon at the time: Christendom, civilization, modernity, the state, the international market, and so on. The premise underpinning this exercise of what Anne Orford (2012) calls "constituting order" is that once people and their surroundings have been secured into their proper places, orderly transitions, development, sustainability, virtuous economic exchanges, and justice can be achieved.[1] This commitment to ordering does not take into account, however, how impossible it is for many communities, nonhuman animals and the natural environment to be "in place" on a planet in which the workings of the international legal order itself have generated, and continue to generate, so much "out-of-placeness." My argument here, then, is that being out of place has become an endemic global condition, one that is *produced by* and *productive to* international law.[2] This condition can be grasped in its fullest in the Global South, a large and diverse geography that has been continually wrecked and disciplined by the international legal order.

My central question, in other words, is how can we start making sense of a world that is founded upon the act of making us out of place? And more to the point here, who can we approach, and how can we even exist when we become aware of this ubiquitous out-of-placeness?

Using a combination of auto-ethnographical reflections and historical analysis, in both cases centered on the constitutive role played by international law in the Global South – as well as in assumedly more Global North locales – I tackle these questions in three moments below.[3]

In the first of these moments, I explain my own sense of being always somehow out of place – not because of any realization about some innate element of my identity but because I was born in that complex geo-historical formation called the Global South.[4] In this first part, I bring up the idea of what it means to be *trigueño* – the idea that people like me are part-Indigenous, part-African and part-Spanish – in order to convey some of the heterogeneous and unstable entanglements that define this part of the world. *Trigueñidad* is a component of many Latin

---

[1] For a general account of this constitutive approach to law, see especially, Brigham (2009) and Eslava (2017).

[2] On international law and the productive function of difference, see also, Knox (2016).

[3] On autoethnography, as a practice of exploring the interconnections between the personal and broader historical and social forces, see for example, Ellis and Bochner (2000).

[4] For an outline of this historical approach to questions of "identity," see, Hobsbawm (1996).

Americans' popular imagery about themselves. It has also been endorsed as an official identity at certain points by many states – including Colombia, where I was born – to refer to the bulk of their citizens.[5] The idea of being *trigueño* functions in my analysis, as a result, as a sort of "thinking portal." It helps us to grasp the out-of-placeness underpinning life in the South and other locations. It speaks, at the same time, of attempts at generating cohesion in a world in which privileges continue to be maldistributed along the "color line" (with whiteness as its horizon).[6] In the second moment, I engage more explicitly with international law and its constitutive role in making *and* managing out-of-placeness in the world. In the third, concluding moment, I suggest a type of global socio-legal approach more attuned to a time when the disorder of the South has – defying 500 years of assumptions – come to be the defining feature of "most of the world."[7] For this final task I borrow from a tradition of ethnographic thinking that is as ambitious as it is agonic. Reflecting from and with the South, it invites us to broaden our epistemological registers when being out of place has become both a global reality and the only ethical position left in a world in permanent convulsion. My effort to describe a *trigueño* international law is, in this context, a call for a different approach to the global order – one attentive to those interconnections, dislocations, and processes of disciplining and resistance that constantly cut-across our landscapes and bodies.[8] But before we get there, let me begin from where I began . . . .

FROM THE SOUTH

I was born in the northeast of Colombia, right on the border with Venezuela. Humid and hot all year around, violent and economically

---

[5] The category of "mestizo" plays a similar function in other parts of Latin America. See, for example, Eduardo Kingman (2002).

[6] I have in mind here W. E. B. Du Bois's (1982) expansive understanding of "the color line."

[7] On the category of "most of the world," see, Chatterjee (2004). On the South and its (dis)order as a global point of reference, see especially, Comaroff and Comaroff (2006, 2012).

[8] As I describe below, my attention to the category of *trigueño* here aims to contribute to a line of analysis that has highlighted the unique and never passive position of (post)colonial/subaltern/Third World subjects in the functioning and making of international law. See, especially, Obregón (2006); Becker Lorca (2014); Parfitt (2011).

volatile, my hometown is one of those dots on maps that are so close to major points of reference – in this case an international border – that they blend themselves into those contiguous, more relevant phenomena. Depending on the size and quality of the map, my hometown is a defined dot or, more likely, it merges, like ink into water, with *la frontera*. In every sense, I was born in a "border town" – a chaotic money-making hive, a place of transit, a nest for all sorts of seedy activities and, above all, an incredibly exciting site in which to learn from the endless forms of (post)colonial disorder on which it thrives.

My city, home of around one million people today, lies just at the southern end of a massive jungle known, rather wonderfully, as Catatumbo. Technically a basin created by the end of the Andes as they branch out from Colombia into Venezuela and encase Lake Maracaibo, the region of Catatumbo – named after the river that flows into the lake – is both atmospherically unique and rich in natural resources. Because of the way the heat and condensation from the lake get trapped by the mountains, the jungle there is thick, green-as-green, and boggy. But perhaps most famously of all, the constellation of tropical forces in this place generates constant lightning activity; lightning so extreme, and so persistent, that it feels like the sky is trying to take revenge on the naughty, destructive humans below, electrocuting all with a messianic cacophony of thunders. Sadly, though perhaps predictably, global warming and recurrent droughts mean that this sublime choreography of lights and sounds may not be around for much longer.

Embracing the poetics of this unique site, scientists have attributed this eerily persistent lightning activity to Catatumbo's location in what they call the Inter-Tropical Convergence Zone. Once well-known to sailors as "the doldrums" or "the calms" because of its monotonous, windless weather, the Inter-Tropical Convergence Zone encircles the globe where the northeast and southeast trade winds converge; where South and North meet. Running alongside the thermal equator, this is quite literally a highway of planetary renewal and the cradle of monsoons; in other words, it is the very spinal cord that connects us all. And in its bosom nestles that restless place called Catatumbo.

In *Tristes Tropiques* (1955), Claude Levi-Strauss famously described the doldrums as a sort of kabbalistic site, whose "oppressive atmosphere" is "more than just an obvious sign of the nearness of the equator" (74). The young Levi-Strauss had crossed this final leg of the very sea route that led Christopher Columbus to "discover"

Trinidad and the coast of Venezuela on his third trip (1498) many times in the 1930s, as he traveled to and from his post as French academic attaché to the recently inaugurated São Paulo University. The Inter-Tropical Convergence Zone was, for Levi-Strauss, a site in which men, "whose greed could no longer be satisfied by their own continent," found their way to the "New World" (74). And, indeed, they did.

The Prussian naturalist and frenzied cataloguer Alexandre von Humboldt, who traveled as a botanical expeditioner across the Americas between 1799 and 1804, described Catatumbo as a place where lights could be seen from more than forty leagues away, as if explosions were taking place "in a throat of mountains" (von Humboldt and Bonpland 1826, 390). Not much later, Agustín Codazzi, an Italian army man, arrived on the continent in 1817, following the wars of independence led by Simón Bolívar (el libertador!). Responding to anxieties widely felt amongst early postcolonial leaders about the fictitiousness of their young nations, Codazzi was commissioned to map out Venezuela and Colombia from top to bottom (Appelbaum 2016). At the peak of his career, Codazzi also remarked on Catatumbo's apocalyptic beauty. It always presented itself with "continuous lightning" which, "located almost on the meridian of the mouth of [the Lake of Maracaibo], directs the navigators as a lighthouse": a lighthouse now serving as an entry point to that world that von Humboldt and Codazzi had – through their expeditions, and on the backs of unnamed Indigenous and African porters – made commensurable, comprehensible, and consumable (Codazzi 1841) .

A complex archive of (post)colonial forms of plundering have thus followed Catatumbo's mundane riches. First of all, of course, there was gold. Many Europeans from the mid-sixteenth to the mid-eighteenth century believed Catatumbo to be one of the places where El Dorado might be found. This attracted wave after wave of Spanish as well as German conquistadores and missionaries, in particular Capuchin Franciscans. The local Indigenous community, the Motilones Barí, as well as the Chitareros located south of my hometown, famously fought tooth and nail against the invaders. Eventually these communities were decimated by disease and war, and resettled in towns. Their resistance restarted when the Capuchin Franciscans were expelled from Colombia following their alliance with the Spanish Crown during the wars of independence. Yet from 1885, the Barí came to face two new monsters: large landowners or latifundistas, and then a new rush, this time for "black" gold. In 1905 the Colombian government signed the first concession for the exploitation of oil in the region with a local general, Virgilio Barco Martínez. This opened the way for the return of the Capuchin Franciscans in 1910, inaugurating a period of formal resistance by the Barí. But with oil now firmly in the picture, in spectacular quantities around and beneath the Lake of Maracaibo, things changed forever.

During the 1920s, and even more so after 1931 when Barco's concession was ceded to the US company Gulf Oil (today Chevron), the struggle of the Barí people reached new heights. The Chaux-Folson contract, which sealed the relationship between the Colombian Government and Gulf Oil, included a clause obliging the government to protect the company from Indigenous aggressions. Over the next two decades, a combination of official violence and the widespread presence of Catholic and now also Evangelical missionaries brutality crushed Indigenous resistance.

As the world got caught up in the Second World War, and accepted its unquenchable thirst for oil, Colombia and, in particular, Venezuela saw oil exploitation skyrocket, bringing with it unthinkable wealth. Following on the heels of this wealth came new migrants from Italy, Portugal, and Spain. They also came from the Middle East, adding to the already existing population from that part of the world – after all, the Kingdom of Castile had "discovered" the Americas just as it completed the *reconquista* of the peninsula from the Arabs after seven centuries of intermingling.

One drop of this oil bonanza trickled down early on into my hometown at the end of the 1940s – a drop that, in the long run, and against this already complex landscape, turned out to be crucial for my family. In 1949, Gulf Oil, in association with its sister company, Colombian Petroleum, established a new neighborhood in my city. Designed according to US standards, and following the imperial tradition of veranda architecture and residential plantation compounds, the neighborhood first served as a sort of fenceless gated community for company workers. It had a church, a soccer field, a playground, a park dedicated to Simón Bolívar (with a massive statue of *El Libertador* on his beloved white horse, *Palomo*) and a plaza dedicated to the black gold, centered around a defunct pumpjack – one of those old-fashioned above-ground pistons designed to dredge up the bounty of oil wells. In 1970, however, Gulf Oil and Colombian Petroleum were brought under the operation of Ecopetrol, Colombia's state-owned oil company (remember that time of nationalizations in the Third World?). This opened the neighborhood to outsiders, losing with it its allure.

It was to this neighborhood, the result of a whole composite of out-of-place elements, that my mother's family came to live in 1971. My grandmother and grandfather – "*nona*" and "*nono*" I called them, in the Venezuelan–Italian tradition – were in themselves quite a bundle of out-of-placeness. My grandfather, almost two decades older than my grandmother, was from Colombia's coffee region, in the center of the country. A salesman who struggled to make ends meet by traveling across Colombia and Venezuela selling items ranging from keyrings and safe boxes to gravestones, was generous, loved *el Partido Liberal*, and had an amazing sense of humor. His mother was from direct Spanish descent (or at least that is how she is described in the family with a sense of pride), as was suggested by my grandfather's distinctive fair skin and light eyes. My grandmother's father, on the other hand, was from a small Venezuelan town nearby, and her mother was from my hometown. Her father was well known because he sold fabric in a shop owned by one of the *familias turcas* that had set up in town at the turn of the century.

My grandmother, darker in complexion, was a force of nature. *Nona* – a woman who never once went a day without walking; who conceded to and depended on no-one; who was (in her own way) political through and through – was ferociously clever and always ready to disrespect conventions. Both mystical and pragmatic, she navigated with all sorts of tricks the difficulties of bringing up five kids on her own while my grandfather traveled. She was doing this at a time when the longstanding war between Colombia's two traditional parties – *el Partido Conservador* and my grandfather's *Partido Liberal* – had momentarily stopped thanks to a power-sharing arrangement known as *el Frente Nacional* (1958–74); while the country started to implement an import substitution industrialization strategy, framed by the US-led anti-communist regional development program, *la Aliaza para el Progreso*; and when guerrilla groups, in particular the Marxist-Leninist *Ejercito de Liberación Nacional* (ELN) and the Maoist *Ejercito Popular de Liberación* (EPL), were consolidating their presence in Catatumbo.

It was against this setting, that my grandmother won the lottery with a ticket she had obtained on credit. With the number 3336 (a lucky number in my family!) she secured the money to pay the deposit for the house in the former Gulf Oil neighborhood, next to the plaza with *el libertador* and *Palomo*.

I spent much of my childhood in that house. Packed with potted plants, birdcages, and a dog called Laika (in memory of the Soviet space dog), my memories of it include playing barefoot with my cousins and watching Hanna-Barbera cartoons on Venezuelan channels (only Venezuela had the money to pay for such luxuries back then, in the early 1980s). I also remember long conversations with my grandmother about the ability of various saints to appear in broad daylight, the witchcraft power of bird feathers, and the possibility of curing all sorts of ailments with local herbs. During these conversations, and in that house, I started to realize how difficult it was to make any kind of straightforward sense of the world. I experienced an intense confusion – fed each day by new rounds of competing explanations, both official and popular – about the place of Colombia, my hometown, and my own self within the broader schema of things. Here the assumed order fostered through the idea of being *trigueño* was as much part of the problem as a partial relief.

As in other parts of Central America and the Caribbean, one of Colombia's foundational myths is that the blood of almost all Colombians – after centuries of interracial relations – comes from three sources: Indigenous, African, and Spanish. We are, in short, *trigueños*. Deeply rooted in the national historiography and psyche, this apparently harmless, egalitarian idea is, however, ridden with problems. To start with, the *trigueño* idea has always had difficulties making sense of a country – and an entire continent – in which five centuries of colonial history have failed to homogenize racial differences, instead leaving a panoply of skin colors even within families. On a more substantive level, the idea of *trigueñidad* has silenced discussions of the uneven distribution of pain and power on a pigmentocratic basis, in which those on the white side end of the color spectrum continue to be favored (Vásquez-Padilla and Hernández-Reyes 2020). As such, it echoes uncomfortably the Spanish colonial *castas* system in assumingly postcolonial times (Obregón 2006).

The idea of Colombia as a largely *trigueño* country became entrenched through the inclusion of skin color on national identity cards, which were introduced initially for electoral purposes at the end of the 1920s and then as a compulsory document in 1962. *Trigueño* was the default option in many parts of the country that were not predominantly Black or Indigenous (like on the Atlantic or Pacific coasts or the Amazons), or predominantly white (as in the usually richer coffee-producing areas) (Forero et al. 2013). When skin color was removed as a category in 1993, it left a profound mark on how the country understood itself in racial terms – a largely mixed society, with incidental small pockets of other skin colors on the margins, and with whiteness, of course, as a horizon.[9]

In families like mine, being *trigueño* was thus a common trope used to account for the paths taken to produce the family's color notation and to circumvent the impossibility of tracing our history very far back. This was particularly useful given my grandparents' different origins and skin shades. Some members of my family had light skin, clear eyes, and blond hair, while others had darker complexions. My grandmother, who saw herself and me in the middle of this color distribution, used to tell me that we two were the real *trigueños* in the family – *trigueños* in the sense of a traffic light at a busy intersection that connects everyone without knowing anyone's "real" points of origin or destination. An extra layer of enigma formed when my grandmother added that she had known immediately, as soon as I was born, that I would share her hue because newborn baby boys' testicles always reveal their future skin color. I was marked from the beginning (and in what a way!) to be of a color that is paradoxically of everywhere but also of nowhere – a residual index of our convoluted history, of the wiping out of Indigenous peoples, of the slave trade, of the European colonial project.

Many questions used to cross my mind back then: how much was I – or my grandmother – Indigenous, Spanish, or Black? And if we were all *trigueños* (if some more than others), how much Indigenous, Spanish, or Black blood did the other members of my family have? And what about other Colombians who were actually Indigenous or Black – were they also a bit *trigueños* too?

The curiosity bubbling beneath these questions, and the impossibility of finding any stable ground on which answers to them might be constructed, only increased as Catatumbo became an even more entangled mass of global flows and destructive forces. In the late 1980s and early 1990s, structural adjustment reforms kicked in hard across Latin America, and Colombia became embattled once again in civil war, this time fueled by other kinds of gold: marijuana first, and then cocaine and heroin. Guerrilla actions against multinational oil companies intensified too, followed by a brutal response from both official and

---

[9] This idea of Colombia as a mixed society is equally present in other countries in the region and still informs governmental programs. On recent criminal identification techniques used in Mexico, see, for example, Delgado (2020).

paramilitary forces. Catatumbo became during these years a hotbed of drug production for the international market, a source of immense wealth and trouble that came to touch all segments of society and the natural environment. Wave after wave of aerially sprayed glyphosate (Monsanto's deadly pesticide, 'Roundup') was used to thwart the region's narcotization, while palm oil plantations became an accepted developmental counterinsurgency measure. Fighting evil with evil further fed the monster of paramilitarism and accelerated the destruction of peasant communities and Indigenous territories. And as if this were not enough, the Bolivarian Revolution that began in Venezuela in 1992 prompted the militarization of the border, which later intensified with Venezuela's economic collapse. Millions of displaced Venezuelans have left their country through Catatumbo, thousands staying in my hometown to start a new life. Millions of Colombians have themselves been internally displaced in the previous decades as a result of the only recently (and precariously) concluded civil war. Many of them, like Venezuelans, have also settled in *la frontera*.

Catatumbo, with its other-worldly lightning and mind-bending humidity, continues to be a prime theater for these tribulations. With such a place always in the back of one's mind, it is difficult to ignore how, regardless of all stabilizing efforts, being out of place is a perennial condition there as well as in many other similar parts of Colombia and the larger Global South. This out-of-placeness does not generate, however, free-floating cosmopolitan individuals. It is, instead, one that – emerging from haphazardly arranged historical forces – generates putative *trigueño* beings, subjects who spin like a tangled-up maze of infinite threads in a tropical throat of mountains. A few years ago, the Colombian cartoonist Vladdo captured this condition in a drawing about the endless reasons behind Catatumbo's constant state of crisis (see Figure 8.1). Like a frantic ball of wool with a thousand beginnings and uncertain ends, Catatumbo and its people are, like many others in the Global South, instantiations of infinitely convoluted global histories: ciphers of the ongoing genocide of Indigenous peoples, reverberations of the slave trade, uncomfortable reminders of the European colonial project. Late modernity gone wild in the tropics.

WHOLENESS AND INTERNATIONAL LAW

From my description above, I hope it is starting to become clear that being *trigueño* is not a hard fact. We can think about it instead as a

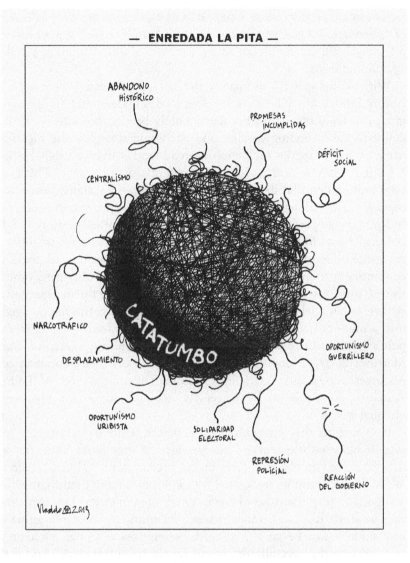

Figure 8.1 Enredada la pita, Vladdo, Revista Semana (2013)

superimposed racial rubric that attends state logics, as well as a short-hand that speaks of the near impossibility of giving an account of many people's rickety histories, of being ever 'in place' in a place like Colombia. In this second sense, it is an ontological condition of coming from everywhere and nowhere, of standing always on a moving ground.

171

But, again, as productive as it may be in its capacity to generate a degree of coherence – a momentary condition of "in-placeness" – the idea of *trigueñidad* still covers up ongoing asymmetrical distributions of privilege and suffering.

With whiteness still ultimately the site of privilege, progress, and history, and with, for example, African-descendent and Indigenous groups in Colombia still disproportionately bearing the effects of the country's never-ending conflict and economic struggles, the *trigueño* category is a capacious middle-of-the-road marker that can signal who is losing, who is winning, and who is potentially in-between. This is a vital point given that in Colombia there has been a sustained effort to officially embrace the nation's plurality via the recognition of Indigenous peoples' and Afro-Colombian communities' territorial and political rights in recent decades. The 1991 Colombian Constitution recognized importantly the ethnic diversity of the country and made a commitment to protecting it: "yes, largely *trigueño*, but also many other things" was the overall message.[10] In the decades since the inauguration of this state model – which in other parts of Latin America has evolved into a more fully fleshed-out call for "pluri-nationalism" – Colombia's political structure has transformed in significant ways (Acosta and Martínez 2009). Notwithstanding these advances, the allocation of resources across ethnicities in Colombia, as in the rest of Latin America, continues to be extremely unequal, in an already very unequal world.[11]

It is due to this pigmentocracy – where whiteness continues to suggest more entitlements – that the idea of *trigueño* denotes, not a specific color but, above all, a nebulous predicament. Whiteness, after all, is also a condition, associated with color but, more than that, with an ability to reap the elusive benefits of the present order. This explains why someone like me – a true *trigueño*, according to my grandmother's inspection – can be very privileged, because many things, including class affiliations, have allowed me to live in a white(r) way. And the same applies for a Black person with close proximity to white entitlements and structures of power. English rapper and political activist, Akala (2018, 306) made this point recently: "while I critique

---

[10] See especially, Colombia Constitution (1991), arts. 1 and 7.

[11] See the cross-regional tracking of this situation by the United Nations Economic Commission of Latin American and the Caribbean (CEPAL/ECLAC): www.cepal.org/es/temas/pueblos-indigenas-afrodescendientes.

imperialism, I also acknowledge the contradiction of my own 'Western' privileges, brought about in part – ironically – by my proximity to whiteness."

Trigueñidad, in Colombia and elsewhere, operates then as a marker that works, sometimes, through soft touches and small gestures. On other occasions, it functions as a hard statement of what someone does not have (Echeverría 2010). Being *trigueño* speaks of a multiplicity of untraceable histories, and on other occasions as a reminder and enforcer of privation, and with this a call to become white(r) each day. It is that mid-road crossing that needs to be crossed if you want to get there (and imagine if your gender or class also works against you!). The further you are from being Indigenous, Black, or *trigueño* (or female, LGTBQ, or lower class), the closer you are to being better off, better able to claim a proper place in history.

Enjoying being "in place," or finding oneself "out of place" are thus not interchangeable states of being, or the result of discovering one's true identity and real place in the world. They are instead specific socio-historical formations with profound disciplinary functions. From an international law point of view this is crucial, given the discipline's traditional role of ensuring a particular kind of order in the world. The reading of global reality and social change that is the foundation of international law departs and ends with an assumption that global history and global life are, by design, organized into neat spaces and along a progressive temporal continuum. If some kind of disruption emerges – in the form of an armed conflict or a humanitarian or economic crisis, for example – it is understood that international legal mechanisms should be deployed in order to bring things back on track. The vagaries of reality, and even mistakes made on behalf of international law, are exceptions, which the international legal order can always readjust into its universal progress narrative. There is always the possibility to "cleanse law," of imperial traces, racism, patriarchy or otherwise (Berman 1999).

A vivid encapsulation of international law's universal progress narrative is contained in the opening lines of Malcom Shaw's (2017, 1) popular textbook *International Law*. Its first chapter, "The Nature and Development of International Law," begins in the following way:

> In the long march of mankind from the cave to the computer a central role has always been played by the idea of law – the idea that order is necessary and chaos inimical to a just and stable existence ... Progress,

with its inexplicable leaps and bounds, has always been based upon the group as men and women combine to pursue commonly accepted goals, whether these be hunting animals, growing food or simply making money... Law consists [in this sense] of a series of rules regulating behavior, and reflecting ... the ideas and preoccupations of the society within which it functions ... And so it is with what is termed international law with the important difference that the principal subjects of international law are nation-states.

For Shaw then at some point we had "the cave," our original place, which as a species we eventually replaced with modern settlements. In this process, law has been diverse at some level, for example in certain aspects of municipal law, but in terms of its aggregated global function, it has put us on the path of civilization. Now, while a Hobbesian chaos has constantly threatened us, the combination of municipal and international law has allowed us to keep on evolving. The cave was replaced by national jurisdictions, which eventually came to be encompassed by the international order. These moves – from the cave to the nation-state to the international – have helped us make the most out of our innate drive to hunt, feed ourselves, or make money. In Shaw's view, this has ensured that today we can collectively claim – across the world, in one go – to be living in the "computer" age. And although environmental degradation, global inequality, and the crystallization of a particular international division of labor that traps "developing" nations in ongoing circles of poverty and violence have also all been the outcomes of this process, these all remain outside the formal purview of law (Linarelli, Salomon, and Sornarajah 2018).

International law's universal, progressive and, in many ways, strikingly optimistic approach to history also jumps out from the United Nations (UN) Charter. According to the Preamble, "we the people," determined "to save succeeding generations from the scourge of war," have left behind the violence that "twice [during the twentieth century] brought untold sorrow to mankind." Reaffirming "faith in fundamental human rights," we have committed ourselves, therefore, "to promote social progress and better standards of life in larger freedom," and "to employ international machinery for the promotion of the economic and social advancement of all peoples." Through the UN "we" have also pledged to endorse "the principle of equal rights and self-determination of peoples," as well as, according to Article 2, to respect the principle of "sovereign equality" and refrain "from the threat or use of force against the territorial integrity or political independence of any state." In the case of a serious threat to these principles, the UN and its members are invested with the right to respond with accepted "enforcement measures."

As we can see, the UN Charter presupposes and strives to realize a global wholeness, one in which each community has its natural place – or, in the language of international law, in which each society has its own state. Through respect for their self-determination – and equality – and via international legal instruments, each of these states safeguards its place in the global order, improving its standards of living through its own laws. The Charter makes no suggestion (any more than does Shaw), however, as to how the international legal order might be involved in undermining the objectives that the Charter tasks itself in upholding. For example, there is no hint of any lack of respect for, or any systematic undermining of the possibility of, some people's self-determination – and thus their ability to be "in place" – as a result of the ongoing effects of the colonial project and its symbiotic relationship with international law (Anghie 2004). There is no trace of the collateral damage resulting, time and again, from international law's explicit or implicit operation (Eslava 2017). There is no mention, as Knox (2016) has put it, of international law's filial relationship to "the expansion of capital *through* racializing certain territories and societies" and "[i]n so doing ... open[ing] them up for ... their control and management" (112 [italics in the original]). The Charter's universalism, chronological historicism, and pragmatic optimism invites us, instead, to see the international legal order as a homeostatic system in which being "in place" is the rule and "out of place" the exception.

In sharp contrast to the conditions of the majority of people in a place like Catatumbo, in particular those *trigueños* and others at the end of the equation, international law sees its subjects as usually living in a grounded and balanced normality. Connected to the global order, these subjects are seen as able to capitalize from their position in this computer age. In case of a crisis, especially one that domestic institutions cannot control, international law can always step forward and use its enforcement measures to ensure peace, progress, and in larger freedom (Charlesworth 2002).

I recently came across an uncanny rendition of this conceptualization of global life in Melbourne, Australia – a city that is in many ways diametrically opposite, geographically and socio-economically speaking, from my hometown, and that has become a global emblem of urban livability and economic prosperity over the last couple of decades. At the entrance to one of the new residential high-rise towers that today dominate the inner city's skyline, a large poster welcomed residents and advertised their serviced apartments to others (see Figure 8.2). Placed within easy view of passing pedestrians, it featured a white couple in formal clothes, softly dancing against an urban landscape at nighttime. Accompanying the scene was a take-away message, "balanced global living," and underneath a further articulation of it: our company provides "a warm and stylish home, with many recreation and lifestyle activities," "because life is about living."

Revealing and to the point, the poster invited viewers to mull over the idea that normal global life is characterized by serenity, beauty, and an effortless ability to do well in today's global order.[12] Like countless similar marketing exercises widespread across the North and South, this poster was designed to interpellate, importantly, not just those who could afford to live in the building – who could find their new "place" in it – but to lay pedestrians who, more likely than not, could not afford such apartments (surprise, in Australia not everyone is rich!). For the few who could purchase these properties, its function was to reiterate their privilege. For those without the means, the message was subtler: in order to be successful in today's world one needs to let oneself be judged and transformed in ways that hardly correspond to who one is and what possibilities one actually has.

Underpinning this worldview of "balanced global living" was again the idea that life is, in its usual state, rounded, stable, prosperous, and harmonic. To ensure this state of affairs there should be a proactive municipal law that facilitates, like in Melbourne, the motions of the market through private and public law provisions for private building initiatives and individual consumption. According to this understanding, international law is seen as being at a distance given that everything is working according to plan: some people can make it; others not; tough luck. Keep dancing or keep dreaming to dance. Your turn will come.

As is the case for Shaw's textbook and the UN Charter, however, the international legal order is tightly enmeshed in this poster's existence and associated tensions. For a start, the apartments it is advertising are built on unceded Aboriginal land – the land of the Wurundjeri people. Legitimating an act of illegal occupation sponsored by the international

[12] I have explored similar marketing exercises in Eslava (2014).

Figure 8.2 Balanced global living
(L. Eslava, Melbourne, 2019)

legal order, then, the poster accelerates this erosion of sovereignty and its ongoing effects on Aboriginal peoples by seeking to multiply the claims over their land through the colonization now of vertical space (Liong et al. 2020). This is facilitated by a global legal order that, through domestic legislation, enables international investment, real-estate speculation, and a particular type of economic growth that has converted Melbourne into a ground zero of the global property bubble that started in the early 2000s and continues today. Meanwhile, this same global legal order takes a lenient approach to the domestic mistreatment of asylum seekers in Australia in order to facilitate a strictly regulated migration system based on economic power. To top all this off, the building, the white dreams this poster embodies, and the consumption signals it sends out bolster a type of "living style" that puts further pressure on the global environment, in particular the fragile Australian ecosystem. The combined background effects of international law silently framing this poster invites us to think about that type of *trigueñidad*, and that type of Southern out-of-placeness, that today runs from Catatumbo to Melbourne's inner city and beyond.

A WORLD IN CONVULSION

The events I have described here in relation to my personal history and to international law's more general role in generating and regulating out-of-placeness are the result of rhizomatic processes. They are multi-tentacular developments that run from the human to the divine, passing through the material to the ontological. They are, Michael Taussig (2001) would put it, instantiations of a "nervous system"; events that can be only understood in relation to the "general economy of the world," using George Bataille's (1991) language. This interconnected nature of global life, and the convulsion that has come to characterize it, is in this sense a widespread phenomenon. However, in some places – like Catatumbo and similar locations – it is so acute as to become an almost palpable experience, and even a lethal affair.

Let me illustrate this point by moving back to Colombia but this time to the Pacific coast. Historically these territories have been home to the highest concentration of Afro-Colombians in the country, and the lowest levels of income, welfare, and security. They first became the refuge of Afro-Colombians during the colonial period, as slaves escaping their masters crossed the dense jungles that separate the central part of the country to the Pacific coast. Victims of some of the same (post-)

colonial forces that shape life in Catatumbo, yet bearing the harshest effects of Colombia's pigmentocratic order, today these communities are still severed from the rest of the country by those jungles that once protected them. Some of these jungles have for centuries received some of the highest rates of rainfall on the globe, although (as in Catatumbo) the rains are becoming more erratic as the global climate crisis escalates. Existing in this unique environment, pressed by poverty and furious weather patterns, many of these communities have seen their young people jumping on the boat of illegal drug production and trafficking in recent years. And with the arrival of drugs since the late 1970s – especially the mighty quantities of *coca* that can be grown and produced in a land that is so environmentally well-endowed and still so remote – things changed forever, just as oil changed things in the throat of mountains where I come from.

Not surprisingly, the dynamics of drug production on the Pacific coast have been driven by global forces, transforming existing constraints into an unfettered calamity. The neoliberal structural adjustments, which started in the late 1980s in Colombia, have evolved in the past decades into a chronic illness, whose pernicious symptoms include high rates of un- and under-employment and the almost total de-industrialization of the economy. In consequence, more and more rural communities have found the production and traffic of cocaine – to the US via Central America or more recently to Europe through Venezuela and then North Africa and Spain – to be the only way they can survive. This situation has only intensified by the ongoing demand for cocaine in the Global North.

The flipside of cocaine's exquisitely "global" form of production and exchange has, of course, been the generation and circulation amongst communities in the Pacific of new global desires attached to the consumption of a very specific, constantly renewed set of "high-end" commodities. Branded sneakers and jeans; iPhones; gold chains; breasts and behinds of a particular size and shape – all absolutely incompatible with the economic possibilities of the average person. Drugs and beauty, and the beastly (symbolic and physical) violence that often result from their interactions, have become a part of the day to day in this part of Colombia, if not of the entire country.[13]

---

[13] On the interaction and beauty and the beastly in Colombia, see especially, Michael Taussig (2012). On the racial dimension of the war on drugs, see especially, Koram (2019).

The result of this explosive cocktail of global forces comes in the form of recurrent waves of violence, each one gorier and more damaging than the last. These cycles of devastation have young people at their core – especially young people belonging to those groups which have always been the victims of historical forms of dispossession and displacement. Young Afro-Colombians and *trigueños* are the ones who have come to be trapped in this deadly economy, in particular young men aged between twelve and twenty-one, whose life expectancy in some areas does not exceed eighteen or nineteen years. These are kids and young adults who, pushed by need and a destructive economy of desires, engaged again and again, with a kamikaze spirit, in the production and transport of drugs in order to buy that crucial pair of sneakers or jeans that would give them a place in this cruel world.[14]

Interviewing some of these young men in the port town of Tumaco, I came to know firsthand about the self-destructive circularity that accompanies their lives.

Located on the southwestern corner of Colombia, near the border with Ecuador, Tumaco – really a very large and complex municipality – has a hot tropical climate that eases at nighttime with the breeze from the Pacific Ocean. Tumaco's extensive territory is inhabited mainly by Afro-Colombians, as well as by Indigenous peoples and by proper *trigueños*, as my grandmother would say. The large part of the municipality is semi-rural, which then merges into the jungles that I described above. In one of my interviews in the actual town, a young rural *Tumaqueño* told me how frustrated he was with the "lack of identity" amongst his friends, and their lack of interest in reconstructing their personal histories, for example, their African roots, through cultural activities. He told me that his friends were obsessed with *tennis de marca* (branded sneakers) and explained to me that this obsession was fed both by social media and by the new fashion stores opening up in Tumaco's town center (see Figure 8.3).

Tumaco's unemployment rate is 70 percent and its per capita income is around 1,000 USD per year. A pair of Adidas or Nike shoes would easily cost a month's salary. As this suggests, very few of its residents other than the *muchachos* who now earn their living through illegal drugs could afford such an item. In order to be part of the illegal drugs trade and with this being able to buy these desired shoes, young males

---

[14] On the "cruel optimism" involved in this economy of desires, see especially, Berlant (2011).

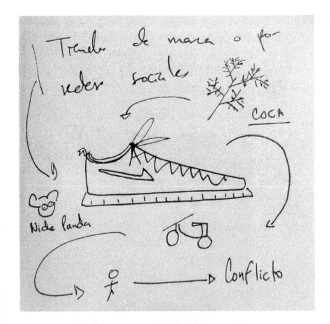

Figure 8.3 *Circuits of devastation*
(L. Eslava, fieldwork drawing, Tumaco, Colombia 2018)

commit themselves initially to perform meager tasks for local gang leaders. Once this first step has been taken, and consumption starts, they quickly tag their desires to bigger items, for example a motorbike, which take them further into the gangs' business and their wars – right into *el conflicto*, as my interviewee told me.

Tellingly, the often self-abrogated nickname given to this type of *muchachos*, now in the thick of these circuits of devastation, is *niche panda* – a label used today across the Caribbean and the Latino community in the US and beyond to refer to dark-skinned young males (*niches*) obsessed with Global North luxury items, for example, four-wheel drive BMWs, which, according to common belief, look like panda bears. Desiring the unaffordable, but committed to getting it nonetheless, *niche pandas* get down and dirty in the business of the cocaine trade, covering themselves and their dark bodies with the illegal white powder – a color combination that reinforces again the *niche panda* image. Dark, racially speaking, but trapped in a world of desires only available through white levels of wealth, my interviewee and his friends are similar to the *trigueños* in Catatumbo: subjects whose lives resemble frantic balls of wool, spinning like a tangled-up maze of infinite threads in the tropical South.

The lyrics of a song that serves as a sort of anthem for *niche pandas*, and that has several versions produced across Latin America, erringly conveys the volatile tumultuousness, and the patterns of destructive consumption, that profoundly mark the existence of these young *Tumaqueños* and many others in their same situation.[15]

> *We send fast boats full of coke and marihuana*
> *Gringos consume like pandas*
> *Niches are packed now with money*
> *The son of El Chapo people call me*
> *I am asked for one thousand kilos of panda*
> *I smuggle coca, ready, watish*
> *I put it in Guadalajara*
> *We have made the trip, and I get paid*
> *In containers, it is taken down*
> *Fast boat drivers wait for their money and chicks*
> *They take them a wrap, and we go to Jardin Plaza*[16]
> *We buy cool neck chains, then we go to town*
> *In one go, in our den, we pop champagne*

It is possible to grasp in this – in many ways limited – translation of the lyrics of this version of *Niche Panda*, what Jordanna Matlon has characterized as the tight dance between global consumerism, commodification, and race today. According to Matlon, international brands and branding are currently "occult expressions of capitalist success" that have emerged as "alternatives to conventional success within the [rapidly disappearing formal] labor economy" (Matlon 2019). In this tragic milieu, dark marginalized individuals put their faiths on these brands while participating in an economy that fetishes them, usually as decadent figures, which enables further extractions of value (Knox 2014). In this process, importantly, darkness has ended up being widely desired, while at the same time rejected by a political economy that intentionally antagonizes with it. The result? "We – all" want to be somehow "Black" but only by proximity or look. "We all" want to be white because that's where security and comfort stills resides. A perpetual *trigueñidad* then is the ethos of our times: white subjects wanting to look "dark," occasionally; "dark" individuals desperately

---

[15] Junior Jein, *Niche Panda (El Último Panda)*, 2016. Official video available at www .youtube.com/watch?v=W6yNv4OnLEM.
[16] *Jardin Plaza* is an up-market shopping mall in the town of Yumbo, also located on the Colombian Pacific Coast.

struggling for "white" benefits to be shared equally; mix-subjects, pulling in both directions depending on the occasion. For young people in Tumaco this is a well-known story – one that is so real and intense that often kills them.

In recent decades there has been a sustained attempt to develop a repertoire of concepts with which to describe the position of these and similar types of racialized mixed subjects within the broader dynamics of international law. Paying particular attention to the Global South, the figure of "creole" legal actors, "mestizo" international lawyers, and "hybrid" figures have emerged in the literature as critical rubrics to describe the unique and never passive position of Southern subjects in the functioning and making of international law (Obregón 2006; Becker Lorca 2014; Parfitt 2011). What I have tried to do here is to continue advancing this series of conceptual frameworks, being attentive to the operation *and* constitutive function of international law across our asymmetrical global order, from the most macro to the most micro. As I hope to have shown, paying attention not necessarily to international personalities, elite groups, international lawyers, or other "key actors," but instead to ordinary individuals facing *and* embodying a world in convulsion – a world created and regulated by international law – gives us a sense of the intense drama underpinning global life for "most of the world." For these subjects being always somehow out of place is a constant. Their place is – evoking Gloria Anzaldúa (2009) again in this final section – el *mundo surdo*, a left-handed world of relational difference, rather than one dictated by right-handed cartesian assumptions about time, place, and the self.[17] As a heuristic, as a thinking portal, the idea of *trigueño*, according to my exploration here, helps us to engage, at least momentarily, with the multiple histories of violent (post-)colonial encounters by which these subjects, and their futures, have already been so profoundly shaped. It brings the material and symbolic, the past and present, the public and most intimate, tightly together, at least momentarily (Hornborg 2020).

As questions of race cannot longer be silenced under the banners of post-racial assumptions. As the world warms or suddenly cools down making the tropics with all of its intensities an increasingly usual climatological feature across the planet. As global health crises remind us that we are all too human although separated by abysmal

---

[17] Anzaldúa intentionally uses "s" instead of the formal "z" to highlight her south Texas, no *Ibérico*, Spanish pronunciation of "zurdo."

inequalities. In these times *trigueñidad* appears less like a curiosity and more like a paradigm of our times. And with this, *trigueñidad*, with its out-of-placeness, is more and more an ethical position to think with.

If the argument that I have presented here makes sense, it becomes necessary to embrace a type of global socio-legal approach that gives an account of our entwined (international legal) present. This, our present, is not one in which being in place is the norm, and out of place the exception. Our today is one in which interconnectivity and profound dislocations run through and through our everyday mélange, in Catatumbo, Melbourne, Tumaco, here and there, and everywhere. We need to learn to pay respect to this immanent interconnectivity and dislocation, because they bring us all together, and they are simultaneously pulling us apart. As Kathryn Yussoff (2018) has put it, "[w]e are all, after all, involved in" global geo-sociological processes, "from the cosmic mineralogical constitution of our bodies to the practices and aesthetics that fuel our consumption" (101). Our desires, aims, and aspirations are "constituted in the underground, shaped in the mine and the dark seams of forgotten formations that one day we will become, that we are already becoming" (101). A *trigueño* international law – and a *trigueño* approach to researching and writing about the global legal order – should start with this impurity and brokenness, and it should aim to help us live, in the most ethical possible way, with the challenges to come. Donna Haraway (2016) has already charted some of the road ahead: "We – all in Terra – live in disturbing times, mixed up times, troubling times and turbid times." So, what to do next? "[T]o become capable, with each other in all of our bumptious kinds, of response … The task is to make kind in lines of inventive connection as a practice of learning to live and die well with each other in a thick present" (1).

References

Acosta, Alberto, and Esperanza Martínez. 2009. *Plurinacionalidad: Democracia en la Diversidad.* Quito: Ediciones Abya-Yala.
Akala. 2018. *Natives: Race and Class in the Ruins of Empire.* London: Two Roads.
Anghie, Antony. 2004. *Imperialism, Sovereignty and the Making of International Law.* Cambridge: Cambridge University Press.
Anzaldúa, Gloria. 2009. "'The Coming of el Mundo Surdo' and 'La Prieta.'" In *The Gloria Anzaldúa Reader,* edited by AnaLouise Keating, 36–50. Durham, NC: Duke University Press.

Appelbaum, Nancy. 2016. *Mapping the Country of Regions: The Chorographic Commission of Nineteenth-Century Colombia*. Chapel Hill: University of North Carolina Press.

Bataille, George. 1991. *The Accursed Share, vol. 1*. Princeton, NJ: Zone Books.

Becker Lorca, Arnulf. 2014. *Mestizo International Law: A Global Intellectual History 1842–1933*. Cambridge: Cambridge University Press.

Berlant, Lauren. 2011. *Cruel Optimism*. Durham, NC: Duke University Press.

Berman, Nathaniel. 1999. "In the Wake of Empire." First Annual Grotius Lecture at the American Society of International Law. *American University International Law Review* 14: 1521, 1551.

Brigham, John. 2009. *Material Law: A Jurisprudence of What's Real*. Philadelphia, PA: Temple University Press.

Chatterjee, Partha. 2004. *The Politics of the Governed: Reflections on Popular Politics in Most of the World* New York: Columbia University Press.

Comaroff, Jean, and John Comaroff, eds. 2006. *Law and Disorder in the Postcolony*. Chicago: University of Chicago Press.

2012. *Theory from the South: Or, How Euro-America Is Evolving Toward Africa*. New York: Routledge.

Coombe, Rosemary J. 1995. "The Cultural Life of Things: Anthropological Approaches to Law and Society in Conditions of Globalization." *American University International Law Review* 10(2): 791, 828.

Darian-Smith, Eve. 2013. *Laws and Societies in Global Contexts: Contemporary Approaches*. Cambridge: Cambridge University Press.

Du Bois, W. E. B. 1982. "The Negro and the Warsaw Ghetto." In *Writings by Du Bois in Periodicals Edited by Others, Vol. 4: 1945–1961*, edited by Herbert Aptheker, 173–6. New York: Kraus-Thomson.

Charlesworth, Hilary. 2002. "International Law: A Discipline of Crisis." *Modern Law Review* 65: 377.

Codazzi, Agustín. 1841. *Resumen de la Geografía de Venezuela*. Paris: Fournier.

Delgado, Abigail Nieves. 2020. "The Face of the Mexican: Race, Nation, and Criminal Identification in Mexico." *American Anthropologist* 122(2): 197.

Echeverría, Bolívar. 2010. *Blanquitud y Modernidad*. Mexico City: Era.

Ellis, Carolyn, and Arthur P. Bochner. 2000. "Autoethnography, Personal Narrative, Reflexivity: Researcher as Subject." In *Handbook of Qualitative Research*, 2nd ed, edited by Norman Denzin and Yoanna Lincoln, 733–68. Thousand Oaks, CA: Sage.

Eslava, Luis. 2014. "Istanbul Vignettes: Observing the Everyday Operation of International Law." *London Review of International Law* 2(1): 3.

2017. "The Materiality of International Law: Violence, History and Joe Sacco's *The Great War*." *London Review of International Law* 5 (1): 49.

Forero, Olga Restrepo, Sebastián Guerra Sánchez, and Malcolm Ashmore. 2013. "La Ciudadanía de Papel: Ensamblando la Cédula y el Estado."

In *Ensamblando Estados*, edited by Olga Restrepo Forero, 277–337. Bogotá: Universidad Nacional de Colombia.

Haraway, Donna. 2016. *Staying with the Trouble: Making Kin in the Chthulucene*. Durham, NC: Duke University Press.

Hobsbawm, Eric. 1996. "Identity and Politics in the Left." *New Left Review* 217: 38.

Hornborg, Alf. 2020. "Anthropology in the Anthropocene." *Anthropology Today* 36(2): 1.

Humboldt, Alexander von, and Aimé Bonpland. 1826. *Viage a las Regiones Equinocciales del Nuevo Continente, volume 2, book V, chapter XVI* (Casa de Rosa, 1826). Reprint: Ediciones del Ministerio de Educación, 1956.

Kingman, Eduardo. 2002. "Identidad, Mestizaje, Hibridación: Sus Usos Ambiguos." *Revista Propocisiones* 34.

Knox, Robert. 2014. "Race, Racialisation and Rivalry in the International Order." In *Race and Racism in International Relations: Confronting the Global Color Line*, edited by Alexander Anievas, Nivi Manchanda, and Robbie Shilliam, 175–92. New York: Routledge.

2016. "Valuing Race? Stretch Marxism and the Logic of Imperialism." *London Review of International Law* 4(1): 81.

Koram, Kojo, ed. 2019. *The War on Drugs and the Global Color Line*. London: Pluto Press.

Levi-Strauss, Claude. 1955. *Tristes Tropiques*. Reprint. New York: Penguin, 1992.

Linarelli, John, Margot Salomon, and Muthucumaraswamy Sornarajah. 2018. *The Misery of International Law: Confrontations with Injustice in the Global Economy*. Oxford: Oxford University Press.

Liong, Ju Tjung, Helga Leitner, Eric Sheppard, Suryono Herlambang, and Wahyu Astuti. 2020. "Space Grabs: Colonizing the Verity City." *International Journal of Urban and Regional Research* 44(6): 1072.

Matlon, Jordanna. 2019. "Black Masculinity Under Racial Capitalism." *Boston Review* July 16, 2019. https://bostonreview.net/race/jordanna-matlon-black-masculinity-under-racial-capitalism.

Obregón, Liliana. 2006. "Between Civilization and Barbarism: Creole Interventions in International Law." *Third World Quarterly* 27: 815.

Orford, Anne. 2012. "Constituting Order." In *The Cambridge Companion to International Law*, edited by James Crawford and Martti Koskenniemi, 271–89. Cambridge: Cambridge University Press.

Parfitt, Rose. 2011. "Empire des Nègres Blancs: The Hybridity of International Personality and the Abyssinia Crisis of 1935–36." *Leiden Journal of International Law* 24: 849.

Shaw, Malcom. 2017. *International Law*. 8th ed. Cambridge: Cambridge University Press.

Shklovsky, Viktor. 2016. "Art as Device." In *Viktor Shklovsky: A Reader*, edited by Alexandra Berlina, 73–96. London: Bloomsbury.

Taussig, Michael. 2001. *The Nervous System*. New York: Routledge.

2012. *Beauty and the Beast*. Chicago: University of Chicago Press.

Vásquez-Padilla, Darío Hernán, and Castriela Esther Hernández-Reyes. 2020. "Interrogando la Gramática Racial de la Blanquitud: Hacia una Analítica del Blanqueamiento en el Orden Racial Colombiano." *Latin American Research Review* 55(1): 64.

Yussof, Kathryn. 2018. *A Billion Black Anthropocenes or None*. Minneapolis: University of Minnesota Press.

CHAPTER NINE

BECOMING A FAMILIAR OUTSIDER

Multi-sited and Multi-temporal Research in Plural
Legal Contexts

Keebet von Benda-Beckmann

At the beginning of our research in West Sumatra in the mid-1970s, we
visited a former member of the district council who had suffered severe
brain damage from an accident. His wife introduced us: "Here are Franz
and Keebet. They are from Switzerland and want to study *adat* (customary law). Franz is German and Keebet is Dutch." "Dutch?," he
exclaimed, his face contorted, "I am afraid of the Dutch!" We had
triggered his memory of the Indonesian War of Independence when he
was active in the resistance. Never during my fieldwork would I feel so
utterly out of place. I wanted to leave immediately, but his wife
reassured me and said this was something of the past. This encounter
made me realize that under the surface, the colonial past was still very
much present no matter how many people would tell us that it was
history and hardly played a role in their lives.

Feeling out of place as a Dutch researcher would keep me on edge
and made me keenly aware of the inequalities that were a heritage of
the Dutch colonial legal system. But my sense of being out of place was
more complex than this. It meant in the first place working in a
scientific field (anthropology of law) for which my Dutch legal education had not prepared me; second, having to operate in foreign languages (Swiss German, Indonesian, Minangkabau, Moluccan Malay);
third, studying societies (West Sumatra, Ambon, Dutch Moluccans in
the Netherlands) as an outsider – one with a particular Dutch colonial
background (with a grandfather who had been an administrator in a
Dutch sugar plantation, a mother who spent the first four years of her
life there, and a father who had served in the Dutch army during the

188

Indonesian War, whose parents had helped to build up the medical faculty in Surabaya between 1946 and 1950). Yet at times I found myself unexpectedly in place. This occurred when my previous research on care and social security at one side of the transnational Moluccan community, on Ambon, provided the necessary trust at the other end of the same transnational community, in the Netherlands, to probe into the sensitive issue of old-age care among Dutch Moluccans.

INTRODUCTION

This chapter offers a reflection on forty-five years of research that included work in Indonesia – West Sumatra and the East Indonesian Island of Ambon – which I shared with my late husband, Franz von Benda-Beckmann, and in the Netherlands among Moluccan migrants that I carried out with two Dutch-Moluccan researchers. Beginning as a total stranger – and with a Dutch colonial background – I slowly turned into a familiar outsider.[1] The central question of this chapter will be how this affected my study of the social working of law under conditions of legal pluralism. This involves two related sets of issues. One is that being "out of place" in my case means more than the general anthropological principle that as an outside observer one generates unique understanding in co-creation between the fieldworker and persons in the field.[2] The disciplinary move from law to anthropology at a time in which there was not a clear understanding of how to do this, contributed to my being out of place.[3] It also meant coming to terms with a colonial background, which put me on edge but also gave me a heightened sensitivity towards legal inequalities. With my Moluccan research in particular, I discovered that one can be at the same time out of place in one sense and in place in another sense. A first section discusses my multiple ways of being out of place – and in place.

A second, related set of issues concerns how over time our work evolved towards multi-sited and multi-temporal research. In West

---

[1] I am grateful for the thoughtful comments of Leisy Abrego, Mark Fathi Massoud, and Lynette J. Chua.
[2] See Bornemann and Hammoudi (2009); Dresch and James (2000, 2); Allen (2000).
[3] See the interviews in Halliday and Schmidt (2009) about the challenges and struggles in finding the appropriate research methods, and the changes in approach developed over the years of empirical studies on law. See Massoud (2016) and Nouwen (2014) for current research on law in fragile states.

Sumatra, the home of the Minangkabau, I began in 1974 with a study of village justice and state courts, a mildly multi-sited research. From 1984–5 we studied social security under conditions of legal pluralism in Hila, an Islamic community on the East Indonesian island of Ambon. This study became part of multi-sited and multi-temporal research, when it turned out to be crucial for research among Moluccan migrants in the Netherlands in the early 1990s. From 1999 onwards, our study in West Sumatra was both multi-sited and multi-temporal.[4] All encounters, serendipity, and the unexpected that I experienced over the years generated various ways and degrees of being an outsider. Becoming more familiar outsiders over time facilitated understanding of some of the epistemological conundrums of plural legal constellations.

Several points stand out. Over time I came to understand the profound difference between the binary mode of argumentation employed by judges in West Sumatra, and villagers' ways of thinking in terms of degree. Multi-sited and multi-temporal research in West Sumatra and among Moluccans also revealed the dynamic and capricious relationships between co-existing types of law.[5] Third, the search for appropriate terms to discuss social security on Ambon facilitated understanding of the graded Moluccan norms of obligation, and of notions of personhood. My research on the Moluccas later helped me appreciate intimate feelings of obligation and neglect that elderly Moluccans in the Netherlands shared with me, issues my Dutch-Moluccan co-researchers shied away from discussing with them. It also helped me understand the different interpretations of relationships within the transnational Moluccan communities.

MULTIPLE WAYS OF BEING OUT OF PLACE

When Franz was asked to apply for a position as assistant professor in legal anthropology in Zürich, we discussed intensively what this would mean for the two of us and decided it would be a great adventure.

[4] Turner (2009, 38) argues that long-time or multi-temporal research opens the possibility of multi-sited research. See Howell and Talle (2012) for the effects on long-term field research among marginalized, peripheral communities that over time became fully entrenched in the modern world.
[5] A similar point was made by Howell and Talle (2012, 5). Forced to change from classical field research to multi-sited research, they could trace the capricious and fragmented dynamics of change and continuity by which some core values disappeared, others showed remarkable resilience, and yet others obtained new meaning.

We were thrilled when he got the job. Professor Lorenz Löffler was developing a regional focus on Southeast Asia at the newly established institute for social anthropology at the University of Zürich. As Franz already had started to learn Dutch, Indonesia seemed ideal for fieldwork. Research in Malawi had acquainted him with societies with a matrilineal social organization and the Minangkabau of West Sumatra drew his special attention. They formed the world's largest ethnic group with a matrilineal social organization, were devout Muslims, had high levels of education, and were deeply entrenched in the Indonesian state and the world market. They seemed perfect to study the social working of law in a setting where people could draw on state law, customary law (called *adat* or *adat* law), and religious law.

This propelled me out of place right from the beginning of our life-long personal and academic collaboration that ended with Franz' premature death in 2013. I had just finished my law degree and had planned to go into social lawyering. For me, moving to Switzerland, also meant having to operate in two foreign languages, German and Swiss-German (*Züridütsch*). My Dutch law degree proved of little use, but I was hired as an assistant to the newly appointed professor in the Sociology of Law, Manfred Rehbinder, and began to think of doing PhD research myself. It took many discussions and as many bottles of wine to overcome my uncertainty as to whether I, as a trained lawyer, could carry out anthropological work on law.

I also felt out of place due to my colonial background. My mother was born in Semarang as a daughter of an administrator of a sugar plantation that could not cope with the colonial racism and inequalities and returned with the family to the Netherlands when she was four. Besides, my father had been recruited to serve in the Dutch army during the Indonesian War of Independence from 1947 to 1949. During that same time his parents helped build up the medical faculty at Surabaya. During my childhood I had heard so many negative stories about the Dutch Indies that Indonesia held little attraction for me; going there even felt inappropriate. In long discussions we explored how we could deal with my reluctance and eventually the advantages of going to Indonesia prevailed. I began to read anthropological studies of law, including the work of the Dutch Adat Law school of Cornelis van Vollenhoven and his students. Thus, within a relatively short period of time I mutated from a lawyer into a researcher studying the social working of law from an anthropological perspective.

My legal background helped me understand the Indonesian state legal system, which was still largely based on Dutch law. While lawyers accepted me as a legitimate participant in discussions, for many anthropologists I would remain a lawyer. At that time, most anthropologists considered law, understood exclusively as the law of the state, as something for lawyers to study.

Sitting between the two chairs of law and social sciences was sometimes uncomfortable, but far more often liberating, interesting, and exciting. In a way being out of place also felt like being in exactly the right place. I never regretted becoming a legal anthropologist, but a sense of being out of place has never left me completely.

MULTI-SITED RESEARCH IN WEST SUMATRA: DISPUTE MANAGEMENT AND PROPERTY RELATIONS

Our first field research was conducted in West Sumatra in 1974–5. It combined classical fieldwork within one village with research in three local courts, making it mildly multi-sited research. This section shows that the combination of observing court procedures, studying court files, and attending cases of dispute management in a village proved highly productive. It revealed that the meaning of *adat* rules in village settings differed from interpretations in court. Thus, parallel versions of *adat* law were in use: Those used by courts and other state institutions, and those developed within each of the village communities. Crucial for these differences were the distinctive modes of argumentation and evaluating evidence, that is, binary in court, and in terms of degree in villages. The village study also confirmed that staying sufficiently out of place enabled guaranteeing confidentiality. This was necessary to obtain the required trust to build up layers of insight in the complex plural legal constellation.

When preparing our research, we had been warned that fieldwork, especially on law, might be problematic in Indonesia. The political situation in Indonesia had become tense and in 1973, the Department of Inner Affairs put serious constraints on anthropological fieldwork. Before these rules had been issued, the governor of West Sumatra had invited the Dutch anthropologist Patrick de Josselin de Jong, an authority on Minangkabau kinship, to carry out research in West Sumatra. De Josselin de Jong refused to work under such constraints and aborted his research. The governor felt deeply embarrassed towards his guest. When we began our research almost a year later, the political situation had relaxed. *Adat* law was an acceptable theme for obtaining a research permit and the only condition was a general monthly report. Officials were extremely cooperative and frequently mentioned how embarrassed they had been about the constraints, and how glad they were that new researchers were coming in. The local police officer visited us a couple of times. After a friendly chat about our research, he quickly turned to the more important fact that he, Franz, and the famous boxer Muhammad Ali were of the same age. No official required details or disclosing names or interfered with our research and this remained so throughout the decades of research we carried out in Indonesia.

We began fieldwork with three months in a small town, Bukittinggi, situated in the central highlands of West Sumatra that formed the core of Minangkabau territory. We took lessons in the local Minangkabau language, improved our skills in Indonesian (*Bahasa Indonesia*), and started research at the local court. Letters of recommendation from the Supreme Court (*Mahkamah Agung*) and the High Court in Padang opened all doors to local courts. The court registers gave us an idea of the kind of issues courts were dealing with. On that basis we selected the village Candung Kota Lawas (CKL), from where several major disputes had been submitted to the court. This allowed us to compare the ways that courts and village institutions dealt with disputes. A district functionary who lived in CKL, where he also was the head of its village *adat* council, found us a house where we stayed for eleven months. From there I frequented the local court in Bukittinggi, and made frequent trips to two other local courts in the core Minangkabau region. Franz focused on property and the socio-political organization of CKL.[6]

The house assigned to us stood on inherited property of a matrilineage. It was one of a cluster of houses in which sisters and cousins (Mo-Si-Daughters) lived with their nuclear family. This opened quite literally a window on the matrilineal and uxorilocal principles of Minangkabau social structure. In the 1970s, women with their husband and children lived as conjugal families, sometimes in a three-generation arrangement, in individual houses that were usually built on family

---

[6] Academic requirements for the acquirement of a PhD and a "*Habilitation*," the prerequisite for becoming a full professor under the Swiss and German system, forced us to select different subjects: dispute management and property and social continuity. This allowed us to use our mutual data for our own work. The two books that came out of the study should be seen in conjunction (F. von Benda-Beckmann 1979; K. von Benda-Beckmann 1984).

property. As a result, sisters and female cousins frequently lived closely together, as was the case with our closest neighbors. As they would fetch water from the well next to our house, we spoke to them every day and could observe from close by the collaboration, avoidance, and tensions that come with living closely together.

The other result was that I, as a woman, became loosely associated with that sub-lineage, in the sense that I joined my neighbors for preparations of rituals such as weddings and funerals, thus learning the rules and obligations, and much more, connected with these events. We became more familiar outsiders but discovered that our neighbors treated us more as insiders than we had expected. In one of the last weeks of our stay I brought the conventional plate of rice that a guest brings to a wedding. This evoked a surprised reprimand. Because it was a wedding of a family member, I should not have brought rice. Thus, my association with this family in various ways gave me insights that I would not have obtained otherwise. However, it was not too close to impair relations with other villagers, the more so since Franz' affiliation as an in-married husband remained unclear.

Being outsiders had certain advantages. After it had become known that we were not potato experts as rumors had it, villagers accepted us as young scholars interested in Minangkabau *adat*. Many families had children pursuing an academic degree and had some idea of what anthropologists did. People wanted to make sure we would not write nonsense, for the books we would write would contribute to the knowledge of their children. A couple of *adat* officials took it upon themselves to instruct us. This happened during long, intensive evenings, for "a black cock flies at night," meaning that lineage heads, who traditionally wear black clothes, may discuss *adat* only at night.

Being outsiders also meant not belonging to one particular camp in the extremely contentious disputes about landed property. This worked well when it became known that we never disclosed names of inter-locutors or shared confidential information with other people. Quite often people came to us explicitly to explain details of a certain dispute because they had noticed that their opponents had visited us, and they wanted to make sure we got the whole picture. To dig deeper, it was important to demonstrate how much we already knew, without disclosing its source. For this we benefitted from our work in court. From the court files we built up considerable knowledge of some of the most challenging and long-standing disputes. If someone was satisfied with the extent of our knowledge, he or she would share details that he initially had kept from us. Most people were appreciative of our confidentiality. Only once, in the last weeks of our stay in CKL, did this end on a negative note. The head from a distinguished lineage wanted us to share tape recorded information. He argued that he was the only one for whom confidentiality did not apply because he actually was the *adat* head of the village. When we refused to comply, he ended the discussion, and we never talked to him again.

On the basis of the work in courts, attending sessions of the village *adat* council and the village council, discussions with the village mayor and sub-district head who also dealt with disputes, and through the numerous informal talks and observations, including those Franz had when mapping a section of the village land, we slowly began to understand the frames of thought, the semantics of *adat* concepts, the intimate connection between property relations and socio-political organization, and the intertwinement of *adat* and Islamic law and state law. Village procedures differed substantially from state court procedures based on Dutch colonial procedural law. The interpretation of *adat* as it was applied by the *adat* council often differed from the court's interpretation. However, I remained mystified by the differences in the way judges and villagers evaluated the evidence of witnesses and *adat* experts, for instance, concerning the most important question of who did and who did not belong to kin groups. With my legal background I could easily understand the courts' ways, but following the villagers' ways of arguing was a different matter. It was not until I was writing up my material back home, that I finally comprehended that courts employed a binary mode of arguing, while villagers argued in terms of degree. The discrepancy of the court's binary mode and the more graded mode of *adat* officials turned out to be at the root of what had been a most puzzling issue throughout my fieldwork.

Thus, in the process we moved from being a total stranger to becoming a familiar outsider with whom more and more intimate knowledge was shared on the assumption that we would not take sides and keep information confidential. This allowed us to develop, from different perspectives, layer after layer of insight into *adat*, its property regime, land conflicts, and modes of dispute management.

CLASSICAL FIELDWORK ON AMBON WITH A NON-CLASSICAL THEME

Much as we valued our research among the Minangkabau, we felt a strong urge to diversify our research on legal pluralism, lest our Minangkabau experience would become a template for all complex legal orders (see, for example, Parkin 2009: 92). Thus, in 1984 we started fieldwork in the village of Hila on the East Indonesian island of Ambon (F. and K. von Benda-Beckmann 2007). This section discusses how our position of well-established academics, and as a family with small children affected our research, making it more into a classical village study than envisaged.

The theme of our research – local forms of social security – proved highly productive for studying legal pluralism, but it also posed several challenges. One was to develop it as an analytical tool for a universal issue rather than for the western welfare state only. Being there as a family clearly was beneficial for discussing care. However, finding the semantically adequate terms to discuss care and need was a challenge that made us feel out of place. Besides, state institutions used notions of deserving need that differed from *adat* and from local Islamic law, which made it even more complicated. Once we found the right approach of addressing these issues, we began to understand the graded notions of obligation in the provision of social security. At a much later stage, this also helped me to understand the Moluccans' relational conceptions of personhood.

Plans to go to the Moluccas began when Mohamad Ohorella, a law professor from Ujung Panjang (Makassar), invited Franz to join him to Tulehu, where he was a traditional village head. Franz found Ambon a great place to study a long history of the relationship between the state, religion, and *adat* under very different conditions from West Sumatra. Once again, my unease with Dutch colonial history made me hesitate. Ambon has a special position in Dutch colonial history. Situated in the middle of the spice islands, it had been incorporated into the Dutch colonial empire in the early seventeenth century when it became a hub in the international spice trade. Islam and Christianity had both arrived in the sixteenth century and half of the population had become Christian, the other half Muslim. The Dutch colonial army recruited a large proportion of its soldiers from Ambon and the surrounding islands. When the Netherlands finally turned over sovereignty to Indonesia in 1949, the Dutch government ordered the colonial army with their families to the Netherlands to protect them from lynching. It had hoped for an independent Moluccan state within an Indonesian Federation, but Indonesia chose to become a unified state. The soldiers and their families remained in the Netherlands, under difficult conditions.

Though reluctant to go to the Moluccas, I was eager to pursue an interest in care and social security that I had developed during my work at the Law Faculty of Erasmus University Rotterdam. It took some arguing to convince Franz that this was also a promising theme for studying legal pluralism. At that time, social security was an unfamiliar theme for anthropologists, who regarded it exclusively characteristic of western welfare states. In our conception, the underlying issue of the arrangements that a society develops to care for those that cannot take care of themselves, addresses a universal problem. The concept that social security served as a suitable analytical tool for a complex legal plural constellation that includes the provision of care and support, but also involved long-term relations, expectations, rights, and obligations. In contrast to the more common concept of care, social security put more emphasis on the temporal and diachronic dimensions. Not only did many feel we had chosen the wrong topic, we were also warned that we would never get research permission for social security, because security was a highly sensitive issue in Indonesia. As it happened, we got our permission in due time.

Our starting position in Hila differed substantially from our first research in West Sumatra. Reasonably fluent in Indonesian, we could easily communicate with people who, except for some very old widows, were well-versed in Indonesian. We quickly picked up the local Malay dialect, *Malayu Ambon*. However, we did not properly learn the original Austronesian language, called *Bahasa Tanah*. Adults mostly spoke *Bahasa Tanah* among themselves, which was understood but not spoken by the children that used *Malayu Ambon*.

Another difference was that we came as a family and had to divide our time between research and the children. We taught them at home with materials from their Montessori school, but they also needed special attention because they missed their friends. "Why can we not live in two places, so that we can see our friends here and back home?" asked my eight-year-old son when he missed his friends in the Netherlands but understood that he soon would miss his friends in Ambon. They enjoyed the friendships they made but were also frequently frustrated because they could not understand others and could not express themselves properly. They felt most comfortable close to our house and disliked traveling to new places, where people would crowd around us and strangers would touch them. Therefore, we decided early on to stay as much in the village as possible, which made our research a classical village study.

Being in the field with children also was an unexpected asset. They brought us into contact with youngsters to whom we alone at our age and status would not have had easy access. On several occasions our children commented on things happening to their friends that were of immediate relevance for our research. However stressful the combination of fieldwork and childcare was, living in a comfortable house owned by a Dutch-Moluccan ex-military man in the Netherlands, and lovingly taken care of by his brother and family, meant enormous support which made our life in the village also very enjoyable. We developed close relationships with the family, observed practices of care in our immediate surroundings, and had numerous talks during the evenings, when we gathered on the cool verandah.

A further implication of doing fieldwork as well-established scholars was that it generated some suspicion. Why would persons in such a position live in a village without running water or electricity? A handful of men, among them the village secretary, avoided us. But most people, in particular women, were more than willing to talk to us about care. In contrast to our research in West Sumatra, as a woman I often was the first person to be addressed in conversations. As in West Sumatra, our knowledge was often put to the test. For example, the head of a leading clan tested our language competence by asking us to translate an old Dutch document into Indonesian, without mentioning that he already had a translation. Satisfied that ours was correct he trusted us and shared many more highly interesting Dutch eighteenth-century documents that his family had kept in a large chest. By attending weddings, funerals, and other rituals, spending time in the state supported widows' shop, and talking to many different people, and observing how decisions were made to distribute *zakat fithra* at the end of the fasting month, we began to understand that the state entertained very different notions of deserving need than embodied in local Islamic norms and practices, or in Moluccan *adat*. We also came to understand the diversification developed to secure care and support. One day a young man explained jokingly that one needed five children: one in trade (to earn much money), one in the army or police (to protect against harassment), one in civil service (to offer access to state services), one in education (to secure access to education), and one to stay home for the care labor needed at old age.

Among the most intriguing problems was finding the appropriate terms for what we call care. Caring obligations proved to be graded: the further distanced kin relations are, the more care is subject to negotiation and reciprocity. Poverty is largely constituted by a lack of close relatives. But it took us much time to understand that for the closest relatives the term care, and its Indonesian equivalents *tolong* or *bantu* were semantically inadequate. People would respond with a blank look when we would ask if they would care for their husband, children, or parents. Care in the sense of *tolong* or *bantu* was not something one did for one's closest relatives; it was something one did for others. Caring for one's closest relatives was something you did as-for-yourself. It took me years to realize that this was based on an extended or relational notion of personhood that includes the closest relatives.

MULTI-SITED RESEARCH IN A TRANSNATIONAL MOLUCCAN COMMUNITY

An invitation from a research institute in Leiden to participate in a study of the emancipation of Dutch Moluccan women in 1990 drew me into research in the Netherlands. Intimately related to rights and obligations of care and support, the theme fitted well into my work on social security and legal pluralism. The research was conducted by a Moluccan sociologist, a Moluccan researcher with a background in Islamic studies, and me. This study put me in a paradoxical situation: I had a stronger sense of being out of place than my research in Indonesia. Yet my experience on the Moluccas made me in some respects more in place than my Moluccan co-researchers. This enabled me to reveal some contradictions in caring relations. Unexpectedly, together with my previous research this study turned into a multi-sited and multi-temporal study of the dynamics of changing notions of care in a transnational community (Glick-Schiller 2005).

Suspicion towards a Dutch researcher in a study paid for by the very government that had let them down so badly, put me out of place right at the beginning. A Moluccan organization probed my motives and attitude before accepting me, and made it very clear that I was an outsider and had to earn legitimacy in a way that had not been necessary in Indonesia. But there was another consequence of being an outsider that I had not anticipated. My co-researchers started out from different understandings than I had. Their background was in Dutch Moluccan society without first-hand experience in the Moluccas; mine was in Dutch dominant society, with considerable knowledge of Moluccan society in Indonesia, but not of Dutch Moluccan society. Initially this caused some tension. They wanted me to abide by what they considered taboo questions. Probing in problems of caring relations of the elderly was inappropriate and would hurt their feelings. As a compromise I promised to be very careful in approaching the issue and stop immediately if I sensed that a person did not want to talk about it.

In practice, most elderly people were rather eager to talk about it with me. But caring for the aged turned out to be an iconic element of

Dutch Moluccan identity. Having lived away from the Moluccas, first in the colonial army and subsequently in the Netherlands, and for a long time prohibited from traveling "back home," they had created an ideal image of the Moluccas according to which "the whole community takes care of the needy." This guided their care for their elderly in the Netherlands, which distinguished them from the Dutch majority that in their eyes all put their elderly into homes.

However, demographic change and the possibility to travel to the Moluccas challenged this ideal. During the early years in the Netherlands, there were few aging persons in need of care. By the 1990s, their number had increased, while at the same time ideas about child rearing had changed and more time was devoted to their education. Women in their forties and fifties who wanted to comply with obligations to parents and children alike came under considerable pressure, while some aging persons felt they did not get the support and care they felt entitled to. Besides, when from the 1980s on Dutch Moluccans began to travel to the Moluccas, they discovered that their relatives did not always receive the loving care they had expected. Care was often subject to contentious negotiations. It was a painful experience, difficult to accept in light of the ideals they had grown up with.

Since I knew the situation on Ambon firsthand, my experience made it easier to address these worries. Some clearly stuck to the idea that care for the needy elderly should be extended unconditionally. Generally, such care was indeed extended, and it was not unusual that a woman gave up her job to care for her elderly parents. Some suffered in silence when care did not live up to standard. Others confided to me that they would not mind living in a home, but that their children would feel ashamed if they did. One elderly lady expressed her relief to be able to discuss these matters with me; it was the first time she could share her feelings of discomfort and confusion. Younger Moluccans felt less stress. For them, adjustments to Dutch society and its more individualistic normative conceptions of care and support generated a sense of freedom the middle aged did not have. They managed to combine adherence to Moluccan norms for support with Dutch modes of deciding how and when this would be extended.

MULTI-SITED AND MULTI-TEMPORAL RESEARCH IN WEST SUMATRA: CONSTITUTIONAL REFORMS

The 1980s and 1990s kept us busy with our Moluccan research and a research project in Nepal, and we visited West Sumatra only on and off. However, we felt an urge to do more substantial research and planned comparative research on social security. But when we visited West Sumatra in 1999, shortly after the demise of the Suharto regime, a unique opportunity presented itself to study at the level of village government the unfolding dynamics of the constitutional reforms that were to turn the highly centralized Indonesian state into a decentralized state. This coincided with our move to the newly established Max Planck Institute for Social Anthropology in Halle/Saale, Germany, that offered facilities for long-term research impossible for universities. This section shows how at that stage in our academic career multi-sited and multi-temporal research took shape.

The period of our first fieldwork happened to become a crucial point of reference for many Minangkabau in discussions about the renewed role *adat* and Islam were to play in local government. This unexpectedly made our research into a multi-temporal study that allowed us to observe and discuss epistemological shifts in the term *adat* that had occurred over the past decades. Moreover, our knowledge of the history of the region had deepened since our first fieldwork. Together, this generated insight into the capricious ways in which the relationship between normative orders of the state, *adat*, and Islam unfolded over a period of two centuries. Covering the whole province also revealed the surprisingly wide range of experimentation with decentralization policies (F. and K. von Benda-Beckmann 2013).

Between 1999 and 2009, we visited the region once or twice a year for up to a month. In collaboration with colleagues from Andalas University, we repeatedly interviewed village officials and members of village councils throughout West Sumatra. We also collected material from newspapers and the new communication media, and numerous draft regulations. Having been engaged with West Sumatra for decades had other advantages. Our counterpart from the 1970s, Dr. Narullah, was now one of the leading *adat* law scholars, heavily involved in *adat* politics, and introduced us to whomever we wanted to meet. We were always warmly welcomed when visiting our old neighbors/family in CKL and discussed the recent developments with leading persons in CKL whom we had known as youngsters in the 1970s.

During the end of the Suharto regime, public debate was dominated by the role of Islam in the mobilization of opposition against the regime. To the surprise of many, *adat* became a prime issue. Many had declared *adat* to belong to a distant past, no longer of relevance. That *adat* became such a driving force had two reasons. Village autonomy implied having to raise revenues from village-internal resources.

Villagers now dared to reclaim dispossessed land and *adat* law promised the best avenue for claiming back village land that had been expropriated – often illegally – in colonial times and under the Suharto regime. Decentralization also assigned decision-making power to village governments and the question arose what role *adat* was to play in it. Young urban elites generally considered *adat* backward, feudal, and undemocratic and rejected a role for *adat* and its leaders. Among the proponents, some envisaged a role for *adat* of precolonial and colonial times, but a remarkable number of people wanted to go back to the system of the 1970s, "when people still abided to *adat*." However, their recollections differed from what our research of that period told us, namely that *adat* at that time was important, but *adat* leaders had little authority.

What is important for the purpose of this chapter is that our perspective on the 1970s had not gone through the filter of the 1980s and 1990s in the way it had for most Minangkabau people. We had visited the region occasionally during this period and knew from the literature about the changes in village government of the 1980s that had reduced the influence of *adat* on village government. This having been "out of place and time" allowed us to pitch our findings against the image of *adat* that especially young and educated Minangkabau held of a time before they were even born. We were struck by the resilience of *adat*, not as a preset and unchangeable set of customary law, but as a set of normative conceptions and regulations adapting to new political and social contexts. Core features had remained and could be mobilized again when the political context allowed this, but the form and embedding in government structures had changed.

The new interest in *adat* also happened at a time when more intensified interpretations of Islam had become dominant. These debates made us realize that the term *adat* for the young generation had undergone an epistemological shift, because it no longer included property relations. Thus, in their understanding *adat* had become obsolete because it no longer played a role in village government. With decentralization it regained its more inclusive meaning. That *adat* applied to landed property relations was undisputed. The most emotional discussions turned about the question whether village government should adopt *adat* or "western" notions of democracy, and old status differences embodied in *adat*.

Our multi-sited research revealed the surprising degrees of experimenting with modes of government and the striking variety in which *adat* and religion were incorporated into village government. The feelings of liberation and enthusiasm within which far more persons than those directly engaged in village government participated, in the debates about local democracy and the possibilities that opened up for a freer life, were deeply impressive. This enthusiasm has largely disappeared, due to subsequent standardization and lacking fulfillment of promises made by the central government. One might cynically comment that nothing really has changed, but this obscures how much did change, albeit for a relatively short period.

REFLECTIONS ON MY DUTCH COLONIAL BACKGROUND

One of the biggest surprises during our first stretch of fieldwork in West Sumatra was that nobody seemed to have a problem with me being Dutch. My unease seemed so much out of place that I wondered whether there was resentment at all about the colonial past. Of course, there was, but colonial violence was one of many violent episodes that included the Japanese occupation during World War II, the War of Independence of 1945–9, the civil war of 1956–7 in which Sumatra was threatened with secession, and the transition from Sukarno to Suharto in 1965 with the violent persecution of (assumed) communists.[7] In the mid-1970s the wounds of 1965 were still raw, and public discussion about these episodes was strictly prohibited; they could only be discussed in private. We never initiated such discussions but once we got more acquainted, it became clear that many still held reservations against the Dutch. Assuming we were Swiss or German, some might occasionally make a denigrating remark or a joke with a bitter undercurrent about colonial times. The event described at the beginning of this chapter was one of the very few occasions in which we saw how the memory of colonial violence caused distress.[8]

In my Moluccan research, my colonial background played a different role. The Netherlands was much more present than in West Sumatra, because of the large Moluccan community in the Netherlands with a colonial army background. In Hila, quite a few had close relatives in the Netherlands and visits by Dutch Moluccan relatives were frequent. This may have fed some of the suspicion in Hila that I mentioned previously. But overall, I encountered little resentment, and I felt less

---

[7] See, for Indonesia in general, van Reybrouck (2020).

[8] That there still was much resentment was confirmed in 1992, when President Suharto severed all development cooperation with the Netherlands because of the human rights conditionalities. Many young Indonesians were surprised at the widespread support from elderly Indonesians (Baehr 1997).

out of place here than in West Sumatra. Having research experience in Indonesia, being there with a family, and reasonably well-versed in Indonesian may have helped. As for my Moluccan research in the Netherlands, I had to earn legitimacy as a Dutch researcher, more than because of my personal colonial background. My research background in Hila accorded me some legitimacy and put me therefore more in place to study social security than my Moluccan co-researchers.

During our research on decentralization, we were accepted as senior academics with considerable knowledge of Minangkabau and its history. Besides, Indonesian historians and social scientists were now free to study the atrocities committed between the 1940s until the 1960s. Colonial injustices became important when illegally expropriated land was reclaimed and we engaged in these issues, without encountering much resentment.

CONCLUSIONS

Over a period of forty years of research in Indonesia and the Netherlands my status changed from being a young total stranger to becoming an elderly familiar outsider. Time, language, career, family, and citizenship all had an impact on our research. I had feared that my colonial background might inhibit my research and a sense of unease never left me completely. However, it did not seem to form a constraint. One reason might have been that during our first bout of fieldwork, my husband was German and that we operated from Switzerland. More important, the violent colonial experience often seemed eclipsed by more recent violent episodes and only on very rare occasions did we get a sense of the personal scars it had left. Being Dutch was conducive to understanding the state legal system and offered easy access to historical documents.

Overall, people seemed to see us as slightly odd, but obviously interested and trustworthy persons, a sense that deepened with every return. The more we showed the extent of our knowledge, the more people were prepared to share further layers of knowledge. This deepened our understanding of the epistemological and normative complexity under which people lived. During the different times in our lifecycle, we were assigned different positions. In the early years in West Sumatra, we were treated, and positioned ourselves, as students. Later on, conducting fieldwork with a high university status evoked some suspicion, but being there with a young family, it seemed natural to us and to our Moluccan interlocutors, to discuss issues of care and support. In our research on decentralization policies in West Sumatra we were seen as experienced and knowledgeable in certain ways, although not in many others. But we now could rely on old friends and colleagues that over time had risen to high positions in academia and government. Our long-time counterpart in particular, who had developed from a young university teacher into a prominent Minangkabau *adat* law expert, helped us with information, understanding, and contacts through his enormous network.

Serendipity played a role in several respects, though it was serendipity within specific enabling contexts. We knew De Josselin de Jong from Dutch academia. But it was pure serendipity that we began our research shortly after he had aborted his research, and that this facilitated our research in the 1970s. Serendipity was again favorable at the turn of the century when we were transitioning to the Max Planck Institute for Social Anthropology in Halle, Germany, that allowed us to do long-term research, when the Indonesian constitutional changes started. Besides, nobody could have predicted that the 1970s would be so vital for the construction of village government under decentralization.

Though unplanned, my research became multi-sited and multi-temporal. This facilitated the co-production of knowledge that a classical field study might not have generated. Having been literally out of place from West Sumatra during most of the 1980s and 1990s had an unexpected effect. We discussed our findings of the plural legal context of the 1970s and the role of *adat* leaders at that time, relatively unfiltered by the changes in village structure that followed soon after we left the field, by which local people perceived the 1970s. Of course, our image was filtered by our own memories and the academic work of analyzing and writing our findings (Howell and Talle 2012, 18). This confrontation proved productive when discussing the role *adat* and Islam might play in the new democratic village government. It also deepened our understanding of *adat*'s resilience and adaptability. *Adat* embodies, as Turner (2009, 43) formulated for remarkably similar changes among the Kayapo in Brazil, "a dynamically co-varying set of relations [and, I should add, norms] that assumes different forms at discrete moments in a diachronic process." Despite epistemological shifts in the notion of *adat*, the entailed ontology shows a remarkable continuity (cf. Howell 2012, 156).

The research in Ambon and in the Netherlands together amounted to multi-sited research that offered insights I would not have acquired with a study in one locality only. It is common knowledge that migrant communities over time adjust to the dominant normative order, and that they usually form transnational communities (Glick-Schiller 2005). Less discussed are the implications of members operating under very different normative conditions concerning care and support on either end of the transnational relationships. Ambonese and Dutch Moluccans were not only subject to different state legal systems; they also entertained different conceptions of both *adat* and Islamic rules about care and support (F. von Benda-Beckmann 1988; K. von Benda-Beckmann 2015). Depending on their position within the transnational community, they operate from presumed common, yet in fact different, understandings of *adat*.

The study in the Netherlands also showed how productive research can be with researchers from different backgrounds, each in place and out of place in very different ways. My co-researchers were, to different degrees, insiders to the Moluccan community and were acutely aware of the sensitive issue of elderly care, a sensitivity I as an outsider lacked. But in relation to the Moluccas, they were more out of place than I was. Lacking detailed knowledge of the Moluccas, they did not fully understand how little the ideals about Moluccan culture matched the reality of Indonesian Moluccan society, and the extent to which this had affected the contentious claims and obligations for care and support among Moluccans in the Netherlands.

Finally, our research experiences fully demonstrated the vital importance of "being there" (Borneman and Hamoudi 2009, 19), not only to ask the right questions, but to capture the semantics of norms and the emotions that normative change engenders. This was particularly the case for sensitive issues such as disputes, decentralization, and care and support that have been the subjects of my research. The more familiar we became, the better we understood that people used normative conceptions of care and property in many ways, now referring to ideals, then to institutions, rules and regulations, or to socio-legal relationships, or even to socio-legal practices. It stimulated us to us develop a layered analytical approach to law that allows capturing legal complexity to its full extent (F. and K. von Benda-Beckmann 1994a). Becoming a familiar outsider also made us realize that intensive fieldwork at the beginning was highly conducive for providing the epistemological and normative understanding necessary to conduct fruitful interviews and evaluate other sources that were more appropriate research methods at a later stage. This was certainly one of the reasons for feeling less out of place with advancing time and age.

References

Allen, Nicholas J. 2000. "The Field and the Desk: Choices and Linkages." In *Anthropologists in a Wider World: Essays on Field Research*, edited by Paul Dresch, Wendy James, and David Parkin, 243–58. Oxford: Berghahn Books.

Baehr, Peter R. 1997. "Problems of Aid Conditionality: The Netherlands and Indonesia." *Third World Quarterly* 18(2): 363–76.

Benda-Beckmann, Franz von. 1979. *Property in Social Continuity: Continuity and Change in the Maintenance of Property Relationships through Time in Minangkabau, West Sumatra*. The Hague: Martinus Nijhoff.

1988. "Islamic Law and Social Security in an Ambonese Village." In *Between Kinship and the State: Social Security and Law in Developing Countries*, edited by Franz von Benda-Beckmann, Keebet von Benda-Beckmann, Eric Casiño, Frank Hirtz, Gordon R. Woodman, and Hans F. Zacher, 339–65. Dordrecht and Berlin: Foris and Walter de Gruyter.

Benda-Beckmann, Franz von, and Keebet von. 1994a. "Coping with Insecurity." In *Coping with Insecurity: An 'Underall' Perspective on Social Security in the Third World*, edited by F. von Benda-Beckmann, K. von Benda-Beckmann, and H. Marks, 7–31. Special issue. *Focaal 22/23*.

Benda-Beckmann, Franz von, and Keebet von Benda-Beckmann. 2007. *Social Security Between Past and Future: Ambonese Networks of Care and Support*. Münster: LIT Verlag.

2013. *Political and Legal Transformations of an Indonesian Polity: The Nagari from Colonization to Decentralization*. Cambridge: Cambridge University Press.

Benda-Beckmann, Franz von, Keebet von Benda-Beckmann, and Melanie G. Wiber. 2006. "The Properties of Property." In *Changing Properties of Property*, edited by Franz von Benda-Beckmann, Keebet von Benda-Beckmann, and Melanie G. Wiber, 1–39. New York and Oxford: Berghahn Books.

Benda-Beckmann, Keebet von. 1984. *The Broken Stairways to Consensus: Village Justice and State Courts in Minangkabau*. Dordrecht and Leiden: Cinnaminson, NJ and Foris Publications, KITLV Press.

2015. "Social Security in Transnational Legal Space: Limitations and Opportunities." In *Transnational Agency and Migration: Actors, Movements and Social Support*, edited by Stefan Köngeter and Wendy Smith, 245–61. London: Routledge.

Bornemann, John, and Abdellah Hammoudi, eds. 2009. *Being There: The Fieldwork Encounter and the Making of Truth*. Berkeley: University of California Press.

Bornemann, John, and Abdellah Hammoudi. 2009. "The Fieldwork Encounter, Experience, and the Making of Truth: An Introduction." In *Being There: The Fieldwork Encounter and the Making of Truth*, edited by John Bornemann and Abdellah Hammoudi, 1–24. Berkeley: University of California Press.

Dresch, Paul, and Wendy James. 2000. "Fieldwork and the Passage of Time." In *Anthropologists in a Wider World: Essays on Field Research*, edited by Paul Dresch, Wendy James, and David Parkin, 1–26. Oxford: Berghahn Books.

Glick Schiller, Nina. 2005. "Transborder Citizenship: An Outcome of Legal Pluralism within Transnational Social Fields." In *Mobile People, Mobile Law. Expanding Legal Relations in a Contracting World*, edited by Franz von Benda-Beckmann, Keebet von Benda-Beckmann, and Anne Griffiths, 27–50. Aldershot and Burlington, VT: Ashgate.

Halliday, Simon, and Patrick Schmidt. 2009. *Conducting Law and Society Research: Reflections on Methods and Practices*. Cambridge: Cambridge University Press.

Howell, Signe Lise. 2012. "Cumulative Understandings. Experiences from the Study of Two Southeast Asian Societies." In *Returns to the Field: Multitemporal Research and Contemporary Anthropology*, edited by Signe Lise Howell and Aud Talle, 153–80. Bloomington and Indianapolis: Indiana University Press.

Howell, Signe, and Aud Talle, eds. 2012. *Returns to the Field. Multitemporal Research and Contemporary Anthropology*. Bloomington and Indianapolis: Indiana University Press.

Massoud, Mark Fathi. 2016. "Field Research on Law in Conflict Zones and Authoritarian States." *Annual Review of Law and Social Science* 12(1): 85–106.

Nouwen, Sarah M. H. 2014. "'As You Set out for Ithaka': Practical, Epistemological, Ethical, and Existential Questions about Socio-legal Empirical Research in Conflict." *Leiden Journal of International Law* 27 (1): 227–60.

Parkin, David J. 2009. "Templates, Evocations, and the Long-Term Fieldworker." In *Being There: The Fieldwork Encounter and the Making of Truth*, edited by John Bornemann and Abdellah Hammoudi, 91–107. Berkeley: University of California Press.

Reybrouck, David van. 2020. *Revolusi: Indonesie En Het Ontstaan Van De Moderne Wereld*. Amsterdam: De Bezige Bij.

Turner, Terence. 2009. "Forty-Five Years with the Kayapo." In *Returns to the Field: Multitemporal Research and Contemporary Anthropology*, edited by Signe Howell and Aud Talle, 25–48. Bloomington: Indiana University Press.

INDEX

Abrego, Leisy J., 38–40
  use of acompaniment. *See* accompaniment
    (Abrego)
Abrego, Leisy J., out of place
  projected by others, 36, 50–1
  as a Salvadoran immigrant scholar, 36, 41,
    48, 54
  in white/male encounters, 38
accompaniment (Abrego)
  in academia, 38–40
  conducting interviews in, 49
  definition, 38–9
  and emotional positioning. *See* emotional
    positioning
  inappropriate uses of, 48
  nurtured by activism, 48
  in participant recruitment, 44–6
  presentations in, 51–3
  in project concept, 44
  in research methodology, 40–1
  writing and analysis in, 49–53
agoraphobia, disciplinary, 144, 145, 155
Akala, on proximity to whiteness, 172–3
alterity, 144, 153
  in Gujurat High Court, 132–5
  transgression as, 125
autotheory, 3, *See also* Cooppan, Vilashini;
    Hartman, Saidiya; Nelson, Maggie;
    positionality; Williams, Patricia

Ballakrishnen, Swethaa S., 149
  Accidental Feminism, 139, 142, 144, 146–8,
    152–4, *See* 'local north' advantages, *See*
    fragility, brahmin or *savarna*
  Invisible Institutionalisms, 10, 149–50
  "long table" methodology, 149–50
  queer methods in research, 144
  research methods, 140
  and Sara Dezalay, 29, *See also* Sara Dezalay
  in vulnerability politics, 156
Ballakrishnen, Swethaa S., out of place(ness)
  in Accidental Feminism, *See* Ballakrishnen,
    Swethaa S.: *Accidental Feminism*
  effect of shifting urban/global/savarna/cis
    positionalities, 146

gender fluidity, queer identity, and
    methodology, 144–5
  and hegemonies, 145–6
  odd/identity to make legal theory, 149
  in privilege. *See* privilege and positionality
  and queer citizenship, 153
  queer failure, and being "in place", 158
  research methods, 144–5
  and shifting identities, 145–9
  in vulnerability politics, 149
Baxi, Pratiksha, out of place(ness)
  during arrival in court, 120–2
  getting permissions, 122–3
  in Gujurat High Court. *See* Gujurat High
    Court, positionality effects
  male secrecy and, 133
  in Nyaya Mandir (district court), 125–7
  in relations with prosecutors, 127–8
  scolding as pedagogical tool, 125
  secrecy and, 124–5, 132
  secrecy, alterity, and, 133–4
Benda-Beckmann, Franz von, 189, 207
Benda-Beckmann, Keebet von, fieldwork
  adat, 192–5
  Ambon, 199
  constitutional reforms, 200–3
  Moluccan women, 199–200
Benda-Beckmann, Keebet von, out of place
    (ness)
  Dutch colonial past and, 203–4
  multiplicity, 190–2
benefits of positionality, 7–13
  bridge from positivism to postmodernism, 11
  commuicating privileges, 13
  connection, 9
  creating space for diverse positions, 9–10
  credibility, 9
  identifying marginality, 7–8
  in social science development, 10–11
Blee, Kathleen, 13
Boittin, Margaret L.
  and Mei Jie, Shenzhen madam, 88–9, 94
  research and fieldwork, 87–9
Boittin, Margaret L., out of place(ness)
  in China, 90–4

Books in the Series

Diseases of the Will: Alcohol and the Dilemmas of Freedom
Mariana Valverde

*The Politics of Truth and Reconciliation in South Africa: Legitimizing the
Post-Apartheid State*
Richard A. Wilson

Modernism and the Grounds of Law
Peter Fitzpatrick

Unemployment and Government: Genealogies of the Social
William Walters

*Autonomy and Ethnicity: Negotiating Competing Claims in Multi-Ethnic
States*
Yash Ghai

*Constituting Democracy: Law, Globalism and South Africa's Political
Reconstruction*
Heinz Klug

The Ritual of Rights in Japan: Law, Society, and Health Policy
Eric A. Feldman

Governing Morals: A Social History of Moral Regulation
Alan Hunt

The Colonies of Law: Colonialism, Zionism and Law in Early Mandate Palestine
Ronen Shamir

Law and Nature
David Delaney

*Social Citizenship and Workfare in the United States and Western Europe:
The Paradox of Inclusion*
Joel F. Handler

*Law, Anthropology, and the Constitution of the Social: Making Persons and
Things*
Edited by Alain Pottage and Martha Mundy

*Judicial Review and Bureaucratic Impact: International and Interdisciplinary
Perspectives*
Edited by Marc Hertogh and Simon Halliday

Immigrants at the Margins: Law, Race, and Exclusion in Southern Europe
Kitty Calavita

Institutional Inequality and the Mobilization of the Family and Medical Leave Act: Rights on Leave
Catherine R. Albiston

Authoritarian Rule of Law: Legislation, Discourse and Legitimacy in Singapore
Jothie Rajah

Law and Development and the Global Discourses of Legal Transfers
Edited by John Gillespie and Pip Nicholson

Law against the State: Ethnographic Forays into Law's Transformations
Edited by Julia Eckert, Brian Donahoe, Christian Strümpell and Zerrin Özlem Biner

Transnational Legal Ordering and State Change
Edited by Gregory C. Shaffer

Legal Mobilization under Authoritarianism: The Case of Post-Colonial Hong Kong
Waikeung Tam

Complementarity in the Line of Fire: The Catalysing Effect of the International Criminal Court in Uganda and Sudan
Sarah M. H. Nouwen

Political and Legal Transformations of an Indonesian Polity: The Nagari from Colonisation to Decentralisation
Franz von Benda-Beckmann and Keebet von Benda-Beckmann

Pakistan's Experience with Formal Law: An Alien Justice
Osama Siddique

Human Rights under State-Enforced Religious Family Laws in Israel, Egypt, and India
Yüksel Sezgin

Why Prison?
Edited by David Scott

Law's Fragile State: Colonial, Authoritarian, and Humanitarian Legacies in Sudan
Mark Fathi Massoud

Rights for Others: The Slow Home-Coming of Human Rights in the Netherlands
Barbara Oomen

www.ingramcontent.com/pod-product-compliance
Lightning Source LLC
Chambersburg PA
CBHW061542280225
22737CB00004B/146